The DialAmerica™ Teleservices Handbook

A Guide to Successful
Inbound and Outbound Telemarketing

ROBERT DOSCHER AND RICHARD SIMMS

NTC Business Books
NTC/Contemporary Publishing Group

Library of Congress Cataloging-in-Publication Data

Doscher, Robert.
    The DialAmerica teleservices handbook : a guide to successful inbound and
outbound telemarketing / Robert Doscher and Richard Simms.
        p.   cm.
    Includes index.
    ISBN 0-658-00399-2
    1. Telemarketing.   2. DialAmerica Marketing (Firm)   I. Simms, Richard.
    II. Title.
HF5415.1265.D67   2000
658.8′4—dc21   00-38662

Interior design by Hespenheide Design

Published by NTC Business Books
A division of NTC/Contemporary Publishing Group, Inc.
4255 West Touhy Avenue, Lincolnwood (Chicago), Illinois 60712-1975 U.S.A.
Printed in the United States of America
International Standard Book Number: 0-658-00399-2

01 02 03 04 HP 19 18 17 16 15 14 13 12 11 10 9 8 7 6 5 4 3 2 1

Telemarketing has always worked because phones have ringers, and the only way to make that annoying noise stop is to pick up the phone and say, "Hello?"

But what happens if phones don't have ringers anymore?

Contents

1 Benefits of Telemarketing   1

2 Successful Outbound Telemarketing 13

3 Designing a <u>Successful</u> Telemarketing Test Plan 33

4 Launching a Successful Outbound Telemarketing Test 67

5 Inbound Telemarketing

6 Fulfillment: The Road to Success or the Bane of Direct Marketers

7   The Rollout   143

8   Business Versus Consumer Telemarketing   155

9   Business and Consumer Markets and Offers   179

Foreword

Direct marketing is *not* about creating awareness. It is *not* about changing attitudes. It *is* about changing behavior and influencing people from afar.

The very first use of the telephone occurred on March 10, 1876, when Alexander Graham Bell spoke those immortal words: "Mr. Watson, come here, I want you." Mr. Bell's assistant, Watson, came immediately. That first phone call not only changed history but changed behavior. In fact, for all the hoopla over the Internet and direct-reponse broadcasting, only one medium is more powerful than the telephone when it comes to changing sales-related human behavior—the face-to-face sales call, currently running at about $350 to $500 a pop.

Aside from the in-person sales call, no other medium allows a marketer to talk directly to a prospect, customer, or donor. A skilled teleservices representative can employ the seven key copy drivers—fear, greed, guilt, anger, exclusivity, salvation, and flattery—to change behavior. What's more, the teleservices rep can hear in real time just how those messages are playing because a good listener can hear inflections of elation, disappointment, interest, and boredom and can react instantly with an upsell, downsell, or soothing promise of satisfaction.

Unlike snail mail—where a change in the offer can take six to eight weeks or more—a telephone marketer can rewrite the script on the spot and try the new pitch in minutes.

For the serious marketer, the telephone is the ideal test medium—especially for the dry test (offering a product that does not yet exist)—far more than the Internet. Although capable of extraordinary razzle-dazzle, the Internet is still essentially a print medium whose words and pictures cannot begin to approximate the warmth and enthusiasm of a human voice. What's more, with the slightest interruption—a telephone call or an irrelevant on-screen message—the interactivity can be cut short with the click of a mouse. In fact, a number of new Internet services are pinned to E-voice, giving the prospect fumbling around on the Web a chance to talk to a live person who will answer questions and take an order.

Notice earlier that I used the term "skilled teleservices representative." That's the key! I cannot count the number of cold calls I receive where the person on the other end—whom I can immediately recognize as a stranger—starts reading a script with all the passion and intimacy of Darth Vader or C3PO.

If it is used to sell products where the arithmetic tallies and is executed by consummate professionals with leading-edge hard- and software at their disposal, telemarketing can be the most effective medium ever devised. That's what this extraordinary compendium by Richard Simms and Robert Doscher is all about—maximizing the efficiency of inbound and outbound telephone efforts, both in terms of the systems themselves and the people charged with making those systems work.

In the pages that follow, you will get the inside skinny from two world-class professionals on all facets of teleservices. They'll tell you when and how to set up your own operation or why you might be better off with an outside service. Among the treasure trove of goodies in the pages that follow, you'll find information on

- eight scenarios for testing outbound telemarketing and three scenarios for testing inbound telemarketing
- seven scenarios in which you *should never* use outbound telemarketing
- price testing and how to find the sweet spots
- creating a trial profit and loss statement
- when to use a formal script vs. a call guide
- the nine basic steps in a telemarketing call

- ten steps to successfully training your reps—from the first day of work onward
- inbound spikes and what results if you're not able to answer within 20 seconds
- offers that work on the phone and how to position them
- working with an agency or hiring a consultant
- the costs to hire a consultant—and what to expect in return
- the differences between scripting a consumer call vs. a business-to-business call
- how to rate the efficiency of reps
- the delicate business of monitoring calls

Above all, you will have at your fingertips actual real-life telemarketing cases describing the product, the offer, the strategy, the script, and, most important, the results.

Do you have an in-house telemarketing operation? *The DialAmerica Teleservices Handbook* is your checklist to make sure everything is working at peak efficiency. It is a manual on how to improve what you've got. Are you thinking about starting an in-house department? Here is your wiring diagram. Do you use an outside service and/or a consultant? With *The DialAmerica Teleservices Handbook* as your guide, nobody will put anything over on you ever again.

This is a book I will keep in my personal library and will refer to again and again. Thank you, Richard Simms and Bob Doscher, for creating it!

—*Denny Hatch* is a direct marketing consultant and writer/designer. The founder of the newsletter *Who's Mailing What!* and former editor of *Target Marketing* magazine, he is the author of *2,239 Tested Secrets for Direct Marketing Success, Million Dollar Mailings,* and *Method Marketing.* He can be reached at www.methodmarketing.com.

Acknowledgments

We are quite sure that many of you are already familiar with the name DialAmerica Marketing. However, for those of you who are not, we feel a few words of explanation are in order.

This book is the collaboration of Richard Simms, an 18-year veteran with DialAmerica, and Robert Doscher, president of Response Innovations. The authors first met as client and vendor in 1992 when Bob was vice president of direct marketing for Western Publishing in Racine, Wisconsin, and Rich was the account executive at DialAmerica responsible for telemarketing programs. The lessons they learned together, both successes and failures, made this book possible.

DialAmerica Marketing has been in the telemarketing business for nearly 50 years. Time Inc., the company's founder began testing outbound telemarketing in 1950. The experiment proved successful, and that led to the establishment of a new company in 1957 called Life Circulation Company, a wholly owned subsidiary of Time Inc. DialAmerica became privately owned in 1976. The company's headquarters is currently located in Mahwah, New Jersey.

DialAmerica has grown and expanded through the years. Today, it is one of the nation's largest telemarketing organizations, with branches in major cities throughout North America. The company offers outbound and inbound services to both businesses and consumers, and provides a broad range of telephone marketing services for the direct marketing industry. Its current capacity is in the neighborhood of one million calls per day.

We would like to thank the ownership of DialAmerica Marketing, particularly Art and Bill Conway, co-CEOs, for their support of this book, and also for their generosity in allowing us to use the DialAmerica name in the title.

Finally, we would like to thank all our friends and colleagues who have shared their expertise and insight with us. Many of them have worked with us as clients. Certainly not everything we tried together was successful. But occasional failure can be a wonderful thing. Thank you all for allowing us to learn so much from our failures—these experiences have provided us with enough material to write this book with the certainty that we finally have a pretty good idea of what works and what doesn't.

Enjoy the book!

Introduction

Telemarketing is the business of using the telephone to establish a direct one-to-one communication between a seller and a buyer for the purpose of moving goods and services from a producer to a customer.

As good as this definition is, it is inadequate to describe the full range of activities that we have come to know as telemarketing. In fact there are at least four subdisciplines that comprise this broad subject. They are *telesales*, *teleadvertising*, *teleresearch*, and *telesupport*. Telesales is clearly the one most closely aligned with our definition. Teleadvertising is close but also includes political campaigning. Teleresearch can include information gathering that has very little to do with moving products and services to market, and telesupport includes all nonprofit fund-raising and membership campaigns.

Within this broad definition an enormous industry has grown. From its infancy approximately 50 years ago telemarketing has burgeoned to the point that the twenty-first century began with more than $500 billion in annual telemarketing sales! Industry experts predict that this number will grow to more than $700 billion by the year 2003. They also report that there are nearly 6 million American jobs related to telephone marketing sales and advertising activities, and that total telemarketing advertising expenditures will grow at an average rate of approximately 6 percent per year to reach $84.5 billion by 2003!

For some time telemarketing has been the number one direct marketing medium in the United States. It's bigger than any other medium, including direct mail, newspapers, magazines, television, radio, or the Internet.

As an industry, it's about as high-tech as you can get. Most big telecenters have predictive dialers, automated call distributors, interactive voice-recognition units, on-line scripting, hot-voice and data transfer capability, fiber optics everywhere, and enough computers to launch a rocket. Technology is definitely the name of the game, and, at its most competitive level, it's a very expensive game to play. Fortunately, all this technology has made us much more productive, and that fact, combined with ever-decreasing telecommunications costs, has actually resulted in lower order-acquisition costs at a time when all the other media have been getting more expensive.

Certainly one of the more compelling questions about the future is what will be the impact of the Internet on telemarketing. No one knows for sure. However, we are encouraged to see so many websites promoting 800 numbers. We expect that over the near term the major impact will be to spur additional growth in inbound 800 services. Many of these new Internet buyers will certainly be good prospects for outbound telemarketing.

Why Use Telemarketing?

As we have noted, the economics of telemarketing have improved steadily owing to higher productivity and lower phone costs. Compare this to direct mail, where we have seen steadily rising paper and postage costs drive many previously successful projects below the break-even point. If it weren't for telemarketing, many of these programs would probably disappear. The simple fact is that, of any media, telemarketing consistently delivers the highest response rates, which leads to low order-acquisition costs, and best of all, high market-penetration rates.

One of the great lessons of direct marketing is that a significant amount of money is made or lost in the efficiency of the fulfillment. There usually is a direct correlation between the speed of product delivery and the percentage of payments versus returns and bad debt. The general rule is that the faster you deliver, the more money you will make. Nothing can beat telemarketing for prompt and efficient order entry. It even beats the Internet much of the time, because with telemarketing a live telemarketer assists the customer in the order entry process, asking all the right questions, and making sure everything is correct.

We will be covering the benefits of telemarketing more extensively in chapter 1. For now, suffice it to say that for many marketers today, the question is not "Why use telemarketing?" but rather, "How can I do more of it?"

Why You, and Everyone You Know in Direct Marketing, Should Read This Book

When we initially considered the possibility of writing this book, we realized that no one has ever written a book about telemarketing from the perspective that we intended to offer.

We wanted to write a really great book about telemarketing, packed with actual case studies that would benefit (1) direct marketers at companies that use "outside agencies" and (2) telemarketing agency executives, managers, and staff who would like to learn how to serve their clients better.

We also wanted to teach direct marketers at client companies who work with outside agencies how to (1) be more successful with initial testing by avoiding common mistakes; (2) be more structured and disciplined in the test planning process; (3) be more successful at problem solving by being more involved in training, monitoring, and creative analysis; (4) achieve more telemarketing success by gaining a better understanding of the special fulfillment, customer service, and billing and collection needs of telephone-sold orders; (5) benefit from an agency's past experience with similar situations; (6) best use the services of a consultant in the planning and execution of a telemarketing test at an outside agency; (7) best define the roles and responsibilities of each of the partners in the effort: the client, the consultant, and the agency; (8) realize the value of maintaining sufficient and stable call volume to allow for a dedicated call environment that is not forced constantly to go up and down the learning curve; and most important, (9) when *not* to use an agency because the application will only work in an in-house environment, probably won't work at all, or should first be tested using other media.

We would like to teach agency executives, managers, and staff how to (1) get more support from their client partners by better defining and implementing the roles and responsibilities for both; (2) establish and maintain a proper relationship with an outside consultant who has been hired by the client to manage a telemarketing campaign; (3) do a better job with initial test planning, script writing, and project execution so as to increase potential for early success; (4) provide the highest quality service possible by respecting customer privacy concerns, and staying in compliance with all the proper ethics guidelines, rules, and regulations; and (5) avoid common mistakes, and say no to bad ideas.

We wanted to write a book packed with case studies, actual examples, sample scripts, and the lessons learned from thousands of telemarketing campaigns—successes *and* failures.

We wanted to encourage direct marketers to be more comfortable and confident with their decision to use consultants and outside agencies versus doing the work in-house.

We are hopeful that each reader will be more successful as a result of reading this book, and that consequently we will have a positive impact on the quality of telemarketing in the industry as a whole.

Benefits of Telemarketing

Direct marketing is an inherently risky business and telemarketing is no different. However, it is by far the most flexible and change-friendly media available. It's also the most responsive. In this first chapter we will show you how that flexibility and responsiveness can be translated into tremendous opportunities for profit.

Generating Incremental Sales over and Above Direct Mail

One of the best and most profitable applications of outbound telemarketing is to follow a mailing with a phone call. You can wait for all the mail response to come in, and then begin your calls. You can even follow multiple mailings and insert your call at a point where further mailings would not turn a profit. In fact, as you will see in a future chapter, it is not unusual for our telemarketing response rate to be 10 times greater than your most recent mailing to that list.

Now it certainly is true that not all of the lists you mail will be available for telemarketing, but it always makes sense to ask— and to test them on the phone if they are.

On the inbound side, we believe that there is no longer any question that providing an 800 number in a mailpiece lifts overall response rate in almost every promotion. The only time the reverse is true is when you don't have the capacity to answer all the calls promptly, which results in customer frustration and lost opportunity.

Conducting Low-Cost, Low-Risk Dry Testing

Outbound telemarketing is the perfect media to use for product, offer, and list testing. It has the mail beat cold. When you test in the mail there is a tremendous amount of up-front planning. A minimum direct mail test cell typically involves using 5,000 names. That requires small and expensive print runs. The copy has to be cleared well in advance, and then it takes time for the response to trickle in. Worst of all, there really is nothing you can do with the results until you plan your next campaign, which may be months away.

Clearly telemarketing has numerous advantages. First and foremost, there is much less time required to launch a telemarketing test than direct mail. There is no minimum required other than what you will need to ensure statistical significance. The only real issues are to ensure that the test-cell names have been properly coded so that you can track the results and rewrite the scripts to include any changes you want to test.

Once you decide which is the winning combination among your test cells, you can move all the remaining names into that group, thus maximizing your profits immediately. You certainly can't do that with direct mail.

Outbound telemarketing is by far the fastest, easiest, and least expensive way to test. For these reasons, outbound telemarketing is very often the media of choice to dry test a new product concept. Dry testing is a market research technique that involves offering a product for sale over the phone while it is still in the development stage (or even the imagination stage). In other words, the real purpose of the call is to determine whether there is a viable market for the product you are planning to launch in the future. You can test price, offer structure, and interest in features and benefits along with lists. Of course, you won't want to take too many orders, since you will still be paying to acquire them. You will also have to send a "sorry, the product's been delayed" letter to the customers, perhaps with a free premium, to make them feel better about not being able to own your great idea right away.

Telemarketing Has the Shortest Start-Up Cycle

"How fast can you get it started?" How many times have we all heard those words? Well, truth be told, we can get it started pretty darn quickly. Think of the time it takes to put a full direct mail package together, or produce a radio or TV commercial. Even space advertising in magazines takes months of planning before your ad can hit the newsstands and those first orders start to roll in. Card decks and free-standing inserts (FSIs) are pretty quick, but there are still copy to write and approve and printing lead times to deal with. Outbound telemarketing can have those first orders on the books within a couple of days (or a few short weeks at the most). Of course, you are a lot less likely to make a mistake if you have some time to think through the process of how you will code the records and transmit the data back and forth. However, it only takes a few hours to write a script. Training takes another few hours. The slowest part of the process for an outbound start-up typically is getting the leads into the callable inventory.

Jim Ahearn, vice president of inbound services at DialAmerica, has a great quote: "In the old days it used to take us at least two weeks to get an inbound program up and running on the phones. Now, with all the added efficiency we've gained from all of this high-tech computer equipment, we can usually accomplish the same task in less than six weeks!"

Well, of course Jim's joke is actually an insightful observation about the current state of inbound telemarketing. In fact, he points out that sometimes you can still start up with just a few days' notice. Other times it may take months. This is because advances in technology have not only added sophistication, efficiency, and enhanced service for the customer, but they have also added time-consuming complexity to the start-up process. With an inbound campaign there are certain telecommunications issues that may be part of a client's program that are completely out of the service provider's hands. For instance, it can take your telco six weeks to get lines installed if you require a dedicated data link to the client's mainframe. If that's the case it won't matter that your service provider has everything else ready within a few days or not.

One for the Record Books . . .

The shortest start-up I've ever seen involved a job where I had my
first call from the client on a Thursday afternoon, and we were
on the phones the following Monday night. It was back in 1986
and we were still calling from hard-copy leads (no predictive
dialers yet). The client was an admissions director at a large city
university, which had been promoting a continuing-education
night school program to nontraditional students. The university
had been gathering leads from direct response radio throughout
the spring and summer. When they called us, it was the end of
August, and registration was planned to take place on Wednesday
of the following week. They had several thousand prospective
students who needed meetings with counselors if they were going
to enroll in the fall semester. So there it was. Could we be on the
phones on Monday night and have all the calling finished by
Tuesday? Ordinarily this would be impossible. But in this case the
client already had all the leads printed out on individual index
cards with phone numbers appended. The client also had a script,
which actually worked, and they could get everything to me by
Monday morning. I wrote up a proposal on Thursday afternoon,
and he had it signed and back in my hands on Friday. We trained
on Monday night. By Tuesday night we had called through the
lead base two times. The client decided to keep us on the phones
for the rest of the week. The project worked great. Sure there
were a lot of people who decided not to enroll, but there were
also plenty of people who would not have gone to school that
semester if we hadn't called.

—Richard Simms

Realistically, an outside agency like DialAmerica normally requires
a minimum of two weeks to start up an outbound test. In a crunch, they
may be able to start it quicker, but if possible it's best to give at least three
weeks to a month of advance notice and planning. Clients who approach
the task in a slower, more thoughtful manner are much less likely to have
a problem.

Offers and Lists Can Be Revised Once the Calling Starts

One of the benefits of outbound telemarketing is that you make the calls one at a time. Unlike direct mail, or any of the broadcast or print media, you can make dramatic changes in offer, price, or list selection to an outbound telemarketing campaign with very little notice or advance planning. You can literally pull everyone off the phones, conduct an update training, and resume the calling 20 minutes later with a new script that incorporates almost any change you want. You do need to be careful if you are making changes that will affect the fulfillment of the product with the right price, etc. In those cases you may need to suspend calling for a day, so that you can recode the records to ensure that the customers are receiving what was promised over the phone. We've seen numerous instances where adding a premium to the offer on the first day of calling made all the difference between success and failure for a new test promotion.

Another benefit of making the calls one at a time is that if a particular list isn't working, you can simply stop the calling on that list and continue with the rest. If the reason for the problem has something to do with the accuracy of the data, you can try to get it replaced or corrected, and then return it to the phone room once you've cleaned it up. Pulling nonperforming lists is a basic strategy in outbound telemarketing management.

This is one area where there is no parallel benefit on the inbound side; it is the other media that drive the calls, and the offers and lists are all pretty much set in stone.

Listening to Your Customers

There is no other direct marketing media that provides you with the opportunity to hear what your customers have to say about your company and products in such a completely spontaneous way.

Silent remote monitoring should be a continuous and ongoing process for all telemarketing campaigns, whether they are inbound or outbound, in-house or through an agency. In most situations you will be able to schedule monitoring sessions in advance, and listen to live calls right from the convenience of your home or office. Neither the customer nor the sales rep will know that you are on the line, so it truly is a revealing look into your customer's purchase decision-making process.

Understanding Why Customers Say No

Refusal analyses and other market research can serve as valuable by-products. When someone doesn't order from your mailpiece or catalog, you can only guess at the reason. When response to your space ads or broadcast advertising is low, there is no way to know if that is because customers are not interested in your offer, or if they just never saw or heard the ad.

Telemarketing is the only medium that actually captures reasons for refusal as a by-product of capturing the order. This is true for both inbound and outbound applications. Very often you can learn more from the refusals than from the sales. A good telemarketing operation will capture, categorize, and analyze the nonsale outcomes as a matter of course. This can be done on a list-by-list and offer-by-offer basis.

A little telemarketing can sometimes answer some big questions as to why the market is suddenly reacting to your offers in strange and mysterious ways. We will cover this in much more depth in chapter 4.

Telemarketing Can Work Even When the Mail Fails

List fatigue can be a very real problem for any direct mail program. Almost all direct mail marketers have encountered the situation in which lists that have worked in the past fall below the break-even point. Very often the reason is that the list is just not regenerating itself quickly enough with new names and, consequently, offers are being mailed over and over again to the same audience. In other words, you've plucked the low-hanging fruit, and now the only people left are those that have already seen and disposed of your mailing multiple times. When you reach that point, the unfortunate result is that too few people are actually opening the envelope to consider your offer.

Telemarketing is very often the answer. Telemarketing is a much more interactive media than the mail. Once you pick up the phone and say, hello, we open the envelope for you. Very few people will say, no, before at least finding out who is calling and what the call is about. Herein lies the central reason telemarketing response rates are so much higher than other media. We've seen it happen time and again where promotions that no longer work in the mail become telemarketing-only success stories.

Of course, list fatigue can also kill a telemarketing promotion, particularly if your customer-contact strategy is too aggressive. When that happens, it is certainly time to rest the lists or reinvent the product and/or offer structure.

High Response and Market-Penetration Rates <u>Maximize</u> Customer Value

As we've already mentioned, telemarketing offers the highest response rates of any media. Moreover, owing to its inherently proactive character, it also offers the highest market-penetration rates.

If your company is primarily interested in capturing market share, outbound telemarketing can be a great solution. As you will see in future chapters, outbound telemarketing can, under the right circumstances, contact and secure a yes or no from as much as 85 to 95 percent of the available universe. No other media even comes close.

It's been proved time and again that adding an 800-number response option to a promotion will almost always lift response, sometimes by 25 percent or more. In addition, inbound 800 selling provides the opportunity to upsell and dramatically increase customer order values.

When to Use Telemarketing and When to Avoid It

Up to this point we have been exploring the obvious benefits of telemarketing. However, this book is also about learning from mistakes and making good decisions about what *not* to do.

Here are some situations in which you should test outbound telemarketing.

- You have a renewal or reactivation offer to "good cancel" customers (particularly if the offer works in the mail for one or more efforts). This one is almost always a slam-dunk.

- You are using a subscription, continuity, or club offer structure.
- You have a new customer-acquisition offer that has a proven track record of success in the mail.
- You need to shorten the time between a customer's response to a lead-generation effort and the follow-up by your sales staff.
- You need to improve the average order value to hit the profit targets by upselling with an additional offer.
- You need to find out why customers are saying no through refusal analysis.
- Your other media have fallen below budget, and there is not enough time left in the fiscal period to bring in orders any other way.
- You have unsold inventory that needs to be turned into cash quickly without resorting to a liquidator.

Here are some situations in which you should test inbound telemarketing using an 800 number.

- You are marketing via catalog, direct mail, space, broadcast, or the Internet, and you are asking customers to respond directly to the offer contained therein.
- You have a program that depends on upselling to reach your revenue targets.
- You need to listen to your customer's "live" response to your offer through remote monitoring for market research purposes.

Here are some situations in which you should *not* test telemarketing.

- You cannot tolerate at least a minimum level of risk. Telemarketing is an inherently risky business. You can lose money.
- The call volume is anticipated to be so low that you will be eaten alive by the minimum costs associated with maintaining/managing a telemarketing staff or paying an agency to do the same.
- You do not have a first-class fulfillment operation already up and running. Telemarketing can generate a large volume of orders in a very short time, and you can lose both your credi-

bility and your shirt if fulfillment, billing, collections, and customer service are not up to the task.

- The average order value is so low that there is no way you can cover reasonable telemarketing order-acquisition costs and still make a profit. (We will talk about the telemarketing price point sweet spot in a future chapter.)
- You cannot offer an unconditional satisfaction guarantee and live with the returns that will result from customers exercising that privilege.
- Your product will not stand up to the price/value comparison that it will surely encounter once the customer receives it.
- You can already get 80 percent to 90 percent response using a less expensive media.

It's always difficult to admit that a project appears to have a fatal flaw, and we are constantly surprised by the many programs that work splendidly despite our initial doubts, but it is a wise direct marketer who tries to avoid the problem situations listed above as much as possible.

If telemarketing generates up to 1,000 percent more orders, and turns poor-performing mail lists around at the same or lower cost than mail-generated orders . . . you win!!!!

Suppose that you are mailing 100,000 pieces, five lists of 20,000 names each. The offer is a basic one-shot promotion with a 30-day risk-free preview on a bill-me basis to outside lists of consumers at their residential addresses. The price point is $39.95 plus $4.95 shipping and handling (S/H), and the cost of goods is $10. The major objective is to bring on as many new customers as possible while still turning a small overall profit on the promotion. Let's assume that the average direct mail response rate for the entire promotion turns out to be 2 percent, and that the response range of the five lists runs from a low of 1.5 percent to 2.5 percent. Furthermore, let's say that the list cost is $100 per thousand and the mail cost (printing, postage, etc.) comes to $500 per thousand. Figure 1.1 shows what we got.

As you can see, our order-acquisition cost ranges from a low of $24 per order to a high of $40 per order. Overall, our direct mail campaign

Direct Mail	List A	List B	List C	List D	List E	Total
Names Mailed	20,000	20,000	20,000	20,000	20,000	100,000
List Cost	$ 2,000	$ 2,000	$ 2,000	$ 2,000	$ 2,000	$10,000
Mail Cost	$10,000	$10,000	$10,000	$10,000	$10,000	$50,000
Total Cost	$12,000	$12,000	$12,000	$12,000	$12,000	$60,000
Response Rate	2.50%	2.25%	2.00%	1.75%	1.50%	2.00%
Number of Orders	500	450	400	350	300	2,000
Cost per Order	$ 24.00	$ 26.67	$ 30.00	$ 34.29	$ 40.00	$ 30.00

Figure 1.1 Sample One-Shot Direct Mail Promotion

generated 2,000 orders with an average cost per order of $30. Once you factor in returns, you probably lost money on lists D and E. List C is close to breaking even.

Now let's consider what happens when we add an outbound telemarketing follow-up to this promotion. The standard list cost for a second usage to the same names is usually around 50 percent of the initial cost. So that puts the list cost at $50 per thousand. Let's assume that the names are available with phone numbers appended to the records from the original source for an additional $70 per thousand. That would put the total list cost at $120 per thousand.

Estimating telemarketing conversions is a tricky business. However, they will usually fall within a range of 5 to 10 times the mail response. It doesn't always work that way, but multiplying the mail response by 7.5 would not be a bad starting point. That would indicate that the phone conversions would run between 11 percent and 19 percent, with an average of 15 percent. These are very reasonable numbers. If you have any doubts, check out some of the case studies in chapter 9.

Of course, you won't be able to reach everyone; the list-penetration goal for most consumer campaigns is around 85 percent. (The last 15 percent or so of the names is usually abandoned after multiple unsuccessful attempts at contact.)

Let's also assume that the telemarketing cost to contact and resolve 17,000 names (85 percent of each 20,000-name list) is $26,444. For the sake of this example, we are assuming that lead usage will average 18 leads used per hour (LUPH), and that the cost of the telemarketing effort is

Telemarketing	List A	List B	List C	List D	List E	Total
Names Supplied	20,000	20,000	20,000	20,000	20,000	100,000
Leads Resolved	17,000	17,000	17,000	17,000	17,000	85,000
List Cost	$ 2,400	$ 2,400	$ 2,400	$ 2,400	$ 2,400	$ 12,000
Telemarketing Cost	$26,444	$26,444	$26,444	$26,444	$26,444	$132,220
Total Cost	$28,844	$28,844	$28,844	$28,844	$28,844	$144,220
Response Rate*	18.75%	16.875%	15%	13.125%	11.25%	15%
Number of Orders	3,188	2,869	2,550	2,231	1,912	12,750
Cost per Order	$9.05	$10.05	$11.31	$12.93	$15.06	$11.31

*Response Rate = Orders Divided by Leads Resolved

Figure 1.2 Sample One-Shot Telemarketing Follow-up Promotion

around $28 per man-hour on the phone with no other fees (17,000 leads divided by 18 leads per hour equals 944.44 hours of calling: 944.44 hours times $28 per hour equals $26,444). Lead usage is a function of the audience you are trying to reach. Eighteen leads used per hour is a reasonable guess for an average consumer campaign, and $28 per hour is in the range of what an agency billing hourly might charge. Hence, these are reasonable numbers, at least for the sake of our example.

Figure 1.2 shows how the numbers look for the telemarketing follow-up.

Wow! 638 percent more orders at just about a third the cost! Can this be true? You bet! It happens all the time. And best of all, you probably have four or five more lists that perform below list E. The response is so poor that you don't even bother to mail them anymore, but they'll work just fine with telemarketing. And with those lists in the mix you are up to 1,000 percent more orders at a fraction of the cost of the direct mail sold orders! Once again, you win!

Summary

- Telemarketing, like other forms of direct marketing, is an inherently risky business. However, the potential benefits outweigh the risks by a wide margin.
- Follow a successful direct mail campaign with phone calls to generate incremental sales.

- It is not unusual to exceed your direct mail response by a factor of 10. A 1.5 percent response in the mail can yield 15 percent or more response on the phone.
- Outbound telemarketing cannot be beat as a method for testing new products, offers, and lists. If your test idea doesn't work you can make changes to offers and lists on the fly or pull the plug and walk away with very little expense, particularly if you are using an outside agency that is working on a flat cost per order (commission) basis with no other fees.
- Outbound telemarketing has a very short start-up. It's a perfect media choice when under the gun to meet a budget goal or other fiscal deadline. However, you greatly increase the risk of error when rushing a program on the phones. It is much wiser to take your time and plan carefully.
- No other direct marketing media allows you to listen to your customers' live response while considering an offer.
- Telemarketing will not only tell which products, offers, and lists are most responsive, but will also explain through comprehensive refusal analysis why customers say "no."
- Telemarketing should always be tested when facing a problem with declining response over time in direct mail campaigns. Very often the issue is list fatigue, and outbound telemarketing could be the only way to save a program that is about to die.
- Outbound telemarketing should be part of your plan if attaining market share is a primary goal for your company. Nothing can beat its ability to combine high conversions with high list penetrations to yield a flood of orders.
- Even though the benefits of testing telemarketing are truly tantalizing, it's not for everyone or every situation. Some things just won't work on the phone. Be careful, you can lose money. The best way to manage those risks is to conduct small initial tests. Follow those tests with larger retests, and then wait for the back-end results before committing to a rollout.
- If you are careful with your planning and do everything correctly, you can wind up with a big, big win.

2

Successful Outbound Telemarketing

In chapter 1 we began with the point that telemarketing, like all direct marketing, is an inherently risky business. We mentioned that there are five essential keys to success. In chapter 2 we will explore how these five keys can turn risks into rewards:

1. A highly targeted list
2. An irresistible offer
3. Excellent fulfillment, billing and collections, and customer service
4. A quality product
5. A professionally trained and managed sales force

Without question, the most important part of any telemarketing equation is the lists. Clearly, the more targeted the list, the better the response. Designing an irresistible offer is also extremely important. Ultimately, however, the product is the determining factor in the success of any promotion because if the perceived value of the product, premiums, etc., does not meet or exceed the expectations of the customer, you will not only be the recipient of a significant number of returns, but it is likely that many of your customers will become bad debts. Of course you will also need to fulfill the product efficiently or you will lose any hope of having the customer respond favorably. And finally you need to deliver the marketing message in a clear and consistent manner every time using a well-trained sales force.

Why are these components so vital for success in an outbound telemarketing test program? Using 10 comparative case studies, let's look at these essential keys individually.

A Highly Targeted List

Schools and libraries have traditionally comprised an excellent market for outbound telemarketing. They have significant budgets, and lists can be obtained that detail the size of those budgets. Of course, while the size of a school's budget is certainly a measure of discretionary spending, you should always test smaller schools along with those with larger budgets.

It all starts with selecting the right list. Consider the case illustrated by Figure 2.1.

As you can see, this was a very clean and highly targeted list. There is absolutely no way that the response would have been this high if the telephone problems, duplicates, and not-eligibles had been 20 percent or more of the list, and 20 percent would not be considered excessively high for other markets under normal circumstances.

Schools and libraries traditionally have low return and bad debt rates. However, as it is with other markets, the returns for outbound telemarketing sold orders are generally higher than what you would see in a comparable direct mail campaign. Bad debts often run less than 5 percent in this market, and returns, of course, are a function of the perceived and actual value of the product, along with whether the buyer is actually the user. For instance, we know that while the response was higher for the principals versus the media specialists, the return rate was also higher. This was because the principal was not the end user. That person, usually a classroom teacher, had the final decision about whether the product could be incorporated into the curriculum, and because that person was not consulted prior to placing the trial order, he or she did not necessarily share the principal's enthusiasm for the offer. However, the response rate was excellent and higher than most school programs. It's certainly a telemarketing opportunity that is generally underutilized.

This telemarketing campaign included calls to both school principals and computer media specialists at the school address. The offer was three software programs for the price of two. The cost was $99.95 plus shipping and handling. Lab Packs, which included five disks and an instructional manual, were also available as an alternate offer for $169.99. If buyers returned the product, the company paid the return postage, which is the preferred direct marketing method.

Names Received:	Media Specialists	8,150
	Principals	29,200
% With Phone Numbers		100%
Number of Orders:		8,725
Response Rate:	Media Specialists	33.7%
	Principals	35.2%
	Primary Offer	35.0%
	Alternative Offer (Lab Pack)	0.5%
Partial		
Refusal Analysis:	Telephone Problems	3.8%
	Already Ordered	3.5%
	Duplicates	1.2%
	Not Eligible (junior & senior high school)	0.5%

Figure 2.1 Educational Software Promotion to School Principals and Media Specialists

Of course, one of the major issues when calling schools or libraries is contact rate. However, even if the contact rate is as low as four to six leads per hour per telephone sales rep, a 35 percent conversion rate would yield approximately 1.5 to 2 orders per rep per hour. This would translate to a very acceptable cost-per-order based on current telemarketing charges.

The example illustrated in Figure 2.1 did not have a large difference in front-end response rates between the two list segments (33.7 percent for media specialists versus 35.2 percent for principals). However, that is probably the exception rather than the rule. Consider the case illustrated by Figure 2.2, in which we were once again calling the school market, but now saw some really significant swings in conversion rates

In this campaign we called second through twelfth grade schoolteachers. We qualified them for both their interest and opportunity to bring a school group to a natural science museum as part of an educational field trip program. The teachers were contacted mostly during their free period in the teacher's lounge or department office. To qualify as prospects they were required to answer yes to the following questions.

1. Do you take school trips?
2. Are you involved in the decision-making process about where to take a school trip?
3. Are you interested in receiving information in the mail about this museum field trip program?

Qualifying teachers also were offered a free admission to visit the museum with their families to preview the program.

Names Received	3,500
% with Phone Number	100%
List Source	House Data Base

Qualified Leads	
Fifth Grade Teachers	358
Science Elementary	141
Science JHS/Middle	64
Science SHS	99
Total	662

Response Rate	
Fifth Grade Teachers	37.7%
Science Elementary	32.0%
Science JHS/Middle	61.4%
Science SHS	41.8%
Total	38.3%

Figure 2.2 Lead Qualification to Private/Catholic School Teachers

from a high of 61 percent to a low of 32 percent based on the list segment we called.

It's pretty obvious that the most responsive target for this offer was the science teacher segment at the junior high and middle school level.

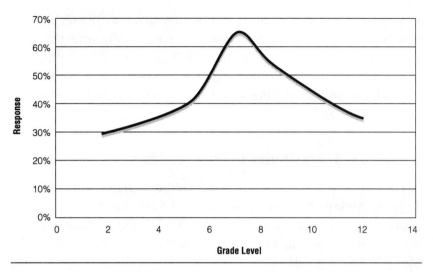

Figure 2.3 Response by Grade Level

Figure 2.3 shows a plot of the response by grade level. It shows graphically the importance of targeting your prospect as closely as possible.

Without question, a highly targeted list is the single biggest key to success in outbound telemarketing. It's been proved many times that if you have a great list, you can often live with an "average" offer, product, fulfillment, and sales rep and still make money—but if you have a poor list, it won't matter how good the other four keys are.

An Irresistible Offer

We will be covering the topic of successful phone offers in great detail in chapter 9. However, the point that we would like to make here is that telemarketing sells without the benefit of pictures and copy. Hence, the offer really does need to be *irresistible* if you expect customers to come to the point where they say to themselves, "Hey, this really is a great deal. How can I go wrong?"

So what are some of the elements of a truly irresistible offer? Well, to begin with, an *unconditional satisfaction guarantee* that is positioned as a *risk-free preview* or trial. This is essential. Very few people will agree to a "hard offer" for a product that is presented over the phone. The perceived risk is too great. Next, you will need a really attractive price point. Finally, you will need a premium if at all possible. Within this context, we're going to examine two cases that illustrate the point. Let's start with one of our all-time favorite irresistible offers, the "ship-till-forbid continuity."

Recipe Card Continuity to Outside Lists

There have been numerous recipe card continuity series during the past 20 years. Almost all of them have received a full direct response marketing effort, which included direct mail, DRTV (direct response television), alternative media, and telemarketing at one or more points in their life cycle. In many cases these various media were fully integrated and ran side-by-side in support of each other. Such was the situation with the recipe card continuity that Response Innovations was involved with a few years back, illustrated in Figure 2.4.

One of the reasons that telemarketing is often planned in coordination with other media is that there can be a significant savings in list costs. The savings on the second use of a list often amounts to 50 percent. The caveat to using the same lists for direct mail and telemarketing is that you must allow at least four weeks between the mailing of the direct mail package and the call. The reason is that when the telemarketing rep calls, the customer can disarm the sale by saying "I still have the package, let me take another look at it." In response, the rep can only say, "OK," and the sale is lost.

The results shown for this recipe card continuity (Figure 2.4) are typical for telemarketing promotions of this type. Keep in mind that these are outside lists, and some of them were converting at more than 25 percent! This program was a huge success and ran for many years. The offer was a winner in every respect. The satisfaction guarantee was positioned as a risk-free preview. The program could be canceled at any time without penalty. There was no minimum number of shipments to buy. The company would even pay for return postage. The cost of the introductory shipment was a low $4.29 plus $2.75 for shipping and handling, and the premiums had a perceived value of at least $15.

The first shipment the customer received included one set of recipe cards, a second free set of cards, a set of category divider cards, and a ring binder. Everything was sent with a 14-day satisfaction guarantee, and the customer could return the preview items and keep the premiums with no cost or obligation. The cost of the first set of recipe cards was $4.29 plus $2.75 shipping and handling. The invoice was sent with the shipment. If the customer paid for the introductory package, he or she would then receive three new card decks every four weeks for $12.87 plus $2.75 shipping and handling. A variety of outside lists were called including buyers of hosiery, women's apparel, cooking magazine subscribers, and sewing and handcraft product buyers.

Names Received	514,175
Names with Phone Numbers (after Matching)	211,675
% with Phone Numbers	41%
# of Orders	25,905
Response Rate	17%

Figure 2.4 Recipe Card Continuity to Outside Lists

The only factor that limited the success of this project was the availability of targeted lists. The recipes themselves were good, and the product leveraged a very well-known brand name for recognition and to establish credibility. In fact, a neighbor of one of the authors was a customer. She would come over every time she got another shipment to show what she had received. She was very excited about building a collection of recipes. It should be noted that this same person has by far the largest collection of paperback romance novels that we have ever seen in one place. It greatly exceeds the average bookstore inventory of this particular genre. Once she starts to collect something, there's no stopping her until she completes the collection. And she isn't alone—that's why we love continuities!

Another of our favorite irresistible offers is the "welcome-back reinstatement." In fact, if we have a choice of which program to test first with a new a client, it's always the "good cancel reinstatement." Here's a case in point.

Negative Option Book Club Reinstatement

One of the areas of opportunity for any negative option book club is the large number of "paid cancels" received at all shipment levels; the earlier the "paid cancel," the greater the opportunity, because of the potential life span and lifetime value of the customer.

The issue is how much you will have to "pay" to reacquire the customer, and what the customer is worth. The calculation is rather simple. The key factor is how many paid shipments per starter you are receiving. The answer for club and continuity programs encompasses a wide range of possibilities. There have been clubs that have averaged as few as 1.8 paid shipments per starter. There have been others that have yielded as high as 8.4 shipments per starter. In the case illustrated in Figure 2.5, it almost didn't matter because the order acquisition cost was so low because of the excellent front-end response.

The most interesting aspect of the case study shown in Figure 2.5 is that there are three offers being tested against each other, each with radically different front-end results.

The most significant observation about this case is that offer 1 had the best response (22.1 percent) and the largest initial financial commitment on the part of the customer. Offer 3 had a significantly lower response rate (12.5 percent) and a lower dollar commitment up front. The educated guess would be that the customers who said yes to offer 1 would buy at least one additional book even without the mention of a future commitment (which appears to have a significant negative impact on the reinstate response). Commitment offers usually will depress response, as many of these people have just recently fulfilled their original obligation and are therefore not interested in assuming another commitment as part of the reinstatement offer.

Here are the three scripted offers.

Offer 1: $1.99 Plus Shipping and Handling, No Further Commitment

There are two reasons for this call. First, I want to thank you for your interest in the _____ Book Club, Mr(s). _____ . Second, we'd like to send you our newest bestseller _____ that sells for $19.95 in most bookstores. We'll send it to you for only $1.99 plus

In this campaign we called "good cancels" from a consumer negative-option book club and offered to reinstate their club membership over the phone. This club offers books relating to military history. We tested three offers as follows:

1. The first book for $1.99 plus shipping and handling with no further commitment.
2. The first book as a free bonus. The customer is responsible for shipping and handling only with no further commitment.
3. The first book as a free bonus. The customer is responsible for shipping and handling only. There is a one-book commitment within the next six months.

Names Received	21,842
Names with Phone Numbers	10,921
% with Phone Number	50%
List Source	House list of "Good Cancels"
Orders	1,399
Response %	16.9%
$1.99 No Commit	22.1%
Bonus No Commit	16.2%
Bonus 1 Book Commit	12.5%

Figure 2.5 Negative Option Book Club Reinstatement

shipping and handling, and because of your special status there will be no obligation to buy another book ever.

You know how the club works. Mr(s). _____ , you will receive the review 15 times a year. That's about every three and a half weeks at no cost to you, and our book prices are discounted up to 35 percent off publisher's prices. We offer the best and newest books recommended by our board of advisors and scholars.

Offer 2: Free Bonus Book, Pay Shipping and Handling Only, No Further Commitment

There are two reasons for this call . . . First, I want to thank you for your interest in the _____ Book Club, Mr(s). _____ . Second, we'd like to send you our newest bestseller _____ that sells for $19.95 in most bookstores, as a free bonus . . . with just a small charge for shipping and handling. And because of your special status there will be no obligation to buy another book ever.

You know how the club works. Mr(s). _____ , you will receive the review 15 times a year. That's about every three and a half weeks at no cost to you, and our book prices are discounted up to 35 percent off publisher's prices. We offer the best and newest books recommended by our board of advisors and scholars.

Offer 3: Free Bonus Book, Pay Shipping and Handling Only, One-Book Commitment

There are two reasons for this call. First, I want to thank you for your interest in the _____ Book Club, Mr(s). _____ . Second, we'd like to send you our newest bestseller _____ that sells for $19.95 in most bookstores, as a free bonus, with just a small charge for shipping and handling.

You know how the club works. Mr(s). _____ , you will receive the review 15 times a year. That's about every three and a half weeks at no cost to you, and all we ask is that you buy just one more book sometime in the next six months. Our book prices are discounted up to 35 percent off publisher's prices. We offer the best and newest books recommended by our board of advisors and scholars.

So, which one was the rollout winner? Before you answer, consider this: The best perceived value to the consumer is offer 2, the free bonus book with no commitment, beyond shipping and handling. The most expensive for the customer up-front is offer 1, the $1.99 plus shipping and handling offer, with no further commitment. The best offer for the company, at least on an expected value basis, is offer 3, the free bonus book, shipping and handling, with a one-book commitment. Here's what happened.

As was shown in Figure 2.5, offer 1, the $1.99 plus shipping and handling offer was the easy up-front response winner at 22 percent even though it was more expensive for the consumer than offer 2. You may not believe that an extra $1.99 in up-front commitment can make such a significant difference, but in this case it did. It was also the winning rollout offer.

Excellent Fulfillment, Billing and Collections, and Customer Service

Believe it or not, our third key, excellent fulfillment, is where a significant amount of money usually is made or lost. Keep in mind that the final sales results depend not only upon your telemarketing partner, but upon the efficiency of your fulfillment system. There's no question that in most cases, the sooner the order is shipped, the lower your return rate and the lower your bad debts.

Several years ago, we worked together on an outbound telemarketing project for a needlecraft continuity series where the customers received the instructions and craft materials required for a complete project. This program appealed to women approximately 55 years of age.

As you can see in Figure 2.6, the results were quite good on the front end. However, over time, we discovered that the real leverage point for profitability was on the back end. Fulfillment speed was essential. Middle-age customers have a different perception of customer service and a different commitment to paying bills. As is the case in most programs, the longer it took to ship the product, the higher the returns.

We offered an introductory package that contained a free set of technique cards, a binder, dividers, and a pattern protector, along with a preview set of pattern cards at $4.79 per set plus shipping and handling. Future shipments of two card packs each were sent about every four weeks at a cost of $12.33.

Names with Phone Numbers	125,000
Orders	19,000
Response %	19%

Figure 2.6 Adult Handcraft Binder and Card Continuity to Outside Lists

We believe that there are two primary reasons for this relationship between fulfillment speed and the rate of returns:

1. Buyer's remorse is a constant threat. The longer it takes to receive the product, the more time the customer has to reconsider the order.
2. The longer it takes for the package to arrive, the greater the likelihood that the customer will forget he or she ordered the product and will simply write "Return" on the package. When this happens, the package will most likely be returned unopened.

As we learned from our "needlecraft continuity" example, this speed-of-fulfillment/returns relationship is even more pronounced with customers over 45 years of age. They generally have a different bill-paying ethic, and feel obligated to pay their bills on time, as their parents did many years ago. Hence, back-end efficiency has greater impact on profitability with this group than it does with other customers.

Next, let's take a look at a business-to-business case—a seemingly successful program targeted to school and public libraries. The offer used a variety of back-end enhancing strategies and ended up failing because of a back-end blunder (Figure 2.7).

On the face of it this would appear to be a generally successful program with more than $1 million in total revenue generated on the front end. Previous campaigns for this client had resulted in a fairly high return rate (40 to 50 percent) and we were experimenting with a new fulfillment process.

However, things did not go quite as well as we had planned. For one thing, we discovered that a majority of school librarians didn't know their fax number. But this was small potatoes compared to what lay ahead.

Approximately two weeks into the project we received a call from the president of the division we were working with informing us that the corporate parent had decided to pull the plug on the operation at the end of the year. Hence our telemarketing project was going to turn into an inventory clearance campaign. We were to accelerate the calling and get every order we could. As you can see in Figure 2.7, we did pretty well. We sold nearly 135,000 books in 10 weeks. What we didn't know was that the fulfillment house, another division of the same company, was not processing any of the orders. They had heard that their sister division was being shut down and they were concerned about who would take responsibility for

In this campaign we called school and public libraries from both house and outside lists to offer them a collection of children's books organized around a particular theme. There were six different themes. The number of books in each set varied from 26 to 31. A free book was used as a premium. The cost of each set was $250 plus shipping and handling. This amounted to an approximate 40 percent discount off the list price. Customers could order up to three packages. Catalog card kits were available at an additional cost. We tested a new fax fulfillment process that would fax an order confirmation plus product information sheets to the customer within a few minutes of the end of the phone call. The customer was asked to confirm the order by signing at the bottom and faxing the "confirmation" back using an 800 number. The purpose of the fax fulfillment test was to build commitment, thereby reducing returns.

Names Received	65,000
% with Phone Number	100%
List Source	House and Outside Compiled

Orders

Libraries Sold	2,409
Themed Sets Sold	4,720
Bought 1 Set	1,005
Bought 2 Sets	500
Bought 3 Sets	905
Average Sets per Customer	1.96
Total Order Value	$1,217,760

Response %

House Lists	12.1%
Outside Lists	6.2%

Figure 2.7 Theme-Based Children's Book Collection Offered to School and Public Libraries

the returns. In fact, they ultimately decided to liquidate the entire inventory. They never shipped a single order from the telemarketing campaign.

This back-end disaster illustrates one of the great truths about the business. If you don't ship the goods and you don't bill the customers, you won't get paid. You may want to laugh at this simplistic observation, but we can't tell you how many times over the course of our careers it's happened that we have placed a test order and discovered that there was a fulfillment or inventory problem only when the product was long overdue and we called to check on it.

A Quality Product

We will be covering the topic of products that sell in chapter 8. However, here is a small list of the product categories that we have had great success with over the years using outbound telemarketing.

Books	Magazines	Financial services
Videos	Software	Children's programs
Educational programs	Telco products	Collectibles

Delivering a quality product is the key to keeping returns and bad debt at bay. It is also the secret to maintaining the future sales potential of your house file. Consider the case illustrated in Figure 2.8.

In this campaign we called active customers who had been receiving monthly shipments and offered them an intro shipment for another similar video continuity program. Customers were to receive the first title in the series for a 30-day examination. Two price points were tested for the intro shipment: "Free" with $3.95 for shipping and handling, and $.95 plus $3.95 for shipping and handling. Some of the customers were also selected to receive several additional premiums that were to be sent with the second shipment (i.e., to those customers that kept and paid for the intro shipment). In all instances the cost of future shipments was $19.95 per video.

Names with Phone Numbers	18,275
List Source	File of Active Customers
Orders	4,498
Response %	**29.2%**
Free + S/H	25.2%
$0.95 + S/H	22.7%
Upsell/Alternates	5.2%

Figure 2.8 Video Continuity Cross-Sell to Existing Customers of Another Series

A 29 percent conversion for a cross-sell promotion is an excellent response, even with an offer as irresistible as the video campaign in Figure 2.8. The normal response range for this kind of promotion is 15 percent to 20 percent. This is a classic situation in which the customers were totally thrilled with their last purchase. In fact, many of them claimed that they did not normally take telemarketing calls, but as we were calling on behalf of *this client* they would be happy to listen to our offer.

In Figure 2.9 we take a look at another situation where the product did *not* quite fulfill the promise.

The day-care market has always been a prime educational target for DialAmerica's clients. It's not at all unusual to see response rates of more than 20 percent, which usually results in relatively low order-acquisition costs.

Given the fact that books are a high-margin product, this should have been a very profitable promotion as long as the returns were less than 50 percent of the total shipped. Unfortunately, that did not turn out to be the case. There were far fewer "critically acclaimed" and "award-winning" books in the assortment than we had led customers to expect. The product that was shipped simply didn't fulfill the promise. It failed to pass the price/value judgment. Returns soared to nearly 90 percent.

In this campaign we called day-care center directors that were current customers with another division of the client's company and offered them a 25-book bulk shipment for a 20-day risk-free examination. The cost was $199.75 ($7.99 per book), which represented 35 percent to 50 percent discount off the jacket price. These were library-bound books purchased on the remainder market. Many were touted as critically acclaimed award winners. The client paid the shipping and handling charges both ways. The customers could pick and choose the books they would like to keep and pay for, and return the balance at the client's expense.

Names with Phone Numbers	5,475
List Source	House Customer File
Orders	1,050
Response %	24.1%

Figure 2.9 Day-Care Center Market for Children's Books

The campaign was a failure. Worst of all, the client wound up damaging its reputation for delivering quality products to this otherwise lucrative market. One of the prime responsibilities of a client in a client/agency relationship is to review the scripts properly to ensure that both the product and the offer are fairly and accurately represented to the customer. If you lead the scriptwriters to believe that your product is better than it really is, you are only setting yourself up for a disappointing back-end failure.

Professionally Trained and Managed Sales Force

We will be covering the issue of training in greater depth in chapters 4 and 5. However, the point we would like to make here is that quality training, motivation, and careful overseeing on the part of management are vital to the success of any outbound telemarketing promotion. Within this context we would like to share with you two final cases (Figures 2.10 and 2.11) that illustrate what can be accomplished when you put all of the components together in one well-planned and expertly executed campaign.

The program described in Figure 2.10 was a great success, on both the front end and the back end. It did, however, require considerable training and management attention. The product itself was complex, and the offer required us to secure a credit card number for every order. As we will discuss in greater detail later on, this is not an easy task. Fortunately, the client helped out with the initial training and product demonstration. Representatives were also on hand to make early script changes in those areas where the content was difficult to deliver and/or not well understood by customers. This allowed us to accelerate the learning curve and achieve our benchmark targets much earlier than would have been possible with a less extensive training process.

We also found that the best management strategy for a complex program such as this was to isolate the program in telecenters that had no other competing programs to divert the attention and loyalty of the staff. Fortunately, the call volume was sufficient to allow us that luxury.

Figure 2.11 offers another example of a successful campaign that benefited from a focused training and management strategy.

In this campaign we called both businesses and consumers who had purchased a software package within the past two years, and offered the latest upgrade on a 30-day trial. This was a highly technical product that required a good deal of explanation as to all of the new features and benefits. Credit card information was secured during the call. After the trial period the customer's account was charged. The software was available on disk or CD in both a standard and a deluxe version. We were also able to upsell and cross-sell several additional products. The price points ranged from $24.99 to $149.99. The average order was $69.75. An inexpensive software program was used as a premium with orders for the deluxe versions. Our call was preceded by multiple mail efforts and a large number of respondents indicated that they had already bought the upgrade.

Names with Phone Numbers	346,000
Orders	26,105
Revenue	$1,821,000
Total Leads Used	260,500
Response %	10%

Figure 2.10 Computer Software Upgrade to House Lists

The campaign described in Figure 2.11 generated more than $2.5 million in revenue, and the order-acquisition cost was less than $600,000. Focused management and a dedicated sales staff were again at the heart of our operational success. We were able to place this program in a telecenter that had become a specialist in selling children's book continuity programs. The reps were already experts at making these types of offers; therefore, the learning curve was nonexistent.

Whenever possible try to place your outbound telemarketing programs with a telecenter that has had previous experience and success with the type of program you are working on. You are always better off if your program is the dominant, or better yet, the *only*, program in the telecenter. Not only will the sales efficiency get better, but the quality of the orders should improve.

In this campaign we called outside lists of parents with children between 8 and 12 years old. We offered them an introductory package from a softcover continuity that contained several premiums including a newsletter, wall poster, and stickers plus several books for a 14-day preview. The books cost $2.95 each plus shipping and handling. If the customer purchased the first set of books, he/she would receive additional four-book shipments about every five weeks. There was no minimum number of books to buy.

Names with Phone Numbers	790,000
Orders	68,100
Total Leads Used	425,500
Response %	16%

Figure 2.11 Children's Softcover Continuity Sold to Targeted Outside Lists

In conclusion, please keep this thought in mind. Successful telemarketing requires a comprehensive testing program that includes offers, prices, premiums, lists, scripts, and more. In many cases, it requires every bit as much imagination and creativity to be successful with telemarketing as it does with media and direct-mail offers.

Summary

- A highly targeted list is the single most important leverage point for success. If the list isn't right, it won't matter how well you do with the rest of the marketing plan.
- The biggest mistake you can make is failing to properly segment and code your lists in advance of calling. Remember, with outbound telemarketing, if one or more of the list segments aren't working, you can pull them out and dramatically improve your results. If all of the leads are mixed together in one big group, your only option may be to pull the plug on the entire campaign.

- An irresistible offer is generally considered to be the next most important key to success. Having an unconditional satisfaction guarantee is mandatory if you are selling over the phone with outbound telemarketing. The customer will always perceive some risk in saying "yes" on an outbound call. The classic solution to a customer's perception of risk is to employ a risk-free offer.

- A poorly executed fulfillment scheme will kill the profitability of any campaign. There is a definite relationship between the promptness of delivery and percentage of payment. Do everything you can to get the product into the customer's hands in the shortest time possible.

- An efficient billing and collections process is equally important to maintaining a profitable back end. We recommend at least eight efforts coupled with a slow-pay phone call.

- Be sure to notify your inbound customer service center whenever you are running an outbound campaign.

- At the heart of every successful direct marketing campaign is a quality product or service. Ultimately, the product must fulfill the promise made in the offer and exceed the expectations of the customer.

- When it comes to telemarketing, training is an investment in enhanced productivity, not an expense to be managed. The more effort you put into training your telephone sales reps (TSRs), the more money you will make.

3

Designing a <u>Successful</u> Telemarketing Test Plan

Chapter 2 discussed how five essential keys provide the framework for achieving success at outbound telemarketing. We will now put those tools into practice as we discuss the requirements of a good telemarketing test plan.

Fitting Telemarketing into an Overall Direct Marketing Strategy

Most often telemarketing is simply one component of a comprehensive marketing strategy that includes direct mail, E-mail, direct-response television (DRTV)/radio, space advertising, free-standing inserts (FSIs), package inserts, co-ops, coupons, catalogs, and retail distribution.

So the obvious questions become

How do I fit it in with all my other customer-contact plans?
What impact will it have on my retail sales channel?
What will be the effect of an outbound phone call on my other media?
Will it *cannibalize* my mail response?
How should I time my various efforts to maximize my results?
What is the right frequency for successive telemarketing efforts?
Are there any seasonality issues?

Will telemarketing add a synergy that actually lifts the response to my other efforts so that the whole becomes greater than the sum of the parts?

These are important questions, and the answers often require a good deal of testing. Circumstances can change over time. What has worked in the past may not continue to work in the future. The point here is that you will need to be disciplined in your continued testing to make sure that your overall strategy is still yielding the desired results.

So, let's take a closer look at the questions.

How Do I Fit Outbound Telemarketing in with All My Other Customer Contact Plans?

This question relates primarily to direct mail, as both outbound telemarketing and direct mail typically utilize the same list universe. It becomes more an issue of time and resource allocation when you are planning to fit your outbound telemarketing campaign in with media such as DRTV, space advertising, and FSIs.

Of course outbound telemarketing will certainly benefit from any positive brand awareness you can build. Because on a phone call there are no pictures and there are limits on the number of words devoted to description of the product's benefits, positive brand recognition can make a big difference in response. In the ideal world, a variety of broad-based media plans are in place concurrently with the telemarketing campaign.

The most important thing to remember is that telemarketing is a completely different channel from any of your other media. We have proved time and again that some people like to buy by mail and others by phone.

What Impact Can I Expect to Have on My Retail Sales Channel?

Retailers and channel sales reps are always nervous about direct marketing. Their argument is that every customer who buys direct means one less customer that bought at retail.

We believe that these fears are generally unfounded. We've seen studies that show that retail sales can jump dramatically, by as much as 100 percent, in the weeks following a large direct mail campaign. In fact, many experts now believe that whatever the direct mail response rate is, another 50 percent to 100 percent of that number will buy through retail. We believe that telemarketing has the same effect. While it can be difficult to isolate the impact of direct marketing on retail sales from other factors (seasonality, price, and other promotional activity), we've seen no real evidence that telemarketing does, in fact, cannibalize retail channel sales.

What Will Be the Impact of an Outbound Phone Call on My Other Media? Will It Cannibalize My Mail Response?

This is a familiar refrain. One obvious solution is to wait until the mail response has peaked and then start the telemarketing program to the nonrespondents.

Over the years, we have done a number of tests wherein we have split the universe of names into three equal parts and tested mail-only versus phone-only versus mail-followed-by-phone. The results have shown that phone-only is a consistent winner on the front end of telemarketing response over mail-followed-by-phone, though there are exceptions. This is not surprising. What is interesting is that the spread between the two usually is larger than what could be achieved by simply adding the direct mail response to the telemarketing response. Even more interesting is the fact that the mail-only segment always seems to finish last when measured by total profitability of the promotion.

How Should I Time My Various Efforts to Maximize My Results?

We've just mentioned that waiting for the mail response to peak before starting your phone calls will eliminate the cannibalization concern. But what about timing the calls to start right as the mail is hitting the recipient's desk? There is no absolute answer to this. Your own testing will show what works best. However, our general guideline would be to keep each of your efforts—phone and mail—isolated into its own exclusive timing window.

Telemarketing Trade Secret:
Never Mention the Mailpiece on the Phone

Only bad things can happen here. Responses will typically include "Send me another," "I saw it and threw it away," "It's on my desk somewhere," "If I want it I'll mail it in . . ." The power of telemarketing is that you get an instant yes or no. Mentioning the mailpiece kills that potential.

Please note that there are two different sets of efficiency issues to consider when planning for the timing of mail drops versus phone calls. There are real cost advantages to dropping your mail in large batches. However, outbound telemarketing occurs one call at a time, and you can sometimes achieve better results if you allow some time to pass from the receipt of the mail before you start your calling. One good approach might be to do two or three large seasonal mailings four to six months apart. You can then start your calls four weeks after the mail drops, and pace your call volume in such a way that it will run uninterrupted until you are ready to call the next group of mail follow-up names.

What Is the Right Frequency to Use for Spacing Out Successive Telemarketing Efforts?

The answer here is directly connected to how frequently your lists are regenerating themselves with new names. The absolute minimum frequency for calling the same person back with the same or similar offer is 90 days. Most agencies have a 90-day suppression program in place that will not allow you to call the same phone number for two different programs from the same company more frequently than 90 days apart. A better plan would be to space out your calls to the same lists by 120 days. This is known in the industry as the 120-day rule, and it usually works well for most programs.

However, even 120 days may prove too aggressive if you are calling your own house file, especially if the offer is essentially the same. In this case we would recommend that you space the calls 150 days apart. This means you will still be able to contact your customers approximately two and a half times per year. All too often we have seen the damage that can be done when the calling schedule becomes overly aggressive, especially with house files.

Are There Any Seasonality Issues to Consider with Outbound Telemarketing?

Outbound telemarketing generally does not have the same seasonal response swings that we see in direct mail, particularly in the consumer market. You can drop your mail according to your best seasonal drop dates, and fill in with outbound telemarketing throughout the balance of the year. People often ask if telemarketing contact rates go down in the summer because so many people schedule vacations during that time. The answer is no, and the reason is that our high-speed predictive dialers allow us to maintain contact even when a smaller percentage of dialed attempts result in a live contact. Of course we do not recommend doing any consumer calling on certain national and religious holidays such as Christmas and New Year's Day. However, we have always had very good success calling during the weeks before and after Christmas. In fact, we've had a lot of success calling on Memorial Day because so many people have the day off work.

Be ready to suspend calling during a national emergency, a time when your customers will not doubt be focused on fast-breaking news events. We suspended calling temporarily during the Gulf War. We've also pulled certain area codes out of the lead inventory when their represented areas have been struck by natural disasters such as hurricanes.

Business-to-business telemarketing is generally the same as consumer calling with regard to the lack of seasonality issues. However, you do need to understand your specific market. There are certain industries that all go out on vacation at the same time because of national labor contracts. It is usually a good idea to suspend calling if there is a big industrywide trade show that will have all of the decison-makers out of the office for several days or a week.

Will Telemarketing Add a Synergy that Actually Lifts the Response to My Other Efforts?

From the standpoint of putting an outbound telemarketing test plan together, we certainly wouldn't recommend that you count on it to make the numbers work. It's very hard to sort out the influence of one media on all the rest, and it will take a good deal of testing to determine the answer.

The balance of this chapter will be devoted to a comprehensive discussion of what is involved in putting together a successful test plan.

Selecting Lists and Achieving Telemarketing Clearance

Outbound telemarketing, like so many of the other direct-response media, always seems to start with list planning. The right place to start is with your own house file, particularly if you are already using it for direct mail or E-mail campaigns.

Using Your House File

The major advantages to using your house file are that there are no additional list rental charges to contend with and the data should be readily available. If you have a direct mail campaign in process, you can simply do a merge-purge to eliminate the responders, and send the remaining names to your call center for a follow-up phone call. Be sure to segment the names and key code them just as you would for your mail campaign. One of the advantages of telemarketing is that you can suspend calling on the unproductive segments and continue with the rest. Of course, this is only possible if you have done a good job of segmentation prior to the start of the campaign.

What to Do If the Data in Your House File Is Incomplete

This can be a problem. However, it doesn't have to be a program killer. Unfortunately, many house-file databases, if they have never been used for outbound telemarketing, lack phone numbers. Fortunately, phone numbers can be appended into the records either by an outside service bureau at a cost of a few cents per name or by your telemarketing agency (DialAmerica provides this service free of charge). However, keep in mind that the match rate is usually only 50 percent, so your callable list will shrink by half.

A larger problem would be if the name and address data are inaccurate or incomplete, or if you have portions of the list that haven't been updated in the last two years. A solution here might be to send the names to one of the large database-management service bureaus that can do a NCOA (national change of address) update. Again, your list may shrink dramatically, but you will save a lot of money by avoiding calls to out-of-date names.

One house-file list source that you should be particularly careful with is electronic "retail" registration names. There are two problems here. The first is that these are not direct-sold buyers. Keep in mind that some people prefer to buy direct and others at retail. Consider the case described in Figure 3.1.

As you can see, the response percentage (Orders Divided by Total Leads Used) for the direct-sold list source was 22 percent higher than the retail source—12.6 percent versus 10.3 percent.

In this campaign we called customers who had purchased a computer software product either direct from the publisher, or through a retail outlet, within the past two years. We offered them the latest upgrade on a 30-day trial.

Orders	20,190
Total Leads Used	183,550
Total Response %	11.0%
Orders from Direct List	7,065
Response % from Direct List	12.6%
Orders from Retail List	13,125
Response % from Retail List	10.3%

Figure 3.1 Computer Software Upgrade to House Lists

In this campaign we called customers who had electronically registered a computer software product with the publisher as a function of installing that product on a newly purchased computer. We offered the customers the latest upgrade on a 30-day trial. Customers were given the option of securing the order with a credit card or paying for it COD.

Orders	49
Orders via Credit Card	41
Orders via COD	8
Total Leads Used	2,075
Total Response %	2.4%
Not Interested	12%
Other Refusal Reasons	15%
Ineligibles	11%
Disconnected Phones	27%
Wrong Numbers	32%
Total Bad Records	70%

Figure 3.2 Computer Software Upgrade to Original Equipment Manufacturers (OEM) Buyers

The second problem with electronic registration names is that the quality of the data can be very poor. There can be a natural inclination for some customers to be a little careless and sloppy in filling out these types of forms. Consider the case described in Figure 3.2, where we had to pull the project after the first day, because the telephone problems and ineligibles were eating us alive. The conversion goal was set at 15 percent, and we were stuck at 2.4 percent.

What a disaster! Seventy percent of the universe was either a telephone problem or an ineligible. This was clearly a case of bad data in the house-file database. Up to this point, the client had no idea why its direct mail wasn't getting better results.

Using Outside Lists

Many direct marketers never even try to use outside lists with outbound telemarketing. They tell themselves that cold-calling to outside lists will never work. This is a big mistake. If you are already using outside lists for direct mail, you should always try to test them for outbound telemarketing.

Another frequently heard complaint about outside lists is that the list brokers have instructions from many of the list owners not to release the names for telemarketing. Unfortunately, this is true a good deal of the time. However, it is not necessarily a dead end. The key here is to keep in mind that there may be an opportunity to swap some of your names for some of the names on the list you want. The other list owner might be just as interested in getting access to your list as you are to his. A good way to approach this is simply to propose a small 5,000-name trade as a test. If the answer is still no, perhaps the owner would be willing to swap inactives or expireds. There should be a lot less concern with that type of trade than there would be for a deal involving hot-line or active customer names.

If all of this fails, you might try to elicit the assistance of a third party, such as your telemarketing agency. Very often the reason that list owners don't want to release their names for telemarketing is that they fear the list will be abused, and consequently its value will be diminished. However, if the list you are interested in is already being called by a trusted agency who will also be handling your test, the owner should have confidence that the agency's TSRs will do a good job, and that the integrity of the list will be protected. There have been many times when DialAmerica has been able to intercede with one of its clients on behalf of another to make available a list for outbound telemarketing, where the list broker originally refused. We've even had cases where we not only got access to the names, but also received permission to mention the list owner's name in the script, and thereby present an endorsed offer. That's a real plus. An endorsement from the list owner can increase response dramatically.

The final step in selecting lists for your outbound telemarketing promotion is to look for synergy between the previous purchase history and the products you would like to offer next.

Product Analysis

Now that you have a handle on which lists will be available, you can turn your attention to the issue of which products to offer. The sequencing of this process is somewhat counterintuitive, since most direct marketers start with a budget goal for a particular product and then move on to the list-selection issue. What we are suggesting here is just the reverse. Start with the lists first. The point is that it is much better to be a customer-centered company, than a product-centered company. In an ideal world you would look at your customers' needs first, and then seek out the perfect product to offer.

Now, all of that having been said, we understand that budgets are budgets and that sometimes you just have to make your numbers on a certain product because of inventory realities, royalty commitments, or pressure from above.

Regardless of how you go about matching lists to your primary offer, the job does not stop there. Unlike direct mail, outbound telemarketing provides live communication between a sales rep and a customer, and that provides for the opportunity to upsell and offer alternates. It is very important that you do everything you can to expand the selling opportunities as much as possible. Very often this can make all the difference between success and failure. Consider the case study described in Figure 3.3.

Upselling usually is considered the name-of-the-game in inbound telemarketing. It is equally important on the outbound side. The difference between success and failure in an outbound telemarketing campaign will often rest on your ability to build the average order value with creative upselling (particularly in one-shot promotions). This is true in both the business and consumer markets.

As you can see from Figure 3.3, a large percentage of the revenue can be generated by upselling additional products after the customer says yes to the primary offer. Tracking the percentage of upsells generated is one good way to measure the performance of your inbound and/or outbound telemarketing operations.

We recommend that you work to expand your upselling opportunities whenever possible. One exception to this would be when you are selling in a club or continuity format. There can sometimes be a problem with higher returns on the intro shipment, when you sell more than one continuity to the same customer at the same time. We suspect that the reason for this is that the low introductory cost advantage is elimi-

In this campaign we called businesses and government organizations and offered them a 30-day free trial of a new computer software product. The primary product was priced at $279.00. Customers who said yes to the primary offer were offered an upsell of a second software product at a discounted price of $79; the regular price was $199.00. A full working version of the product was delivered with an invoice in the package.

Total Customer Orders	3,037
Primary Software only	1,085
2-Product Upsell Bundle	**1,823**
Downsell Alternate only	129
Total Leads Used	23,361
Total Response	**13%**
% of Upsells	**60%**

Figure 3.3 "Upselling" to Customers Who Accept the Primary Offer: Business Computer Software to Outside Lists

nated when you bill for two intro packages simultaneously. Given the importance of maximizing "pay and stay" on the intro of a continuity, you certainly don't want to do anything to jeopardize that situation.

Another exception would be when the price of the primary product is at the upper end of either the customer's ability to pay or your ability to carry them on an open line of credit.

Now let's take a look at Figure 3.4, a case study that shows the importance of building alternate selling opportunities into your plan.

This project would never have worked without the opportunity to sell an alternate offer. There was a large segment of the list that was not a viable target for the primary offer. In this instance, most of the prospects were using a different computer operating system from the one that the book featured in the offer discussed. Whenever you are putting together a telemarketing promotion, you should always try to include one or two alternates that would appeal to someone for whom the primary offer isn't relevant.

In this campaign we called a house list of mechanical engineering customers who had purchased computer programming books in the past, and offered them a 30-day preview of a new book on X. There was an alternate offer for a new book on Y for customers who were not using X. The price of the X book was $79.95, and the Y book was $49.95. More than 90 percent of the orders were for the alternate offer. An engineering pocket guide was used as a premium.

Orders	525
Primary Offer for Book X	50
Alternate Offer for Book Y	**475**
Total Leads Used	2,030
Response %	**25.9%**

Figure 3.4 One-Shot to Computer Programming Professionals at Home

Pricing Analysis and Testing

One of the interesting things about outbound telemarketing is that it does not seem to have the same sensitivity to price that direct mail has, at least not on the front end (during the phone call). This is owing to the fact that the customer only *hears* the number rather than seeing it in print. Now, don't get us wrong; we are not saying that you won't see a difference in front-end telemarketing response if you increase your price point. What we are saying is that the spread will probably not be as great as what you would see with the same price test in the mail. Moreover, price will still play a big part in the ultimate purchase decision (the back end) once the customer has the product and the invoice in hand.

Consider Figure 3.5.

As you can see, price was not nearly as big a factor as the list in determining the response percentage. Figure 3.6 shows another case where there was an even larger spread in the price, but the front-end results were surprisingly close.

The price spread between A and B was $60, a 70 percent increase. Yet the response rate was only 1.9 percent lower, an 8 percent difference. Even in C, where the price was $208 higher, a 240 percent increase over

In this campaign we called both house lists and outside lists of parents of children under the age of six and offered them a 14-day examination of an educational product containing 10 softcover storybooks and five matching audiocassette tapes. We tested two price points, $29.95 and $24.95

Orders	1,068
Total Response %	12.3%
House Lists	19.9%
Outside Lists	6.4%
$24.95 Offer	12.7%
$29.95 Offer	12.3%

Figure 3.5 Children's Book and Audio Cassettetape Set Sold to Parents at Home

In this campaign we called safety managers and offered them a 10-day preview of a safety training video. We tested three price points; $84.95, $144.95, and $292.95.

Orders	**982**
A. $84.95	534
B. $144.95	264
C. $292.95	184
Response %	**22.2%**
A. $84.95	24.5%
B. $144.95	22.6%
C. $292.95	17.1%

Figure 3.6 Training Video Sold to Industrial Safety Managers

A, the response rate only fell 7.4 percent, a 30 percent difference. Of course, it is generally true that businesses are usually less price sensitive than consumers. However, this doesn't tell the entire story. It turned out that cell A was the only one that actually turned a profit. Almost everyone in C returned the product because they thought it was overpriced.

This very interesting case illustrates the danger of making decisions strictly on the front-end response. If the client had immediately rolled out with one of the higher prices in B or C, it would have been a disaster. Always keep in mind that the customer will be making the final purchase decision once the product is received. If your product fails to meet your customer's price-value judgment, you will get it back as a return.

Finding the Sweet Spot

We believe that price is one variable that should always be tested when using outbound telemarketing. This is the only way you will be able to determine the pricing sweet spot for your particular products. However, here are some general guidelines.

- Consumer one-shots usually need to be over $25 to work with outbound telemarketing at all. Response usually falls dramatically once you get over $50 ($29.95 + S/H is a sweet spot).
- Business one-shots usually need to be over $50 to work on the phones at all, and have a top-end at about $500 under most circumstances if you want the customer to give you an order on the first call. When you get above $500, you will probably need a multistep process, perhaps involving a face-to-face sales meeting ($99.95 + S/H is a sweet spot).
- Consumer ship-till-forbid continuities work great when the intro price is under $15 ($7.95 + S/H is a sweet spot) and ongoing shipments (10 to 12 per year) are under $20 ($14.95 + S/H is a sweet spot).
- Business ship-till-forbid continuities work great when the intro price is between $75 and $250 ($149.95 + S/H is a sweet spot) and ongoing shipments (4 to 6 per year) are under $75 ($49.95 + S/H is a sweet spot).
- Reinstates for business and consumer negative option clubs usually need low welcome-back price points under $10 for the first shipment ($1.95 + S/H is a sweet spot).
- Reinstates for ship-till-forbid continuities work well at full price as long as you include a premium such as a free unit of the product (one unit free plus one unit at full price is a sweet spot).

The Offer

Offering a free trial or a risk-free preview with an unconditional satisfaction guarantee is considered an absolute requirement for most outbound telemarketing sales campaigns, particularly when you are dealing with outside lists. This is known as a soft offer. Most reasonable people who receive an offer via an outbound call will have legitimate concerns about whether the product is truly as good as it sounds over the phone. They will wonder if it is really worth the price, and if they will actually find a use for it. The classic marketing response to a perceived risk on the part of the buyer is to develop a risk-free offer.

Free trials are not nearly as pervasive in inbound 800 campaigns (although they are used frequently), because customers will have been exposed to a full sales and marketing message, usually complete with photos and extensive copy before they are asked to pick up the phone and place an order. More often than not, a credible satisfaction guarantee is more important than a free trial on an inbound telemarketing call.

We will examine the basic offer types (one-shots, continuities, subscriptions, etc.) in considerable detail in chapter 9; however, we would like to define to some extent the basics required for a *successful* offer.

The offer described in Figure 3.7 was a great one. It featured an excellent product that would have a lot of value for most people teaching children in a day-care setting. It was offered at a reasonable cost, payable in easy installments. It was presented on a risk-free 30-day examination basis and even included a valuable—but low-cost—premium.

But, believe it or not, one of the biggest reasons that this program worked as well as it did was because it included an *alternate* offer. You are probably wondering, "how could an alternate offer that only pulled in six-tenths of 1 percent of response be all that big a deal, when the primary offer pulled 18.7 percent?" Well, that 0.6 percent equaled 235 orders and $90,000 worth of revenue!

Now let's take a look at an offer that didn't work.

This offer in Figure 3.8 had lots of problems, starting with the fact that $300 is a lot of money to pay for a 20-minute video with no other supporting materials. However, the real problem was that we were asking the customer to pay $40 just to preview the product.

In this campaign we called both house and outside lists of day-care, preschool, and Head Start centers, and offered them a one-shot shipment of an instructional activity program on a 20-day risk-free examination basis. The total cost was $395. The customers were billed in either 5 or 10 installments and received an interactive game as a premium. There was an alternate offer for another product that also included reproducible worksheets and a teacher's guide.

Orders	7,506
Response %	
Primary Offer	18.7%
Alternate Offer	0.6%
Total Response	19.3%

Figure 3.7 Day-Care Center Market for Supplementary Teaching Materials

In this campaign we called an outside list of accounting department managers and offered them two employee training videos. The videos were offered on a paid-preview basis ($40 for one or $49 for both). The purchase price was $299 for each video and $499 for both. The client planned to conduct follow-up calls using an in-house sales force to negotiate the final sale.

Orders—Paid Previews	12
Total Leads Used	1,100
Response %	1.1%

Figure 3.8 Finance Training Video

After several days of poor results we added an alternate offer, which permitted us to send out the videos on a no-charge basis for a 10-day examination, if customers said that they were not permitted to preview on a paid-preview basis. This helped a little, but it wasn't enough to make a difference. Perhaps a premium might have helped, but the client didn't want to do it. It's our understanding that none of the previews turned into a full purchase. The lesson here is that most customers are not going to accept a hard offer, sight-unseen, over the phone from a company that they have never heard of before and have never done business with.

In this campaign we called a house list of active continuity club members and offered them a book for a 30-day examination. We tested two offers, a discounted price, $22.99, versus full price, $29.99, with a second softcover book for a premium.

Orders	**8,865**
Discount Price	3,625
Full Price with Premium	5,240
Response %	**39.3%**
Discount Price	31.4%
Full Price With Premium	46.9%

Figure 3.9 One-Shot Offer to Continuity Club Members

Discount Versus Premium

We really like premiums when it comes to outbound telemarketing, because they can be used in so many ways. They help gain the customer's attention. They help close the sale. They help change customers' minds when their initial reaction is no. And best of all, they add value to the transaction when the customer is making the final purchase decision after receiving the product. But what happens when you actually test discount versus premiums on the phone? Consider the the case shown in Figure 3.9.

Yes, those numbers are for real! We got 39 percent response (orders divided by total leads used). But the real story here is the fact that selling at full price with an inexpensive premium beat the discount offer by a wide margin. That premium definitely cost less than the $7 we were giving away as a discount. Premiums always beat discounts.

Terms and Conditions

We've made the point that an unconditional satisfaction guarantee, positioned as either a free trial or a risk-free preview, is essential for success in any outbound telemarketing campaign. Most companies already offer their customers some sort of product or service guarantee, and our experience is that outbound telemarketing can usually work with whatever you already have in place.

Therefore, the only real question becomes, how long should we let the customer have to preview the product to make the final purchase decision—10 days, 15 days, 30 days, or longer? The answer here is that it depends upon how long you believe the customer will need to fairly examine the product and make a positive purchase decision. If your preview period is too short, you will force your customer to return the product without even trying it out. If it's too long, your customer may realize that they are not using it sufficiently to warrant the cost. We believe that, under most circumstances, 15 to 30 days is just about right.

Now, let's take a look at some of the other issues relating to the terms and conditions needed for a successful outbound telemarketing test plan.

Certainly, one of the biggest decisions you will have to make is whether or not to take the orders on a bill-me basis, or whether you will require your customers to secure the orders with a credit card in advance.

Let's take a look at Figure 3.10, a case study for an outbound telemarketing project that never would have worked without a bill-me option.

Securing an order with a credit card is always a challenge on an outbound telemarketing call. The issue, of course, centers on the fact that many people are afraid to surrender their credit card numbers over the phone to a person they have never spoken to before, especially when they have not initiated the call. This is not the case with an inbound 800 call, since the customer is responding to an advertisement with an expectation to place an order and often approaches the call with credit card in hand.

If you were calling a house list, where the customer had a preexisting business relationship with your company, it would not be unusual for 70 percent or more of the customers who said yes to the offer to change their mind when you asked them for their credit card number over the phone. In the example in Figure 3.10, 90 percent balked when we asked for their credit card number. With calls to outside lists, this credit card refusal rate can jump to 99 percent.

One of the most successful strategies for dealing with this problem involves taking advantage of the previous purchase payment data. It works like this: If the customer has previously made a direct purchase and there is a record of the previously used credit card number and expi-

In this campaign we called existing customers and offered them a newly released computer software product as the primary offer. A second product was used as an alternate offer and as an upsell. The price of the primary product was $54.75, and the price for the upsell/alternate was $19.75. An older software product was used as a premium to encourage customers to secure the order with a credit card. Customers who declined to use a credit card were offered a bill-me option but would not receive the premium.

Customers Sold	**2,544**
Bill-Me %	90%
Credit Card %	10%
Total Leads Used	**21,200**
Response %	12%

Figure 3.10 Bill-Me Offers Versus Credit Card Secured

ration date in your database, you can send the last six or eight digits (only) of the card number along with the expiration date through to the rep terminal. Once the customer says yes to the offer, the sales rep suggests that the customer can use the same card as last time. ("We just need to verify the last six/eight digits of the card number to make sure it's the same one and to update the expiration date.") The customer is not asked to read the full number out over the phone, and the sales rep has no access to the complete card number. The balance of the number is then appended into the record after the sale either by the telecenter's mainframe computer or the fulfillment house. In either case the full security of the credit card number is maintained.

There have been numerous instances where this approach has been able to cut the 70 percent to 90 percent order loss down to a much more manageable (and profitable) 10 percent or 20 percent. A bill-me option is absolutely essential if you are using outbound telemarketing to call outside lists. Figure 3.11 shows a case in point.

What a difference a simple thing like having the credit card number on file can make! Be sure to keep all that data from your previous purchase history.

In this campaign we called customers at home who had previously purchased a software product. We offered them a 15-day trial of an educational reference product. Some of the records had credit card data on file and we were able to verify the last six digits and post the new purchase to the previously used card. Customers refusing to use a credit card were offered a bill-me option. The offer carried a 15-day satisfaction guarantee for return at full credit. The price points ranged between $29.95 and $49.95.

Total Customers Sold		38,411	
Revenue		$1,150,000	

Names *WITH* Credit Card Info		Names *WITHOUT* Credit Card Info	
Total Sales	7,461	Total Sales	30,950
Bill-Me Sales	1,521	Bill-Me Sales	25,375
Credit Card Sales	5,940	Credit Card Sales	5,575
Response Rate	17.2%	Response Rate	16%
Bill-Me Orders	20%	Bill-Me Orders	82%
Secured with a Credit Card	80%	Secured with a Credit Card	18%

Figure 3.11 Bill-Me/Credit Card Offer (Some with Credit Card on File)

What About Installment Billing? As we mentioned earlier, adding installment billing as a payment option also can have a big impact on overall profitability. We always recommend installment billing for "consumer" programs, whenever the cost of the product exceeds $50. Our experience is that this tactic can lift the initial front-end response by as much as 20 percent. This will also allow you to sell at much higher price points than would otherwise be feasible.

However, this is not the case with business-to-business applications; businesses generally prefer to pay all at once, as long as the cost is a few hundred dollars or less. It actually costs more money to process multiple payments.

Who Should Pay the Return Postage? There is no easy answer here. This question comes up all the time on the phone. It's not a very big issue in business-to-business campaigns, because the postage is relatively small and the company picks up the tab. However, on the consumer side the customer both pays for it and has to deal with the inconvenience of taking the package to the post office to send it back. Furthermore, the offer is no longer risk-free if the customer has to pay money to return an unwanted product. In terms of crafting an irresistible offer, paying for the return postage is definitely a plus. However, you will attract more premium bandits if you pay for returns, and as a marketer you don't want to do anything to encourage returns. Paying the return postage can lead to higher front-end response, and lower order-acquisition costs, but it can also lead to higher returns. Clearly, this is an issue that should be decided by testing.

Should We Credit the Customer for the Outbound Shipping and Handling Charges When the Product Is Returned? The answer here should be, and usually is, yes, because of the importance of maintaining the risk-free nature of the offer. However, some companies do require the customer to pay outbound shipping and handling even if they return the product. They feel that a customer who is willing to pay for shipping and handling is a customer who intends to keep the product. However, most companies that have this policy do not rigorously enforce it, since the cost to send out invoices is usually more than it's worth in return. Moreover, they would rather have a happy and satisfied customer who will buy again in the future. If you force customers to pay this charge, that's probably the last money you will see from them.

Direct Mail History Is a Predictor of Telemarketing Response

The next step in the test planning process is to make a reasonable prediction as to what kind of response rate should be expected from the campaign under consideration, thereby setting a goal that can be translated into anticipated orders for the sake of a preliminary profit and loss statement.

One of the best ways to go about this is to consider previous outbound telemarketing history—either your own or your agency's—with similar programs. However, if this is your first experience with outbound telemarketing, and there is no relevant history available, then the thing to do is look at the direct mail history. There should be a direct connection between the phone and the mail response rates. Lists that do above average in the mail should do above average on the phone. As we mentioned in chapter 1, one of the rules of thumb the authors have used over the years is to take the direct mail response and multiply it by a factor of 5 to 10 to make an initial estimate of the telemarketing response rate. This rule of thumb usually works well if the mail response is between 1.0 percent and 2.5 percent. When the numbers are higher or lower than this range the formula usually breaks down. Obviously, if you are getting 8 percent response in the mail, you won't get 80 percent on the phone, but you might get 30 percent. Similarly, when you are only getting 0.2 percent in the mail, you'll probably have a problem on the phones as well—in fact, you may not get any orders at all.

One of our purposes in writing this book is to provide you with a large number of case studies that we hope will help you to find a parallel to your own situation. However, if you don't have either previous telemarketing or mail response experience to use as a predictor, we definitely recommend that you start with a small test and wait for the back-end results before committing to a rollout.

Setting Front-End Test Goals and Making an Initial Prediction

Once you have made a reasonable prediction as to what the telemarketing response rate could be, you are in a position to set a goal for the number of test orders you'll generate.

We always recommend that you start out with a small test. You should look at how many test cells you will have and then decide how many orders you will need in each cell to have statistical significance. From a telemarketing perspective, we often recommend that you start with one thousand orders on a consumer campaign, and a few hundred to a thousand on a business-to-business campaign. This will give your telemarketers enough calling to go up the learning curve and achieve a good level of efficiency by the end of the test. That should also allow them to make a good prediction regarding what it will actually cost to acquire an order in a rollout environment.

In chapter 1, we introduced some of the issues that play into what it might reasonably cost to acquire an order. If you are working with an agency like DialAmerica that uses a performance-based pricing formula, they will simply tell you what they will charge you on a flat-cost-per-order basis for the test. This type of arrangement limits your risks considerably. This is also known as working on a PI basis (PI = per item or per inquiry). You can plug this PI number directly into your trial profit and loss statement, and you are ready to go. One of the major advantages to this pricing strategy is that you will have a fixed rather than variable order-acquisition cost. In fact, your agency will be sharing some of the risk for the test.

If, on the other hand, you're planning to do this test in-house or with an hourly billed agency, you will have a variable order-acquisition cost that is dependent on the daily swings of the contact rate and conversion percentage.

Fundamentally, a good guess will need to be made as to how many orders can be generated for each man-hour spent on the phones. This is usually referred to as sales per hour, or SPH. To calculate the SPH you need to multiply the estimated contact rate or leads used per hour (LUPH) by the estimated conversion percentage. You then divide the full cost to maintain a sales rep on the phones for an hour's time (including supervision, overhead, and everything else) by the SPH to yield the estimated order-acquisition cost. Here are the formulas.

SPH (Sales per Hour) =   estimated Leads Used per Hour (LUPH) × estimated conversion %

TCPH (Total Cost per Hour) =   Either the hourly rate plus all other fees divided by the anticipated number of hours required to complete the test, or the full cost of the telemarketing operation calculated on an hourly basis

OAC (Order Acquisition Cost) = Telemarketing Cost per Hour (TCPH) ÷ Sales per Hour (SPH)

Given the variable nature of hourly rate billing, we highly recommend that you find an agency that will work with you on a PI basis. Then you won't have to bother with any of this math on a per-hour basis. Your only concern will be to maximize the conversion percentage and the number of orders that can be generated from the list universe. Moreover, testing is a lot less risky when you have a fixed order-acquisition cost.

Setting Back-End Test Goals and Making Initial Predictions

We'll say it again: Telemarketing is an inherently risky business. Estimating payments, returns, and bad debt is always the trickiest part of dealing with those risks. In general our experience shows that the returns of phone-sold orders are higher than mail-sold to the same list. However, the percentage of bad debt is often lower. We believe that there are two reasons for this. First, the number of fraudulent orders is usually less on the phone than in the mail, and second the customers know that we have their phone numbers and can always call them if they are delinquent in paying the bill or returning the product.

There are many factors that will influence the back-end payments, returns, and bad debt. The major ones are

List selection

Promptness and efficiency of the fulfillment, billing, and
  collections

Price (the higher the price, the higher the returns)

Quality of the product (is it as good as was promised over the
  phone?)

Nature of the sales support materials included with the shipment
  (welcome letter, brochures, user guide, etc.)

Customer service and product support

Terms and conditions of the offer and level of commitment that
  the customer was asked to acknowledge in agreeing to the
  offer

Level of quality-control standards in place at the point of sale
  (i.e., sales rep supervision, remote monitoring, training,
  scripting, and order-verification procedures)

Here again, if you have some direct mail history to work with, you can probably bump up the mail return rate by 50 percent, reduce the bad debt by 50 percent, and have a reasonable guess. (Example: if mail = 20 percent returns + 10 percent bad debt, then phone = 30 percent returns + 5 percent bad debt.)

Why Are Returns So Much Higher with Outbound Telemarketing Than All Other Media?

Outbound telemarketing has relatively high return rates because the response rates are so much higher to begin with. As you increase the percentage of the market that accepts your offer, you are sweeping up a much larger group of people, some of whom will ultimately discover that they have a lesser need for your product. See Figure 3.12.

If you have no history to work with, you might be able to use the numbers from the tables in Figures 3.13 through 3.17 as a starting point. Please understand that there are many programs where the actual back-end result falls outside of the ranges noted below, particularly for specialized markets.

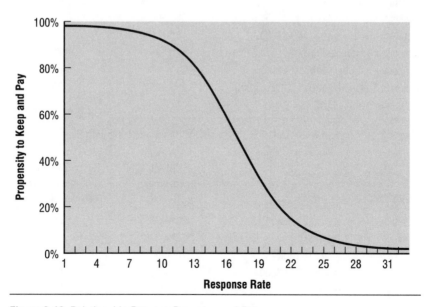

Figure 3.12 Relationship Between Response and Returns

Remember, always do small tests, and don't roll out until you know what is actually going to happen on the back end.

Outside Lists: Bill-Me Orders	Bill-Me Payment Range	Bill-Me Payments Reasonable Guess
Consumer one-shots @ $25 to $50	35%–65%	50%
Consumer one-shots @ $50+	20%–50%	35%
Business one-shots @ $75 to $125	30%–50%	40%
Business one-shots @ $125 to $500	10%–40%	25%
Consumer Continuity Intro @ $10 to $20 Average 3.5 Shipments per Starter	50%–75%	65%
Business Continuity Intro @ $100 to $200 Average 2.5 Shipments per Starter	20%–40%	30%

Figure 3.13 Telemarketing Back-End Estimates for Outside Lists with Bill-Me Offers

House File Lists: Bill-Me Orders	Bill-Me Payment Range	Bill-Me Payments Reasonable Guess
Consumer one-shots @ $25 to $50	45%–65%	55%
Consumer one-shots @ $50+	30%–60%	45%
Business one-shots @ $75 to $125	35%–60%	50%
Business one-shots @ $125 to $500	15%–50%	35%
Consumer Continuity Intro @ $10 to $20 Average 3.5 Shipments per Starter	55%–80%	70%
Business Continuity Intro @ $100 to $200 Average 2.5 Shipments per Starter	25%–45%	35%

Figure 3.14 Telemarketing Back-End Estimates for House File Lists with Bill-Me Offers

Credit Card Secured Orders	Bill-Me Payment Range	Bill-Me Payments Reasonable Guess
Consumer one-shots @ $25 to $50	80%–95%	90%
Consumer one-shots @ $50+	70%–90%	80%
Business one-shots @ $75 to $125	70%–95%	85%
Business one-shots @ $125 to $500	50%–80%	65%
Nobody Joins Continuities on a Credit Card Secured Basis		

Figure 3.15 Telemarketing Back-End Estimates House File and Outside Lists with Credit Card Secured Offers

If Your Selling Price Is	Reasonable Guess Payments	Reasonable Guess Returns	Reasonable Guess Bad Debt
Much lower than average	70%	25%	5%
Lower than average	60%	30%	10%
About average	50%	40%	10%
Higher than average	30%	60%	10%
Much higher than average	20%	75%	5%

Figure 3.16 Telemarketing Back-End Estimates for Bill-Me Offers

If Your Selling Price Is	Reasonable Guess Payments	Reasonable Guess Returns	Reasonable Guess Bad Debt
Much lower than average	95%	5%	0%
Lower than average	90%	10%	0%
About average	85%	15%	0%
Higher than average	80%	20%	0%
Much higher than average	75%	25%	0%

Figure 3.17 Telemarketing Back-End Estimates for Credit Card Secured Offers

Figures 3.13, 3.14, and 3.15 show estimated back-end payments for a variety of program types. The implication is that the balance of the orders are a combination of returns and bad debt, returns being two-thirds to three-quarters of the difference, and bad debt being the rest.

If you really have no clue as to what to expect on the back end, Figures 3.16 and 3.17 offer two other generalized rule-of-thumb tables based on selling price that you can use as a prediction of payments, returns, and bad debt.

Creating the Trial Profit and Loss Statement

Creating a trial profit and loss statement (P&L) for a telemarketing test is very similar to what you would normally do for a mail test. Consider the following example.

We're going to start with a small 1,000-order test and then wait for the back-end results before making any decisions about additional testing and/or a rollout to the balance of the universe.

We will select the top 10,000 names with phone numbers from our house file to maximize our potential for success. This should be more than enough names to generate 1,000 orders if all the assumptions are correct. We might be able to get by with 7,000 names or less, but we don't want to run out of names in the middle of the test.

The offer will be a basic one-shot cross-sell promotion targeted to consumers at their residential addresses with a 30-day risk-free preview on a bill-me basis. We will add an upsell and several alternates to the promotion to maximize the selling opportunities. The price of the primary-offer product will be $34.95 plus $4.95 shipping and handling. A second product priced at $14.95 will be used as an upsell. We will also have three alternate products priced at $34.95, targeted to other interests, so we should have something to offer just about everyone we speak to regardless of their situation.

Our goal will be to have 20 percent of the customers who place an order for a primary or alternate product also accept the upsell. Therefore, the average order value is expected to be $42.89 ($34.95 plus 20 percent of $14.95 plus $4.95 shipping and handling).

If 20 percent of the customers take the upsell, the average cost of goods shipped will be $10, including an inexpensive premium.

Based on our earlier direct mail testing, and using the rule of 10, we are going to predict that the average telemarketing response rate will turn out to be 20 percent.

We are going to use an agency that works on a performance-based pricing formula rather than an hourly rate. They are proposing to do the 1,000-order test at an $8 PI with no other fees. We will review the results with the agency after the first 1,000 phone calls (approximately day 2 or 3 of the test). If the conversion and all other front-end results are in line with expectations, they will complete the 1,000-order test within three weeks. If something is drastically wrong, they will pull the plug on the calling, and we can try to fix it. If it can't be fixed, our only exposure will be for $8 per order generated to that point.

We are going to be conservative with our back-end assumptions. Our pay-ups are usually good in the mail (80 percent to 90 percent), and our fulfillment company has a well-written eight-effort collection series that is being revised to reference the phone call as the source of the order.

However, all that notwithstanding, we have decided to go with the assumption that 55 percent will pay, 35 percent will return, and 10 percent will turn into bad debt.

We are not going to make any allowance for the value of the returns being restocked into inventory, since we will have return-processing costs, and we expect this to be a wash item. We are now ready to put it all together into a trial P&L. (See Figure 3.18.)

Our only up-front out-of-pocket expense is the $8,000 telemarketing charge and the $10,000 for cost of goods shipped. We stand to make $5,590 if all our assumptions prove correct, and even more if we do better on the back end than our conservative projection.

What we need to do now is work up some numbers to see what happens if our back-end assumptions aren't correct and figure out where our break-even point is. Fortunately, we are using an agency that works on a performance-based pricing model. So the $8 PI is in the contract as long as the conversions are meeting our expectations. If they aren't, then

Names Supplied	10,000	
Projected Orders	1,000	
Projected Response (Orders/Total Leads Used)	20%	
Projected Total Leads Used (All Resolved Leads)	5,000	
Projected Average Order Value	$42.89	
Total Projected Gross Revenue		$42,890
Telemarketing Order Acquisition Cost @ $8 PI		$8,000
Precost of Goods Contribution		$34,890
Cost of Goods Shipped		−$10,000
Postcost of Goods Contribution		$24,890
Projected Returns/Bad Debt (45%)		−$19,300
Net of Returns Contribution		$5,590
Net of Returns Contribution Per Thousand		$559.00

Figure 3.18 Trial P&L—Proposed Outbound Telemarketing Test

Payment %	Gross Revenue	Post-COG Contribution	Returns & Bad Debt %	Returns & Bad Debt $	Net Contribution
35%	$42,890	$24,890	65%	$27,879	($2,989)
40%	$42,890	$24,890	60%	$25,734	($844)
42%*	**$42,890**	**$24,890**	**58%**	**$24,890**	**$0**
45%	$42,890	$24,890	55%	$23,590	$1,301
50%	$42,890	$24,890	50%	$21,445	$3,445
55%**	**$42,890**	**$24,890**	**45%**	**$19,301**	**$5,590**
60%	$42,890	$24,890	40%	$17,156	$7,734
65%	$42,890	$24,890	35%	$15,012	$9,879
70%	$42,890	$24,890	30%	$12,867	$12,023
75%	$42,890	$24,890	25%	$10,723	$14,168

* Break-even point

** Best guess point

Figure 3.19 Break-Even Analysis

we will have the option either to pull the plug and pay them $8 for each order generated to that point or to renegotiate the PI based on what has actually occurred and continue the calling under the new arrangement. Either way it's our choice. (See Figure 3.19.)

Even at 35 percent payments, which is very unlikely, our loss is under $3,000. We'll get at least that much value in market research information from the refusal analysis alone, plus we'll be able to remote monitor the phone calls and hear what our customers think of us.

It looks like a great idea to test telemarket! It's now time to see the boss.

Assessing the Risks and Selling Management on the Test

Once you have your telemarketing test plan and trial P&L in hand, you are ready to secure the internal support and approvals. The only remaining piece is to prepare a vision statement, which will show what the long-term potential is if your test should prove successful. You should start by outlining the potential benefits of using telemarketing based on the material in chapter 1 of this book. You will also want to make a projection of the sales potential in a rollout to the total universe of names. This number is usually very impressive because of the high response rates and market-penetration opportunities that can be attained with outbound telemarketing.

Be careful in working out your rollout projections. You won't be able to access all your mail lists for telemarketing. Not even all of your house-file names will work on the phone. Don't count any names that are more than two years old. If your lists don't have phone numbers already appended you will only get about a 50 percent match rate with telematch services, and reasonable list penetration goals are 85 percent for consumer calling and 65 percent for business-to-business. (See chapter 8 for a detailed discussion of list-penetration issues.)

We've said it before, and we'll say it again: Telemarketing is a risky business. You should always include a risk-assessment section in your presentation. It is important to make sure everyone knows there are no guarantees of success. There are too many factors in play. However, unlike direct mail testing, your up-front, out-of-pocket, costs are low because you are making the calls one at a time, and you can always pull the program if it's not working. Furthermore, your risk is even less if, as illustrated in the case in the previous section, you are paying for the orders on a performance-based pricing basis. On the other hand, if you are working with an hourly billed agency or an in-house operation, you will have more risk in the nature of a variable order-acquisition cost and possibly some start-up fees.

What If There Is Someone in the Company Who Is Opposed to Telemarketing?

In every company there will be some people who are just plain uncomfortable with outbound telemarketing. Sometimes these people are right at the top of the organization. The best way to overcome this resistance is to point out that you will be starting with a small test only. Everyone with an interest in the test will be able to monitor the calls right from their office, or even from home. If you don't like what you hear, or if there are any complaints, you can easily pull the plug on the whole thing. Show them the trial P&L and the potential rollout projections and point out that if all of this is successful, you will be able to grow the business dramatically.

Which Departments Within the Company Are Likely to Be Most Affected by the Telemarketing Test?

The operations group, warehouse, computer center, finance, and customer service departments are all likely to be affected by your test. Very often there is one person to whom all of these departments report, perhaps a senior vice president of operations. This person will either be a key ally or a determined obstacle. If the latter is the case than you will need to build support from above and below. Making friends with customer service and warehouse managers is an excellent idea.

Remember, it's just a small test. Even if the whole thing bombs, the actual financial risks are very low and the potential financial rewards are great. Most senior managers are going to be excited about a marketing idea with this much potential.

In our next chapter we will take a look at what is involved in "launching" a successful outbound telemarketing test.

Summary

- Telemarketing works best when it is part of a comprehensive marketing plan.
- Outbound telemarketing need not interfere with either direct mail or retail channels. A properly planned and executed campaign will enhance the impact of other media and distribution channels.
- Timing and frequency are very important issues to consider when integrating outbound telemarketing with other media. It is best to give each media its own exclusive window. The exception to this rule is a coordinated multichannel, multimedia campaign, such as a phone-fax-phone-appointment strat-

egy to market a business-to-business high-value product or service.

- The 120-day rule is a good starting point for any customer contact strategy using the same list for multiple outbound telemarketing efforts.
- Outbound telemarketing doesn't exhibit the same seasonality dynamics as direct mail. Except for certain vertical markets such as schools where everyone is out for the summer, it doesn't display any perceptible seasonality.
- Your house file is usually the best place to start when planning for an initial outbound telemarketing test.
- A highly targeted outside list can often work as well as your house file.
- Always include upsell and alternate offer opportunities in outbound telemarketing plans.
- Always test price, but never change your control offer until you have all of the back-end results in hand. Outbound telemarketing isn't nearly as price sensitive as direct mail.
- Always save credit card payment data. You may be able to use it in future outbound telemarketing efforts, thus allowing customers to make credit card purchases without the risk of giving their card numbers over the phone.
- Never start an outbound telemarketing test without doing a comprehensive trial P&L and break-even analysis.
- Always assume that your test will be successful, and be prepared to make a case for a retest and ultimate rollout.

4

Launching a Successful Outbound Telemarketing Test

In chapter 3 we explained how to put together a telemarketing test plan that will both have a high potential for internal approval and also a high possibility for success because it was based on the five essential keys.

In chapter 4 we will examine how these issues come together in the actual launch of a telemarketing test.

The Hardest Part Is Always the List

The very first thing you should do once you have decided to launch an outbound telemarketing test is to order the list. The second thing you should do is put someone in charge of making sure that the names get delivered to your agency or telecenter on time and then hold that person accountable. The third thing you should do is insist on receiving a photocopy of the record layout and a partial dump of the first 50 records so you can check everything for accuracy.

There is no question that simply getting the list into the hands of the telecenter is the slowest part of the start-up process. It is also the area where the most mistakes are made. Therein lies the value of securing a copy of the record layout and partial dump. It's quicker to solve the problem at that point. Don't wait until the telecenter calls you with the news that your list bombed when they tried to load it into their inventory.

In our experience 90 percent of all delays in telemarketing start-ups are caused by lists that are either late in delivery or arrive with the wrong data. This is particularly true for first-time tests, where the database managers are unfamiliar with the specific needs of outbound telemarketing. Very often they simply assume that they can run the same output as they have done in the past for direct mail campaigns.

Whenever you are using a house file, we highly recommend that you do RFM (recency/frequency/monetary value) segmentation, using a table similar to the ones shown in Figures 4.1 and 4.2.

You can carry this a step further by adding a monetary value marker to each of the entries in the table in Figure 4.1, in essence creating a three-dimensional segmentation process, or in a simpler two-dimensional format, as illustrated in Figure 4.2.

By assigning a separate and unique key code (list segment identifier) to each of the entries in the table you will be able to identify the

Last Purchase	1-Time Buyers	2-Time Buyers	3+ Multibuyers
0–6 Months	A1	A2	A3
6–12 Months	B1	B2	B3
12–18 Months	C1	C2	C3
18–24 Months	D1	D2	D3

Figure 4.1 Three-Dimensional RFM Segmentation

Recency/ Frequency	Monetary Value (1) = $1–$50	Monetary Value (2) = $51–$100	Monetary Value (3) = $101+
A1	A11	A12	A13
A2	A21	A22	A23
A3	A31	A32	A33
B1	B11	B12	B13
B2	B21	B22	B23
B3	B31	B32	B33
C1	C11	C12	C13
C2	C21	C22	C23
C3	C31	C32	C33

Figure 4.2 Two-Dimensional RFM Segmentation

most responsive segments. Most often segment A33 (the most recent purchase, 3+ multibuyer, and highest monetary value indicator) would be the logical top-performing group. However, there are times when the 6–12 month segment will outperform the 0–6 month group. This happens often enough in both business and consumer telemarketing campaigns that you should not be surprised if it happens with your program. It simply means that your customers would like a little more time to get comfortable with their last purchase before they order anything else. They may still be exploring all of the features and benefits, or they may not yet have had enough time to use it as much as they intended.

It is amazing how often telemarketing projects fail because of lack of advance planning with list segmentation. One of the great problem-solving techniques to cure a project that is not meeting expectations is to stop calling the list segments that are performing poorly. The more succinctly you have sliced and diced the lists in advance, the more finely you can split out the names that aren't generating orders. If you have simply blended all the names together, there is nothing left to do but pull the plug on the entire project when the numbers fall below break-even. Remember that this is vastly different from direct mail in that you are making the calls one at a time, as opposed to dropping the entire universe into the mail in one fell swoop.

Splitting the list into three- or six-month slices is about right for most recency segmentation needs. The "1-time, 2-time, 3+ multibuyer" segmentation works well under most circumstances for tagging frequency characteristics into the record. You can segment monetary value in a number of ways. Popular segmentation methods are based on "total lifetime value," "value in the last 12 months," and "value of the last purchase." Remember, the point is to segment the lists in such a way that you would reasonably expect to see a response difference to the offer, based on what you know about these customers' past responses.

Many available-for-telemarketing lists come with phone numbers included. You should always get the phone numbers included, even if your telemarketing agency will append numbers at no cost. The reason for this is that if the name comes with a phone number there is a good possibility that it was captured using telemarketing, either inbound or outbound, and that means that the customer is more likely to be responsive to telemarketing.

Some agencies, such as DialAmerica, maintain an in-house national database of addresses and telephone numbers. These companies append the phone numbers to your lists at no charge. Always check with your telemarketing agency regarding phone look-up before you pay to send your lists to an outside source for phone number appending.

Dealing with Duplicates in Business-to-Business Lists

One of the inherent problems with many business lists is the incidence of semiduplicate listings. This is when there are several (or many) records for different people all within the same company, at the same location, and with the same main phone number. This is not a problem for direct mail because the mailroom delivers each envelope as a separate item. However, it may be a very large problem for telemarketing if all of the calls are routing through the same switchboard operator or department phone screener. It can clearly be very annoying for the receptionist to have to handle call after call when all of the decision makers are out of town or unavailable. Many agencies, DialAmerica included, use a suppression routine to limit the records within any particular campaign to one listing per phone number. This eliminates the multiple-phone-call problem; however, it also means that you may lose a large part of your list, and you will probably have no control over which of the records actually stays in the calling inventory.

Record Layouts, Programming, and Testing Transmission

As we mentioned earlier, whenever you order a list to be sent to a telemarketing agency, you should ask to have a partial dump and a record layout attached. A large agency such as DialAmerica typically receives hundreds of tapes and cartridges per week from every source imaginable. If your names come in without identifiers on the label, and no layouts or dumps, the operations staff will just file them in the library and wait for someone to come looking for them.

In most instances you can use the same file layout for business and consumer records. The business records will probably have three or four extra fields, one for company name, one for title, one for the fax number, and perhaps an extra address line to handle suite/mail-stop numbers. The balance of the record can usually be the same regardless of whether it is a business or residential listing, unless you are also coding purchase history.

Many large agencies will probably want to have the data supplied to them in a fixed record length with fixed length fields. This means that each piece of individual data within each customer/prospect record is always expected to start in the same position. It is very rare that there will be a problem with the format if the list comes from a list broker or data management specialist. These companies usually format the list in any way the telemarketing agency requests.

The situation can become much more interesting when it comes to house-file names. Very often there is no unified database available for telemarketing. It is not unusual for customer service, accounting, and the fulfillment system to each have their own database—with no coordination between them. This can present a real challenge when you want to pull a list that uses data from two or more of these independent sources all embedded in the same record. For example, you might need previous purchase information and phone number from the *customer service database*; payment history (including credit card type, number, and expiration date from the most recent purchase) from the *accounting database*; and basic name and address information from the *fulfillment database*. The data needs for an outbound telemarketing campaign are usually more substantial than for direct mail. Direct mail does not need a phone number, credit card data, or information about the last purchase to print out a mailing label. However, one or all of these items could be critical to the success of your telemarketing campaign.

Another issue that often comes up with house-file lists is the computer format in which they are available. Many companies are now using PCs rather than mainframes to manage their in-house data. That means that the lists may have to be reformatted by the telecenter to meet the needs of the mainframe computers. In this case, you may need to plan for an extra 10 days to two weeks of lead time for programming reformatting before the calls can start.

Figure 4.3 shows a simple record layout that DialAmerica has been recommending to many of its clients for several years.

Fixed file length

Fixed length fields

Record layout to include: Record size and block size specified

Each field's starting and ending position

Each field's size length

Field	Length	
Name	max 30	in first name, then last name order
Title	max 30	business title or gender prefix
Company name	max 30	
Street address	max 30	should contain the house number, PO Box
Second address	max 30	second address
City	max 17	
State	max 2	state abbreviation
Zip code	max 5	zip+4 not required
Canadian zip	7	
Key code	max 30	can be alpha/numeric
Account number	max 30	can be alpha/numeric
Other	max 30	can be alpha/numeric (can have as many other fields as necessary)
Phone number	max 10	10-digit numeric preferred, can handle dashes (-) or parentheses ( ) or spaces as long as they exist in the same position of each and every record on the file
Credit card no	max 16	16-digit numeric preferred, can handle dashes (-) or spaces as long as they exist in the same position of each and every record on the file
Credit card exp	max 04	4-digit numeric preferred in MMYY format, can handle dashes (-) or slashes (/) as long as they exist in the same position of each and every record

Figure 4.3 Simplified Record Layout for Outbound Telemarketing

This is a good simple format that almost every telemarketing agency should be able to handle with little or no problem. Regardless of the format you are using for "names-in" and "orders-out," we believe it is imperative that everyone on the marketing side of the project should become familiar enough with your record layout that they can easily read the data from a partial printout. It is truly amazing how many times the data you get is not what you expected. You will definitely save yourself a lot of time and aggravation if you can ferret out the problem yourself before you get the engineers and programmers involved. This advice remains true for everyone in the marketing side of the business, whether a client or an agency.

The other piece of programming that must be done prior to the start-up is to plan how the orders should be reformatted once they are generated by the telecenter, so as to accommodate the needs of the order entry and fulfillment systems. You will want to use the same record layout that is being used by your current order-entry group. This might be an inbound-800 customer service department, your fulfillment agency, or whoever is currently processing your direct mail response.

Regardless of who will be receiving the outbound-generated orders, it is very important that you do a test transmittal of simulated orders prior to the campaign's launch. Unless you are using a fulfillment agency that has prior experience with processing orders from the telecenter involved, you can expect some rejects at this point. It's quite a rare event when these tests run perfectly the first time, especially with an in-house fulfillment operation. Part of the reason for this is that the programming for these systems has usually been in place for many years, and no one really knows all the ins and outs anymore.

Script Writing Made Easy with a Trade Secret Formula

All good sales calls have the same common elements. They begin with a friendly introduction, gain the attention of the prospect, qualify the prospect for suitability to the offer, *make an irresistible offer*, and ask for the order. Of course most contacts do not result in an immediate acceptance, so the next step is to respond to questions and objections and ask for the order again. If the customer says yes to the offer you will then need to confirm the order in a clear and comprehensive fashion. Finally, every call should be terminated in a friendly and positive manner, regardless of the outcome. This is true for both business-to-business and consumer scripts.

Call Guides Versus Formal Scripts

The first step in the outbound process is to decide how tightly you want to script the call. Call guides can work very well in an in-house setting where there is one set of customer service policies in place, and the call volume is stable and predictable. This allows you to make a more substantial investment in rep training, since the TSRs are dedicated to one (or, at most, a few) programs, and won't be assigned to any other company's campaign. A good call guide will have suggested dialogue for an introduction, plenty of facts about the product or service being offered, and a full list of potential questions and answers. The strength of the call guide approach lies in the open-ended and interactive nature of the call. The weakness lies in the fact that it requires a great deal more training and is heavily dependent on the skill of the individual sales reps. Moreover, a TSR using a call guide will probably take longer to ask for the order than one who is using a regular script. This results in lower contact rates, and can lead to lower productivity and higher order-acquisition costs.

In an agency environment formal scripts work best. We are firm believers in tightly structured scripts for both consumer and business-to-business telemarketing in an agency environment.

The best way to begin is to gather up all the marketing materials you can get your hands on, including direct mail pieces, space ads, and product sell sheets. Starting with a blank piece of paper, write down every feature, benefit, and detail about the product or service that you find in those materials. Organize them into groups according to whether the item is a feature, a benefit, a detail of the offer, or a description of the premium (if there is one).

If there is a mailpiece, start with the outer envelope and write down each of the teaser copy points. Write down anything that appears in bold print or is included in a headline. These points are usually the most important ones. Pay special attention to how the guarantee is worded. You may be able to position the guarantee as a risk-free preview or a satisfaction-guaranteed trial in some sections of the script.

Structure is the key to success in script writing. The process illustrated in Figure 4.4 represents nearly 50 years of ongoing testing and experience. This is the DialAmerica approach to script writing.

Preintroduction (Ask to speak to the prospect.)
Introduction (Introduce yourself and the reason for the call.)
Gain Attention (Mention the best part of the offer and qualify for eligibility.)
Offer (Explain the product, terms, and nature of the commitment.)
Close (Ask for the order.)
Sales Continuation (Agree, change subject, sell benefits, close.)
Up/down/Cross-sell (Explain the offer in the briefest terms possible.)
Confirmation (Review the terms and conditions of the offer.)
Final Close (End on a positive note. "Thank you and good-bye.")

Figure 4.4 DialAmerica Script

Our heading for this section is a bit misleading in that it promises to make scriptwriting "easy." Unfortunately, we can't completely deliver on that pledge. If we could we would be taking all the creativity out of the process. One of the worst ways to write a script is to take a successful presentation for another product with a similar offer and simply change the names and insert a few benefits into the proper spots. Unfortunately, this is exactly how it is done much of the time. This simple fact is paramount: *Structure* is the key to script-writing success.

Let's look at structure's impact on the script section by section.

Preintroduction. You probably won't need a preintroduction for consumer offers, but you will need one for business-to-business endeavors, as you will need to move through one or more intermediaries before you get the prospect on the line. The best approach is to be polite and say as little as possible about why you are calling until you are actually speaking to the prospect. The more you reveal about the nature of the call, the more likely it is that you will receive a refusal from someone other than the decision maker. Regardless of how you respond to the screener's questions, you should always end up with, "So may I speak with Mr(s). _____ , please?" We will cover the differences between consumer and business scripts in much greater detail in chapter 8.

Introduction. The introduction should always be simple and direct: "Hello, my name is _____ , and I'm with (or I'm calling for) (company name)." Federal and state regulations require that all consumer telemarketing calls begin with complete disclosure as to who is calling and why the call is being made. This early disclosure can actually work to your benefit in that unqualified prospects will reveal themselves early on in the call and allow you to move on to the next lead.

What about the infamous line, "How are you today?" There are many people who believe that these words should never be used, as it's very hard to deliver this line with any real sincerity. Here's a good sub-stitute, which seems to work a bit better: "Can you hear me OK?" The essential purpose for using a qualifying question in the introduction is twofold. First, you want to find out if your prospect understands what you are saying, and second, you need to know whether he or she is in a proper frame of mind to consider your offer. You also need to give your prospect the opportunity to either terminate the call or grant you per-mission to continue. At a more subtle level, you also would like to ask an easy question that will result in a positive response. Building a series of positive responses throughout a conversation is important to the ulti-mate goal of getting a *yes* at the close. So, regardless of the words you use, you should always end the introduction with a simple question that is designed to elicit a positive response in 99 percent of prospects.

Gain Attention. Gaining attention has often been called the most impor-tant part of any script. Its purpose is very similar to the teaser copy you find on the outside of most direct mail envelopes.

The function of teaser copy in direct mail is to get prospects to stop what they are doing, open the envelope, and consider the offer. The "gain attention" section in telemarketing is designed to pull the prospect's attention away from whatever he or she was doing when the phone rang and instead listen to your offer.

Telemarketing is different from direct mail in that our phone call is always an interruption, whereas the mail is much less intrusive, and the prospect usually reviews it on his or her own terms.

Clearly, gaining attention requires you to introduce the most appeal-ing components of your offer. That would include the premium, if there is one, as well as the satisfaction guarantee and anything else that you believe makes your offer totally irresistible. You will definitely lift your response rate if you can position your guarantee as a risk-free preview.

A good way to start the dialogue is to thank the prospect for taking the call and then promising to be brief. Very often a qualifying question can be used at the end of the section, as both a bridge to the offer section and another opportunity to secure a positive response to an intermediate question. Here is an example of a well-written script from a computer software cross-sell promotion:

> **Great! Thanks for taking my call Mr(s). _____ .**
> **I'll be brief. I'm just calling to thank you for being one of our good customers, and to let you know that we'd like to send you/we're sending you a free CD-ROM containing 5,000 Xxxxxxxxx Graphics *just* for previewing our brand-new Yyyyyyyyyy at a 50 percent discount for 30 days risk-free. But first, may I ask, are you still using Zzzzzzzzzzzzz?**

Offer. If you have done a good job of introducing yourself and gaining your prospect's interest, confidence, and attention, you can reasonably expect the customer to listen carefully, and seriously consider, the offer you are about to make. Even so, there is a limit to the amount of time that you will have to make your case. It is a good idea to limit the number of features and benefits that you will describe to the top three or four, and then finish up with the line, "It's really too much to describe on the phone, and that's why we send it out to you on a risk-free preview basis. You can try it out, share it with your staff, and then decide."

The most common reason for script failure in the offer section is that the dialogue is simply too long. As we will discuss in more detail later on, shortening the script can be one of the easiest and most effective ways to improve an ineffective presentation.

Normally, you would specify all of the terms and conditions in the offer section. However, if you are selling at the upper range of your pricing sweet spot you may elect to leave the price out. What you are trying to do is force the customer to ask the question, "How much is it?" This is obviously a buying signal. Moreover, it is a perfect setup for making a price-value comparison that is favorable to support your high price point. Here's an example of how that can work.

How much is it? That's the best part Mr(s). _____.
If you were to purchase this at the store, the cost would be
well over $1,000; however, because you are a valued cus-
tomer, we can offer you the upgrade, for only $195 charged
right to your credit card. And remember, you can use it for
30 days and then make your decision. . . . OK?!

Close. If you don't ask for the order, you will never get the sale. The concept of assuming the sale has been at the heart of DialAmerica's success
for many years. "Assuming the sale," means that the TSRs are trained to
believe that every single person they speak to should say yes to the offer.
When you ask for the order with the basic assumption that the customer
will say yes, you create a very positive environment that often becomes
a self-fulfilling prophecy.

Just as you would if you were writing the closing paragraph of a
direct mail offer, you should mention the premium and the risk-free
nature of the offer and ask for the order with a strong assumptive "OK"
at the end. Here's an example.

It's a great offer and if you're not *totally* satisfied, just return
it within 30 days and keep the free *Graphics* CD-ROM, a
$14.95 value, as our gift. OK?!

Sales Continuation. Of course, most people will still say no, even if you
have done an excellent job in every respect. The worst thing you can say
at that point is "Why not?" *Never ask the customer to verbalize the objection.* If you do, this will force the customer to take ownership of the
objection and defend it against whatever subsequent arguments you
might present. In all our years of managing telemarketing campaigns,
we have never once seen a TSR get an order after asking the customer
"Why not?"

The secret to overcoming objections over the phone is not to attack
them head-on, but rather to recognize them as valid, but not necessarily of central importance, and then to redirect the customer's attention
to the benefits of the product and the irresistible nature of the offer, and
then close again.

The DialAmerica sales continuation success formula is this: Agree, Change Subject, Sell Benefits, and Close. When someone offers an objection, the first thing you need to do is agree, by saying something like: "That's OK, I understand exactly what you are saying Mr(s). _____ ." The next step is to change the subject by directing attention to a key benefit or perhaps the risk-free nature of the offer. The third step is to resell one or more of the features and benefits and then ask for the order again. Here's an example of a very effective sales continuation.

> I can understand your reluctance Mr(s). _____ , and that's just why we offer it to you on a 30-day preview:
>
> (Pick one or two benefits.)
> - The 5,000 color photos are royalty-free and are a $149 value all by themselves.
> - The 2,000 fonts will let you customize every document you create.
> - The full-color 1,000-page catalog is the best you can find.
>
> We're so convinced that this is the best xxxx package ever, that if you're not *100 percent satisfied* for any reason, you can return the software to us and we'll cancel the charge . . . no questions asked! So, I'll get your *free* gift and xxxx out to you for 30 days, and then you can decide. Either way, you keep the free gift. OK?!

Upsell-Downsell. The secret to successful upselling is to keep it brief. Both the customer and the TSR have invested a lot of emotional energy to get to this point (where they are ready to negotiate an order for the primary product). Neither of them will be able to tolerate a long-winded second sale. One of our favorite strategies is to suggest that the customer is eligible to preview an additional product on the same terms. Experience shows that if the upsell product is closely tied to the primary product, and the offer is simple and risk-free, you can reasonably expect to convert approximately 20 percent of the primary orders into upsells. Here's an example of what we would normally consider to be the upper limit for dialogue in an upsell. (By the way, the conversion on this upsell was 63 percent!)

> **That's great. Now we're permitted to send out up to two previews at one time, so I could also send you our Xxxx program. It's the perfect solution for anyone who needs a quick and easy way to store and retrieve information, track performance, and perform many other duties traditionally involving tedious paperwork. Xxxx uses a multilevel password system for complete confidentiality and security. It's normally $149.00, but we can bundle it with Yyyy for just $49 more. And of course it's all part of the same 30-day free trial offer, so you can check it out and then decide. OK?!**

Downselling requires a similar selling strategy in that brevity is a virtue. Generally, we do not recommend transitioning to the downsell before you have made a full presentation of the primary offer and received a specific refusal reason that you believe will be overcome by the alternate offer. The two best reasons to offer a downsell are that price is an issue and/or that the primary product is not really the best one for the customer. Here's another good example of what we are talking about.

> **Well, in that case you might be more interested in our regular version. It has fewer features than the deluxe version, but it's only $29.95. OK?!**

Cross-selling works best when the transition is made to the alternate offer very early on in the conversation. This is one of the main reasons why you should include a qualifying question in the gain-attention section. That way you can move to an alternate product before you have spent any time at all on the primary offer. One of the best ways to transition into the alternate offer is with the words, "Well, in that case, I think you would be more interested in our (*product or service*)." At that point you can transition over to the alternate offer.

Confirmation. While we generally believe that it is a very bad practice to have the TSRs read a script word-for-word, the confirmation is one section where very tight script adherence should be enforced. Many, if not most, telecenters are now tape-recording the confirmations of their orders and then passing those tapes on to a verification staff for review and approval prior to processing the order. Hence, asking for permission to tape-record the balance of the call is usually one of the first things that happens after the customer says yes. If you need to capture a credit card, that is usually done before the tape is turned on. A good confirmation will verify the identity of the customer along with the specifics of the terms and conditions of the offer. It's also a very good idea to ask the customer to acknowledge his or her understanding and acceptance of the offer. The confirmation should always finish up by asking the customer if there are any questions and then thanking the customer for his or her time.

> Great, and which credit card would you prefer to use
> Mr(s). _____ —Visa, MasterCard, or
> American Express? And the card number and expiration
> date? I'll be happy to hold while you get your card.
> (Capture data.)
>
> Now to avoid clerical errors, I'd like permission to tape-
> record the confirmation of our offer, OK?! . . . Great, now
> I show your full name and address as (repeat full name
> and address). Is that correct?
>
> Fine. Just so it's clear, along with your gift we'll send
> you:
>
>> 1. Xxxxxxxxx for $49.95 plus $5 shipping and
>> handling and sales tax if any.
>> 2. Xxxxxxxxx & Xxxxxxx for $69.90 plus $6.50
>> shipping and handling and sales tax if any.
>
> *IF CREDIT CARD*: This will be billed to your (credit
>   card type). And I have the number
>   and expiration date as
>
> _____ .

> *IF BILL ME*: An invoice will be included with the
> shipment.
>
> Mr(s). _____ , if you are not completely satis-
> fied, please return it to us within 30 days for a full
> refund, but please keep the gift as our thanks. Do you
> understand and accept our offer? (Wait for response.)
> Fine, do you have any questions? Great, the package
> should arrive in 2 to 3 weeks. Thank you again for taking
> the time to speak with me. I'm sure you made a great
> decision.

Final Close. Every call should end on a positive note, regardless of whether or not the customer has bought anything. In fact, DialAmerica trains its TSRs to end every call with the final close, even if they believe that the customer has hung up and is no longer on the line. There are two reasons for this. First, it allows the TSRs to end the call in a positive way, which sets them up for their next call. Remember, our fundamental strategy is to assume the sale, meaning that the TSRs approach every call believing that the prospect will say yes. The second reason to end with the final close is that we want to leave the customer also feeling positive about the time they have spent on the phone with us, so that they will listen the next time we call.

> *Final close for sale*: Thank you again for your time.
> Mr(s). _____ . Please call us at 1-800-xxx-
> xxxx if we can answer any questions or be of any help in
> the future. Have a good day/evening.
>
> *Final close for nonsale*: That's OK, Mr(s).
> _____ , perhaps next time. Please call us at 1-
> 800-xxx-xxxx if we can answer any questions or be of any
> help in the future. Have a good day/evening.

No script is complete without a comprehensive fact sheet on the company, its products, and customer service policies, along with a full list of answers to frequently asked questions. Here's a list that should be a good starting point for your own question-and-answer script.

Frequently Asked Questions

1. *I don't have any money in the budget . . .*
2. *Can you send me some information . . . ?*
3. *I am not interested . . .* (go to *sales continuation*)
4. *We don't have a need for that kind of product . . .*
5. *How much is shipping and handling?*
6. *How does the guarantee work?*
7. *How is the product shipped?*
8. *How do I make a return? Who pays for return postage?*
9. *I've never heard of your company . . .*
10. *How much is it?*

It's important to remember that a script is delivered by real live people speaking to other real live people. What sounds right in vocal conversation can look terrible in print. People don't speak the way they write. We always caution clients not to get hung up on any particular sentence or set of words that they might find awkward or grammatically incorrect when they are doing the initial review. Most scripts are going to change on the second day of calling anyway, so there is no point in trying to find the perfect words. In fact, we believe that if you haven't revised your script in the last 90 days, you are probably not spending enough time listening to the calls with remote monitoring. Market conditions are constantly changing, and your script needs to change with them.

Rep Training

It may be the fifth key, but from the standpoint of telemarketing operations, it is the single biggest point for success.

TSR retention is the key to telemarketing profitability, and training is the key to retention. Without high-quality training, no telecenter can survive for long. Training is an ongoing process, particularly in an agency where there is a constant stream of new clients, programs, and applications.

DialAmerica uses a structured training regimen for outbound tele-marketing that always allows the TSRs the opportunity to make at least a few phone calls on the first day. Clients are encouraged to visit the branch and help out with the training in a number of ways. A typical training outline for launching a new outbound telemarketing test in an agency setting might look like this:

1. **Introduction.** Introduce the client and any corporate staff that may be visiting the telecenter that day.
2. **Introduce the test objectives.** Everyone needs to know what the real purpose of the test is. Sometimes that is to generate a predetermined number of orders or qualified leads. Other times it is to determine if there is a viable market for a new product or service that is not yet even in the development stage (a dry test).
3. **Introduce the company and the product or service to be offered.** This is the perfect opportunity to get your client involved in the training if he or she is on site. It is also a good place to show a PR video on either the company or the product. A good enthusiastic product demonstration by a knowl-edgeable product or marketing manager can go a long way toward building the sales reps' confidence in the product and its promotion.
4. **Review the script, fact sheets, and Q&A.** A good slow read-through with emphasis on how to deliver not only the words, but also the punctuation is the best way to introduce a script. We like to think of our TSRs as actors in a repertory theater. Another metaphor that we often use is to ask the reps to think of the script as a musical score. Just as musical notes can have different values in terms of length and volume, so do the words in the script. We train the reps that when they see punctuation, boldface type, italics, or capitalization, they need to speak those words differently to give them the proper emphasis. Another tactic we use is to have the TSRs slow

down the pace of delivery whenever they feel that the dialogue is long. This runs somewhat counter to the normal inclination to speed up the pace of delivery whenever the scripts are long. But, in fact, long or complex material delivered too quickly will not allow customers to keep track of all of the ideas being presented.

5. **Ask for questions from the TSRs.** We usually ask our reps to hold their questions till the end of the training session, as many questions will be answered along the way. If you have done a good and comprehensive job of training, you won't have many questions at the end.

6. **Role-playing and demo calls.** Depending upon the size of your training class and the complexity of the project, you may want to split the TSRs up into pairs and let them role-play through the script with one another. An even better way to give them a sense of script flow is to have the person who wrote the script or did the training go out on the sales floor and do demo calls that can be monitored in the training room. Demo calls are the best tool you have for showing the TSRs how to deliver the dialogue, respond to questions, and close orders.

7. **Live phone calls.** It's now time to put the TSRs back on the phones. We have found that letting the reps get a few calls under their belts on the first day is the best thing you can do to get off to a good start. Good salespeople are a little like thoroughbred horses. You can't let them stand at the starting gate too long. They want to make sales.

8. **Setting goals for the first day of calling.** There is really no way to know how a new program will work until you start the calling. Given the fact that the TSRs will be on the phones for only a short time on the first day, we recommend that you set the goal for that first day for everyone to get just one sale, regardless of what you ultimately expect the program to do in terms of conversion. This will take the pressure off and should allow the TSRs to deliver the dialogue more confidently.

9. **Residual training and feedback from live calls.** There are many advantages to getting the TSRs on the phones right away. One of them is that you can bring everyone back into the training room for the last 15 minutes of the shift and get some feedback as to what they encountered. It also allows the account managers the opportunity to remote-monitor calls and see which sections of the script are working and which aren't. Here's a good list of questions you can use as discussion openers for your first residual training session.

- Who got sales? Tell us about the call. Why do you think the customer said yes?
- Did anyone have a question come up that wasn't on the Q&A sheet?
- Was there an objection that you felt was impossible to overcome?
- Did any of the customers interrupt your presentation and have an early disconnect? If so, at what point in the script did that happen? Did anyone else have a similar experience?
- Did anyone get a sale from someone who initially said no but then changed his or her mind? What did you say? Did you use the sales continuation dialogue?
- Are there any parts of the script that feel awkward? Can you think of any script changes that would help?
- How does this compare to the last project you were on?

Based on the rep feedback and the remote monitoring, you should in most instances be able to make positive script changes in time for the start of day two of calling.

The training process is somewhat different for new hires in that you may not want to put those people on the phones the first day. You may want to team them up with a veteran rep to do extended monitoring and demo calls. They will also need additional training on how the rep terminals work and the proper way to key in data. You should always start new hires out on a regular ongoing program where the performance benchmarks are well established. Never start a new hire out on a new test.

Remote Monitoring, Making Improvements, Making Money

The ability to remote-monitor the phone calls, without either the sales rep or the customer knowing that you are listening in, is one of the biggest benefits that telemarketing offers versus other media. You are literally able to eavesdrop on the buyer's decision-making process. Within the context of launching a new project, you should plan to begin your monitoring from the first calls on.

If the script is awkward or ineffective, you will discover this right away; hopefully, you will be in a position to make prompt changes. Here are some things to look for.

- Are the TSRs getting down to the close, or are the customers interrupting with early refusal signals?
- Are there any words or phases that sound awkward?
- What questions do the customers have?
- Does the sales continuation work?
- Do the customers really understand the dialogue/offer?

As was mentioned in the previous section, it makes a lot of sense to get the TSRs on the phones for at least 45 minutes to an hour on the first day of any new test. It's also a good idea to pull them off the phones for the last 15 to 30 minutes of the shift, so that you can have a residual training session to get ideas on how you may want to change the script for day two of calling.

Making improvements is the key to making money with outbound telemarketing. However, don't panic if the response is slow at first. Remember, there is always a learning curve that the TSRs will have to maneuver. We generally consider it a positive sign if there are *any* sales on the first day of calling. If there are no sales at all on the first day, you should take a close look at everything before you resume calling on day two. It is not unusual to have a half a dozen or more script changes during the first two weeks of a test. The important thing to remember is that you must be able to track the impact of each change you make on the overall response. It is usually not a good idea to run multiple script tests simultaneously with different reps.

Identifying and Solving Problems

Most programs do not just fly high and straight right out of the box. One of the things that makes telemarketing so interesting is that you are making the phone calls one at a time, and thus you have the opportunity to identify and solve problems as you go.

The first thing you should look at is the response on a list-by-list basis. It is probable that some of the segments are outperforming others. These are of course the ones that you will want to penetrate the deepest. Conversely, there may be segments that are doing very poorly and dragging down the overall results. You may want to abandon these altogether.

Another problem to watch for is the incidence of an early-interrupt, where the customers are interrupting the TSR before the close to offer a refusal signal. This can be an indication that your script is too long. Sometimes you will find that customers are interrupting at the same place in the script. If this is happening, you have inadvertently placed a refusal trigger into the dialogue. The easiest and best solution is to eliminate those words from the script. Sometimes that's not possible because the dialogue that is causing the problem is critical to the integrity of the offer. An alternate solution is to move the offending words as close to the end of the script as possible.

The most frequently used method for identifying and solving problems is simply to conduct a good thorough review of the refusal analysis stats. You should always consider in advance what you believe are the most likely reasons why customers might say no to your offer, and then assign a unique tracking code to each of those reasons. If your initial remote monitoring reveals any additional reasons, you should add those to the list. Telemarketing is the only direct media that can identify why people say no.

Consider the case illustrated in Figure 4.5. This was a project to call previous customers who had purchased a computer software product and offer them the latest upgrade version at a discounted price of $99 versus the regular retail price of $849 for first-time buyers. There was no alternate offer and no premium.

Our goal for this upgrade offer was to achieve a 20 percent conversion rate. As you can see, we weren't even close. There were several major problems to contend with.

Sales	129	3.3%
Refusals		
Not Interested	1,011	25.8%
Already Purchased Upgrade	474	12.1%
Miscellaneous Other Refusal	150	3.8%
Send Literature	120	3.1%
Happy with Previous Version	84	2.1%
Can't Afford/No Money in Budget	54	1.4%
Hang-up Early Disconnect	51	1.3%
Unhappy with Previous Version	18	0.5%
Product Too Expensive	12	0.3%
Customer Service Problem	9	0.2%
Total Refusals	**1,983**	**50.6%**
Ineligibles		
Doesn't Use Product	132	3.4%
Duplicate Lead	42	1.1%
Other Ineligible	18	0.5%
Total Ineligibles	**192**	**4.9%**
Telephone Problems		
Disconnected Phones	849	21.7%
Wrong Numbers	765	19.5%
Total Telephone Problems	**1,614**	**41.2%**
Total Leads Used	**3,918**	

Figure 4.5 Upgrade Offer to Previous Customers

1. The percentage of telephone problems was at 41.2 percent. Because this was an upgrade promotion and the list was a house file of previous buyers, the implication was that many of the names were more than two years old. The source for many of the names was retail and on-line registration cards. Clearly, the data entry was not nearly as clean as it should have been. Unfortunately, the client did not key code any of the list

segments separately. As a result there was no way to sort out the worst and dirtiest portions of the list. We had no solution for this problem other than to pull the plug and recommend starting over with a better segmentation plan.

2. Another 12.1 percent of the customers told us that they had already purchased the upgrade at retail or through the mail. In many ways this is actually a positive statistic—it indicates that many people do like the product and are interested in upgrading to the latest version. These customers might have been very responsive to a cross-sell offer for another compatible product that would leverage and enhance the value of the product they already owned. Unfortunately, we did not have an alternate product to offer them. Remember, you should always maximize the selling opportunities by including upsells and cross-sells in your offers whenever possible.

3. "Not interested" is usually the refusal category with the highest response rate for most programs. It is also the largest target of opportunity. One of the recommendations we made to the client was to add a premium to the offer, which would add some extra value, and set the offer apart from what was available in the other media (catalogs, retail, direct mail).

4. Price turned out to be an issue even though the upgrade version was heavily discounted versus the regular retail price. It turned out that some of the independent software catalog companies were offering the product at $89 and essentially positioning it as a "loss leader." We picked this up from our monitoring sessions. The customers who mentioned this wound up in a number of different refusal categories. If we hadn't done a good job of remote monitoring, we wouldn't have picked up on this key issue.

The combination of good refusal analysis matched up with comprehensive remote monitoring can be a powerful tool in identifying and solving problems.

After–Call Quality Control

Prior to the advent of predictive dialers and electronic transmission of data, telemarketing agencies such as DialAmerica would routinely call back each customer who placed an order to verify the accuracy and validity of the sale prior to transmitting the record to the fulfillment center. This was known as 100 percent live verification. The calls typically were conducted by a separate staff, which had no access to the TSRs, so that there would be no possibility of collusion between them. These verification calls usually would occur 24 hours after the initial sale was recorded, and the cancellation rate would average 5 percent to 15 percent. The most frequent reason for cancellation was simple change of mind. The balance of the cancels was usually due to a misunderstanding between the TSR and the customer as to the terms and conditions of the offer.

Today however, creating an audio tape recording of the confirmation of the order has become the new standard for maintaining quality control in an outbound sales environment. As was noted earlier in this chapter, it is now common practice to ask for permission from the customer to tape-record the balance of the conversation once the customer has said yes to the offer. The orders are then transferred to a verification center where a staff of verifiers will review each order, both voice and data, to ensure that record meets the standard for quality established for the program.

Much of the time 80 percent to 90 percent of the orders might be expected to clear the verification audit with no corrections. The balance (10 percent to 20 percent) might need either a data correction based on what the verifier heard in the audio record, or a live call back to the customer to reverify the confirmation in its entirety. It wouldn't be unusual to have a small percentage (perhaps 3 percent to 5 percent) of the orders cancel during this taped-confirmation verification process.

As you can see, the cancel rate has dropped dramatically now that we are taping the confirmations. The major reason for this is that the TSRs understand that each recording will be reviewed and critiqued before the order is a processed. They are clearly doing a much better job of ensuring that there is a perfect record of the confirmation on the tape.

They see to it that the customer is left with a complete understanding of the terms, conditions, and commitment inherent in their acceptance of the offer. Furthermore, the customers seem to be doing a better job of paying attention to all the details of the transaction. They know that a tape recording is being made that can be reviewed at a later date to settle any dispute that may arise as to the nature of the transaction, how it was presented, or what was promised over the phone.

Another of the advantages of taped confirmations is that the program managers and/or client can review them at any point in the future, which will come in handy should there be a customer complaint or a high return rate.

What about third-party or hot transfer verification? Another popular method of order verification involves bringing a third party into the phone call to act as an impartial verifier of the authenticity of the order. Sometimes this is a supervisor on site; at other times this person actually is employed by a completely different company. This is the required method of verification whenever the merchandise or service is going to be billed directly onto the customer's phone bill. Telephone companies are required to use third-party verification whenever they are taking an order to switch long distance service.

Processing Orders, Delighting the Customer, Fulfilling the Promise

As we pointed out in chapter 2, prompt and efficient fulfillment is critical to the ultimate success and profitability of any telemarketing campaign. It has been proved many times that there is a direct connection between the speed of delivery and the rate of returns (particularly on bill-me orders). Electronic transmission of orders, which can be downloaded directly into the fulfillment center's order entry system, has had an enormous impact on speeding up the process. It has also solved much of the problem of inconsistent data entry.

Recognizing this important connection between fulfillment efficiency and profitability, many companies are now sending out a welcome/order acknowledgment letter via fax or first-class mail to bridge the gap between the time the order was placed and receipt of the product by the customer.

Another important point to remember is that you will probably need a slightly different fulfillment package for phone-sold versus mail-sold orders. There should always be some sort of welcome letter sent with the package that ties the delivery of the product back to the phone call. Keep in mind that with outbound telemarketing the customer doesn't have anything in print to hold onto until the product arrives. This welcome/acknowledgment letter should always start with the line "Dear Mr(s). _____ /Valued Customer, Thank you for taking the time to speak with our telephone sales representative. Please find enclosed. . . ."

In many ways this letter serves the same purpose as a prospecting letter in a regular direct mail campaign—to sell the product. As we mentioned earlier, outbound telemarketing is different from all other media in that the selling doesn't really start until the customer has the product in his or her hands. Hopefully, your product will delight your customer and exceed his or her expectations. If this all happens the way it should, you will have fulfilled the promise, and you'll be well on your way to a very successful and profitable promotion.

Reporting and Analyzing the Test Results

There are two important sources of information for your final report. The first is the compilation of notes and comments from your remote-monitoring sessions. The second is the tabulation of the statistical results as to how many orders were generated and the specific breakdown of the nonsale outcomes into refusal reasons.

The statistics should be shown on a list-by-list basis as well as with a cumulative total. The breakdowns should be as specific as possible. Watch out for category "Other." This group should never be more than 5 percent of the total.

All too often we have seen final reports that are packed with statistics, but completely devoid of insightful analysis as to what really was happening on the phones, and what actions can be taken with the next campaign to improve the results or test new ideas. Compiling stats off a computer is easy. Anyone can do this. It takes a real professional to see through the numbers and make meaningful recommendations for the future. Don't settle for just the numbers. Ask questions: "What does this mean?" "Why is this happening?"

We have two last words of advice. First, never proceed directly from a small initial test directly to a full rollout of the available universe without first conducting a "confirming retest" using a sample 2 to 10 times the size of the initial test. Second, always back-test whenever you are adopting a new control offer.

We will be shifting gears in the next chapter to look exclusively at inbound telemarketing. Hopefully you will find many parallels between these two related yet quite different telemarketing disciplines.

Summary

- List-related problems are the single greatest cause of outbound telemarketing delays and failures.
- Everyone involved in a campaign should be able to read the record layouts and partial dumps. Checking these documents carefully in advance will save a great deal of time and prevent headaches later on.
- Formal written scripts work best for outbound programs in an agency environment.
- Using call guides rather than tightly written scripts offers more flexibility in interacting with the customers, but also requires more training and provides less control over what is being said. They are better suited for in-house telecenters.
- As in most other issues relating to direct marketing, script testing should be an ongoing process. If you haven't tested a script change in the last 90 days, you probably aren't doing enough call monitoring.
- Role playing and live demonstration calls made by trainers for the benefit of TSRs are invaluable learning tools.
- Always save a little time at the end of a shift for TSRs to provide feedback and ask questions when launching a new test.
- Analyzing refusal reasons can be a powerful tool for solving problems. Matched with a comprehensive call-monitoring plan, you should be able to identify the cause of almost any dilemma you face.
- There is a direct connection between the speed of the fulfillment process and profitability of the campaign.

- Phone-sold orders require a different fulfillment package than mail-sold orders. Always include a welcome letter in your fulfillment package that refers to the phone call and actively sells the product.
- A single page of insightful analysis is much more valuable than 100 pages of statistics. Never accept a final campaign report without a clear, reasonable explanation of what the numbers really mean.
- Be careful when moving from a test to a rollout. It's wise to conduct a confirming retest of 2 to 10 times the initial test size before committing to a full-scale rollout.

5

Inbound Telemarketing

"Otherwise known as the Science of Unknown Numbers"

—JIM AHEARN

W_e would like to begin this chapter by thanking Jim Ahearn, DialAmerica's vice president of inbound services, for his generous assistance in providing ideas and thoughtful insights that were so essential in writing this chapter.

Our initial plan in writing this book was to weave inbound and outbound telemarketing together wherever such parallels and comparisons could be made. However, as the book began to take shape, it became apparent to us that the only way to cover many of the most important inbound topics was to devote a separate chapter to this subject.

A Technology-Driven Business

The face of inbound telemarketing has changed dramatically in the last decade or so. Where years ago you might have just worked with an in-house programmer to set up an order screen for the TSRs to work from, today's inbound environment might require the participation and assistance of dozens of technicians and programmers from a variety of operating units, both within and outside your organization. This technology has changed every aspect of the business, from the ease with which the TSRs respond to callers' requests for service and products, to the consumers' comfort and satisfaction with the transaction.

Setting up your inbound program in today's environment might require:

- Special ACD (automated call distributor) arrangements that involve the participation of the ACD manager
- IVRU (interactive voice response unit) applications requiring the assistance of an IVRU programmer
- Telecommunications issues requiring support from the phone company
- On-line data issues that necessitate a direct data link to the client's database

There are other things to keep in mind as well.

- You may need to download files that have you working on a retrieval basis.
- You could potentially be linked to the home office (agency or client) mainframe—either for data retrieval or reporting requirements.
- And of course there are still the original programmers who will be generating the screens that the TSRs will be working from.
- Your screens could be a simple GUI (graphical user interface) that the programmers are building from scratch, or you may be tapping into a client's mainframe with no GUI. The client may just have regular green screens or mainframe screens that are not written in visual basic; your programmers have to develop a GUI from as many as 50 or more mainframe screens.

So you have all of these technology groups that may or may not be involved in setting up your inbound program.

The biggest mistake that inbound marketers make is to put the marketing plan together first and then bring in the technology after the fact. This often causes one of three things to happen:

1. The marketing plan goes up in smoke when the marketer learns that the technology doesn't work the way it had expected.

2. It's going to take a tremendous amount of resources on either the HR (human resource) side, or in actual dollars and cents with respect to the cost of the technology itself.
3. The customer gets lost in the technology and gives up on the call without fulfilling the original purpose for the call.

To devise a program that is going to utilize today's sophisticated inbound technology to the best advantage, it is important for the marketing people to recognize that they do not necessarily know enough about the technology to make the correct decisions about what will work and what won't. You need to bring the technology in first, and then put the marketing plan together.

We hear stories all the time about callers being put into a VRU that has not been properly programmed; because of technical problems, these callers wind up in a black hole that goes in circles and never takes them where they want to go. In the end, they get confused and hang up.

So what is the solution for this problem? Well, the answer begins with understanding who your caller really is. For instance, a typical bank may not want to assign live operators to help customers check on their account balances and answer simple customer service questions involving the location of branches and hours of operation. It's quite probable that customers calling for those purposes will be willing to spend more time interacting with a VRU than would someone who is calling to respond to a marketing offer. That person is much more likely to get tired of the VRU and simply hang up in frustration. Different people calling for different purposes are going to have different tolerances for dealing with an interactive VRU.

Of course, all of this technology costs money. You can invest 600 to 1,000 hours of programming to develop a GUI so that reps do not look at 50 mainframe screens with thousands of pieces of information but rather work from four or five very user-friendly screens with a bunch of buttons they can click on to access information. The good news is that everyone benefits from the technology. If the agents had to deal with a very confusing set of mainframe screens, the calls would take much longer. The marketing costs would be higher, and the customer satisfaction would be much lower.

Good technology makes the agents more proficient, provides customers with better service, and shortens the length of the call, which drives down the costs for the inbound marketer. It's a win-win situation!

Establishing Levels of Service

A *level of service* is a predetermined percentage of calls answered within a specific time frame. It is a measure of the promptness of response.

One well-known rule of thumb in the industry (which does not, and should not, apply to everyone) is the 80 percent-in-20-seconds rule (80/20 service level). This means that 80 percent of the calls are being answered within 20 seconds of the first ring. This level of service should typically (but not always) result in 97 percent of your calls being answered. The remaining 3 percent hang up before the agent answers the phone. This is known as the abandonment rate. In fact, the average speed of answer and the abandonment rate are both by-products of the service level in place.

Of course, it is important to remember that this 80/20 rule may not be appropriate for every inbound situation. For instance, if you are running an ad in a business-to-business computer trade magazine for mainframe computers that have a minimum cost of $500,000 dollars, an 80/20 service level might not be satisfactory. In that instance you might want 100 percent of the calls answered immediately, because the potential value of the calls is so high.

On the other hand, there are times where you may want to staff for a 60 percent-in-50-second level of service. This could be appropriate if you have reason to expect the vast majority of people who did not get through on the first attempt to keep calling back—for instance for a sweepstakes offer with no other obligation.

Historical Note

The 80/20 service level was first established by the phone company in the mid-1940s as an appropriate level of service for their operators who were responding to operator assistance calls.

The questions you need to consider when you are trying to decide what the service level should be are:

- Who are these people that are calling my toll-free number?
- What value do these calls have from a marketing standpoint?
- Does it make sense on average to have them wait on the phone for a longer-than-usual amount of time?

Remember, your service level is never set in stone. You can change it by adding or subtracting call-handling capacity once you see how the customers are reacting to the current level of service.

Earlier in this section we made the point that the abandonment rate is a by-product of the service level in place. However, this is not an absolute one-to-one lockstep relationship. For instance, if you had a 911 emergency response line that was operating on a 60 percent-in-50-seconds service level, you might still have a zero percent abandonment rate because the callers would be so highly motivated to hold on until they could speak with a live operator. On the other hand, if you were running a DRTV ad for a kitchen gadget, the 60/50 service level might translate into a 30 percent abandonment rate.

Author's Note

I recently had the opportunity to call my motor club's toll-free road service hot line, because my wife's car had broken down in front of our church on a Sunday afternoon. I was first put into a VRU designed to filter out the customer service calls and then advised to hold on the line to request roadside assistance. I waited 9 minutes and 40 seconds for a live operator. Every 20 seconds I was played the same recording: "All of our counselors are still busy. We will be with you as soon as possible." I can assure you, I had no intention of hanging up and losing my place in line. I'll bet their service level that day was 10 percent in 100 seconds or worse. But I'll also bet that their abandonment rate was almost zero.

—Richard Simms

So Who Determines the Service Level, and How Should It Be Set? The client should establish the service level with input from the inbound service provider. Consider the following hypothetical case: My boss just said, "I'm spending $2 million on this advertising program. I want all of these calls answered. You better make sure you are talking to these people when they call in." This can be interpreted as a request to set the service level at 100 percent of the calls answered immediately. Well, this may result in a lot of unnecessary cost to overstaff the program, when in fact, an 80/20 service level might be very acceptable to the callers and much more cost effective for the company.

What Are the Determining Factors That You Should Consider When Making Decisions About Service Level? They are:

- What are the costs associated with maintaining various levels of service?
- What is the service provider's experience in managing similar programs?

One mistake that we see time and again is that a company will look at the service level in its own inbound customer service department and simply assume the same level for its marketing effort. The reason this may not work is that callers who are on hold for customer service may be much more tolerant than those that are holding for a marketing effort. If you have no prior experience to draw on, you're not sure what level of service is appropriate for the callers, and you have no idea what will be cost effective for the program, you should set the service level at 80/20 and run it for a few days. See what the average speed of answer is. Track the abandonment rate. Then make an estimate of how much more it will cost to move from 80/20 to 90/10 (or down to 70/20). At that point you can decide what's best for the program. We believe that 80-in-20 is always a good starting point to look at the reaction of the callers and the realities of the costs.

You can usually make an educated guess as to what will happen at a different service level, but remember, both people and programs are different under different circumstances. There can even be seasonality influences. The only way you can truly determine what the actual customer reaction and costs associated with a service level change will be is to run a test. We've seen programs where people had a tolerance of 15 seconds before they hung up. We've seen others where they will hold on happily for several minutes or more.

Exploding One More Myth About Abandonment Rates. Marketers have typically viewed abandoned calls as lost revenue. However, this is not always true. Consider another hypothetical case:

- One hundred phone calls have been offered in a spike exceeding the capacity of the call center to respond to all of them promptly.
- Thirty callers have hung up equaling a 30 percent abandonment rate.
- The calls have a $50 average order value.
- Thirty calls times $50 equals $1,500 lost revenue.
- The product has a 20 percent profit margin.
- The marketer assumes a loss of $300 in profits ($1,500 × 20 percent).

It is not necessarily true that the marketer lost $300. If the marketer went back and looked at the ANI (automatic number identification) for each of those calls, it might turn out that 20 of the 30 actually called back at some point during the remaining time of the promotion. So in fact, those 30 customers were not really lost—only 10 were lost. This is important to remember when you are considering a change in service levels to reduce the abandonment rate.

You should be able to get copies of the ANI reports from your call center, and if they can't provide them, your telco surely can.

The actual abandonment rate is always lower than what your ACD tells you because of callbacks.

Remember, determining the service level establishes how quickly you will respond to the people who are calling. It really has nothing to do with the marketing aspects of the program, other than the fact that you don't want to impact your marketing effort negatively by not having enough people on the phones to answer the calls.

Of course, maintaining the proper level of staffing to achieve a consistent level of service is easier said than done, particularly in a service bureau environment. An in-house customer service facility might have a relatively predictable and stable day-to-day call volume model that looks like Figure 5.1.

An agency on the other hand that is handling calls for a large number of marketing programs driven by a wide variety of media will be in a much less predictable situation.

It is precisely for this reason that we sometimes refer to inbound telemarketing as the science of unknown numbers. You just don't know what is going to happen when you walk in to work on any given day. In an agency setting you may have client A driving inbound calls with direct mail. Client B is running space ads in magazines. Client C is doing the same in regional and national newspapers. And client D is using syndicated direct-response radio with unpredictable call spikes. Sometimes you don't even know when the ads are going to hit. Sometimes you are told that they will hit on a certain day and time, and they don't. You might be expecting 5 percent response to your mail drop and get only 1 percent, or you may be expecting 1 percent and get 8 percent.

The unknown numbers are not only the number of calls that you are handling at any particular moment, but also the amount of talk-time it takes to satisfy the customers, plus the amount of customer hold-time. If you've anticipated a three-minute call and the actual talk time is four minutes, you've just had a 33 percent increase in the talk time for your program. You may have created unexpected questions or confusion about the offer based

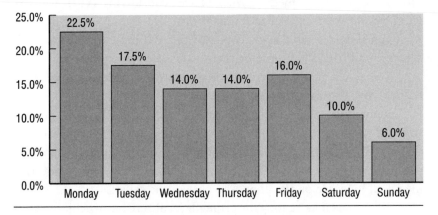

Figure 5.1 Percent of Calls Received per Day

on how you phrased the copy in the ad, a situation that requires the TSRs to put customers on hold while they get help from a supervisor.

Of course, the central question that every marketer wants answered is the one for which there is no guaranteed answer, namely, "How many calls will I get, and how many of those calls will convert into orders?" Telemarketing is a risky business, even on the inbound side, because it is after all the science of unknown numbers. You need to test, test, test, before you roll out.

On the other hand, once you have established a sufficient level of previous history for your campaign, your telecenter managers should be able to develop a relatively sophisticated model that will be capable of predicting the daily (and hourly) call volume for the duration of your campaign. However, keep in mind that those predictions are only going to be valid as long as you are comparing apples to apples. Even a small change in the marketing plan can make a big change in the inbound telemarketing dynamics. So it is always wise to run a small test before you make a major commitment to your telecenter.

Dedicated, Semidedicated, Shared: What's Right for You?

Let's start with some definitions.

- **Dedicated environment.** Agents handle calls for only one client program. This usually has a higher cost per call associated with it. However, if the call volume is sufficiently large (in the neighborhood of 25,000 talk minutes per week), those additional costs can be relatively low. The TSRs are expected to have detailed knowledge about both the products and companies that they are representing.
- **Semidedicated environment.** Agents handle calls for a handful (perhaps two to six) programs. These programs may all be very similar. For instance, the TSRs may be member-save specialists working on member-save programs for a variety of clients across a number of different industries. Their mission on each call is very similar. The TSRs generally are expected to

have slightly less detailed knowledge about each product or
client, than those in the dedicated environment.

- **Shared environment.** Agents handle calls for 10, 20, 30, or
more different programs. There are some shared-environment
agencies where certain reps handle calls for several hundred
different programs simultaneously. In a lot of cases, those
TSRs may not even receive training for individual client programs. The agents may show up for work and discover that a
familiar screen layout is now populated with information for a
new product or client. In this environment, the reps typically
have very little detailed knowledge of the products or clients
that they are representing. Their mission is usually restricted
to capturing basic information and providing a minimum of
client- or product-specific information.

What types of programs would best be suited for each environment? An outsourced shared environment is best suited to basic order
taking, dealer-locator, and simple lead-generation programs. These are
programs where the products or services are simple and the data collection is limited to such requirements as name, address, and credit card
number. The reps probably lack the kind of detailed knowledge that
would be required to explain complex products or do sophisticated
upselling and cross-selling.

Working in an outsourced semidedicated environment would allow
you to field calls for somewhat more technical products or complex services that required some sales ability in addition to basic order processing. This would be a good choice for programs where you would like the
benefit of having TSRs who know a good deal of specific product or
client knowledge, but where you don't want to incur the higher costs associated with operating in a fully dedicated environment.

A program should be in an outsourced dedicated environment
when the judgment is made that there needs to be an absolute focus on
the program to achieve success. Obviously, there are various levels of dedication. In one instance the TSRs are dedicated to one program, but
there may be more than one "dedicated" program running in the call center. In other instances the entire center may be dedicated to the project,
including the supervisors, managers, and clerical staff. It really is a matter of deciding how much focus you require to be successful.

There are even times when a program is so complex, and the nature of the calls is so sensitive, that it should not even be outsourced. These types of programs require an in-house dedicated environment. Jim Ahearn tells a story about one such program that came to his attention a few years back.

An Anecdote from Jim Ahearn

We were invited to visit with a consumer products company that sold hair-coloring products via retail. These products used strong chemicals, and there was need to set up an inbound help hot line for customers who had gotten themselves into trouble in the middle of the coloring process. (A typical problem was, for example, the customer was trying for auburn, but the color was coming out purple.) The plan was to have trained hair-coloring specialists available to help the customers diagnose the problem, and provide a solution on the fly that would save the day. We decided there was just too much risk associated with making a mistake on the phone and possibly giving out the wrong corrective advice. Our primary recommendation was that this program should be handled strictly in-house. We stated further that if the client really insisted on outsourcing the job, there had to be at least one or more of the company's most qualified staff on-site at all times to assist in answering the most problematic calls. In our view this was a program that should have been done only in an in-house dedicated environment.

Disaster Recovery

Disaster recovery is a much more critical issue for inbound telemarketing than it is for outbound. If your outbound system goes down, you simply suspend the calling until the problem is fixed, and then schedule extra calling to make up for whatever time was lost. However, with inbound, depending upon the circumstances, you can lose thousands and maybe even millions of dollars if you were unfortunate enough to have a very expensive DRTV ad flood your network with calls at the exact same moment that a backhoe is slicing through your call center's phone lines.

Fundamentally, you need to make sure that the call center that is going to handle your calls is capable of getting its systems back up and running as quickly as possible when a disaster does occur.

Disasters can come in every stripe and color, and there are different levels of disaster. Here are just a few of the bad things that can happen in the life of an inbound telecenter.

- The server just went down and there is no back-up.
- The power just went out all over town, and you don't have a back-up generator.
- You just got hit by a hurricane/tornado/earthquake.
- There's a major snowstorm or flood. All the roads are shut down. Your systems are up and running, but your people can't get to work.
- You can even be affected by natural disasters that occur outside your near geographic area. For instance, if your telco's central office gets knocked out 100 miles away, you'll go down with them.
- If you are on-line with your home office computers, or the client's mainframe, and they have problems, then you have problems too.

There are so many levels of disaster that you are always at some level of risk in the inbound business. Some of these issues are under your control. Some are not. You obviously need to have enough redundancy in place so that if a disaster is caused by something you can control, you can be back up and running quickly. For instance, if a card in the ACD goes bad, is there redundancy in the ACD? Do you have another card to replace it? If the power goes out, do you have battery back-up? How long will the batteries last? If the batteries run out do you have a diesel generator?

Various companies have different levels of support for their ACD, VRU, servers, and so on. The question for clients and marketers is: How much disruption will my programs experience, and how much disruption can I tolerate if a disaster occurs and my inbound service is interrupted?

DialAmerica, like most other large agencies, tries to put itself in a strong position to recover from the kind of disasters that we have discussed here. Listed below is a profile for what we believe is an excellent disaster recovery plan.

- The ACD should be fully redundant. This means that the cabinet is really split in half so that if a card goes out on one side, the card on the other side automatically kicks in and no service is lost. (A card is a piece of hardware like a circuit board or a chip that controls certain aspects of the ACD such as call routing.) Of course, if the same card goes out on both sides of your cabinet, then the ACD will go down, but, fortunately, the odds of that happening are usually quite slim.
- The power should be backed up by a battery, which is backed up by a generator, which can run long term.
- The VRU system should also be redundant and backed up by a battery and then a generator.
- Power in the building should be backed up by a generator.
- There should be redundancy of phone lines on the telco side. Your call center should have dual access with two sets of phone lines coming into the building, so that if a backhoe cuts through one set you still have service through the other set.
- Your long distance provider should be able to provide you with redundant service so that you can still operate even if they have a break in one of the phone company lines.
- If your telco's CO (central office) goes down, you will go down with them unless you have installed a second set of lines to a back-up CO in another location. (This can be very expensive, but it is also very expensive if you are losing a million dollars a day in revenue while you are waiting for the worst flood of the century to recede.)
- You should also have redundancy on the network side, so that if there is an outage on the network level you can still get a message out to the callers letting them know that there is a technical problem and giving them directions as to what to do (when to call back, another number to call, a website or an

E-mail address to communicate with, whatever the client or the marketing department feels is appropriate).

- If there is a weather emergency and the employees cannot get to the call center, you will need to get a network message out, or perhaps arrange to reroute the calls to another site or sites that can absorb the additional call volume.
- Regional weather issues and quality of road access should be a consideration when selecting the site for a new telecenter. Will these roads be among the first to be cleared if there is a weather disaster?

Disasters occur every day. Prepare yourself as best you can, and then be prepared to live with the cost implications of your decisions.

Recruiting, Training, and Staffing

Recruiting is the effort you make to draw in new employees for your program. *Training* is the process of teaching people to accomplish the task of speaking with the callers in such a way that you achieve the goals of the program. *Staffing* is the process of determining how many people are required on the phones to maintain the established service levels.

Just as you do when you run ads to recruit people for any other position in your company, you will need to specify in the ad the talents and skills that you are looking for to meet the inbound program's objective. For instance, if you need to staff for a member-save program for an ISP (changing the mind of a customer who has called in to cancel Internet service, and getting him or her to keep it instead), you will want to hire people with computer backgrounds. You will be looking for people who are knowledgeable about PCs or have had an education in a technical field. The reason of course is that a person who is calling to cancel his or her Internet service may be frustrated because of inability to get the service to work, and the real problem is that the person is not using the computer or the service itself properly. Your TSRs may need to provide some simple technical support to save the sale.

You also will be looking to hire people with sales skills and a strong positive attitude about themselves. People who call in to cancel a service are calling because of some negative issue that they have had with the product or service. Every member-save call starts out in a negative fashion. Your agents need to be able to thrive in a negative environment and maintain a positive attitude. This certainly requires a different sort of person than the one you would need for a dealer-locator or basic customer service call.

From a client/marketer's perspective, when you are talking about recruiting, training, and staffing, a client/marketer wants to see that you have appropriate measures in place to provide quality call management. Of course, it's always beneficial to both the staff and the reps if the client/marketer wants to be involved in the training process. However, in most cases clients/marketers prefer to leave the training details up to the telecenter management team.

So let's take a closer look at the training process, starting with a cross-training for existing agency-based employees to a new client program in a shared or semidedicated environment. Listed below is a brief outline of a good comprehensive training process.

- Start out by introducing the company. Give a little history and some background about who they are and what they do.
- State the company's goals for the program. Make sure that everyone is aware of the expectations of the relationship between the telecenter and the client or marketing team responsible for the program.
- Introduce the product or service to be offered.
- Review the on-line scripting, the various screens that have been created for the program, the Q&A and customer service policies, and the advertising material that will be driving the calls into the telecenter.
- Review the upsell and cross-sell techniques that will be required to achieve the program's goals.
- Role-play to build comfort and ease with the various tacks that the call can take.
- Have the supervisors pay close attention to the agents as the first calls are being received. Look for any deviations from the expected results.

- Prepare quality-assurance checklists on each rep, and conduct residual training sessions either one-on-one or as a group, as appropriate.

A good training program may take three hours, three days, or three weeks. It all depends on the nature of the program. In the past, 90 percent of all inbound programs could be trained in four hours or less if the TSRs were experienced. However, that won't be the case in the future. Inbound telemarketing training is becoming much more complex because of the Internet. It's not just call handling anymore. Those same TSRs are going to be answering E-mail and pushing Web pages back and forth and will need to be fully trained in that technology as well. It's no longer simply a matter of learning about the written material or advertising connected with the campaign; now the agents must be trained in the navigation and details of the client's website. All of this adds up to a great deal more information. The rep stations in the modern customer contact center will all need to be Web accessible.

Q&A material used to be printed out on hard copy. Today, this same information is typically on-line and is very often written in coded computer language so that the rep can click on a specific question or issue and have the answer instantly.

Customer service and maintenance are becoming more complex every day. In the future your inbound customer service call might sound something like this: "I'm calling today on your 800 number regarding an E-mail that I sent you two days ago. The E-mail was discussing a problem with a Web order that I placed two weeks ago." In order to handle this call properly your inbound agent will need access to the customer's E-mail along with whatever response your company may or may not have sent, as well as a copy of the original Web order with specific shipping and delivery information. The agent may also need access to full purchase history, as well as information about the current availability of the product in question. There are certainly significant training issues connected with having the agents function properly in all those systems.

Training new hires adds even more complications and time to the process. As we mentioned earlier in this chapter, the people and the programs for which they are hired need to be a good match if you are going to have successful training. However, you also need to be flexible enough to realize that the program you hire them for today may not be the one that they are working on in two weeks, either because the program is over, or because they couldn't be successful on the original program.

First-day training in an agency setting will include an orientation on the agency's policies, procedures, expectations, and human resource issues. It will cover how and when people are paid, the bonuses that may be earned, and how performance is evaluated, including the use of remote monitoring and quality-assurance checklists. Next, more specific issues relating to the client and program that the TSR will be handling calls for will be covered. Finally, the reps will be introduced to the technology. They will learn how to deal with the headset, the phone, and the PC. DialAmerica uses an 18-position training facility with multimedia capabilities that allows us to simulate the live-call experience. The training positions are linked to the active telephone systems, but in a test mode. This allows us to demonstrate the various situations that may be encountered in a live-call environment. The facility is also equipped with live-call remote-monitoring speakers so that the reps can get a sense of what is really happening in the center at that point in time. They will then be paired up with an experienced agent for residual training and mentoring. That all happens on day one.

Day two for a new hire will probably take place on the phones in a special training agent group. Here the supervisory ratio may only be one to five, instead of the normal one to ten. The new hires will receive a great deal of attention and close remote monitoring. The call volume may be paced down to this group to give them time to consider and discuss with the trainers how they handled each call.

Days 3 to 21 are the critical first three weeks of the new employee's relationship with your company. This is a time when the agents should receive a good deal of personal attention, including personal conferences with the management team to help the new hire learn to enjoy the job. It's also during this time that good work habits can be encouraged. Most unsuccessful new hires will leave in the first three weeks, so it is important that every effort be made to retain as many good people as possible during this time frame.

Successful staffing, or the process of assigning the proper number of agents to a particular program to meet the service level requirements, is greatly influenced by the quality of your training programs, and your efforts at retaining competent employees.

As we mentioned earlier in this chapter, it's not always possible to predict how many calls will come in for a particular program, or how long those calls will take on average. However, once you have sufficient history to draw on, you should be able to create a model that accurately predicts the call volume and talk minutes on an hour-by-hour basis for the duration of the campaign. Once you have that model in place you can determine how many agents you will need for each project on any given day.

A Selling Mentality in an Inbound Environment

Ten years ago inbound agents were generally looked upon as nothing more than the customer service part of the fulfillment industry. Inbound agents were viewed in the same way as the people who opened up the mail. They were seen as order takers. That mentality still exists in some companies today. When you are asked to handle tens of thousands of calls in a 15-minute period because of a national ad campaign, you might like to have the focus, training, and sales-oriented mentality in place to convert all those calls into sales, but you will probably need to be satisfied to simply handle a high percentage of the calls in the most efficient way possible. A campaign such as this would probably best be placed in a shared environment telecenter, where the focus is mainly on answering as many calls as quickly as possible to minimize the abandonment rate.

If you are using DRTV and it's driving large spikes of response into your telecenter over a short period of time, it's probably not realistic to expect a real outbound sales mentality on those phone calls, because the bulk of the people that are employed in a broadcast response telecenter are still order takers. They'll take the name, address, credit card number, and the item number of the product being ordered, and then they need to move on, because the calls are backing up.

On the other hand, if you are using nonbroadcast media to drive the calls, you then have the option of placing your program in a dedicated or semidedicated environment, which will give you the opportunity to try and create an "outbound sales-oriented mentality in an inbound environment." This has been one of DialAmerica's inbound secrets to success. Of course this will add to the length of each call as the agents use strong cross-selling and upselling techniques to convert the calls at a higher rate, perhaps turning a three-minute call into a four-minute call, which does add to the cost. However, it will also add many more orders with a higher conversion rate, and additional revenue from larger value orders as a result of the stronger sales effort.

Operating an inbound facility with an outbound mentality is not just a training issue. It's also a recruiting issue, and a communication issue, because when you are hiring people for an inbound center, you have to be very clear with those people that they will be expected to use outbound sales techniques on inbound calls to convert those calls to sales.

A classic example of this practice of creating an "outbound mentality in an inbound environment" is when you train your reps to handle both inbound and outbound calls. These TSRs are usually referred to as either blended or universal agents.

A universal agent is a person who is trained to move from a dedicated inbound to a dedicated outbound environment as the needs of the program require. However, the TSR will stay on one or the other formats for several hours or days at a time. They will not be asked to move back and forth between inbound and outbound with each call on a random basis.

A blended agent is one who is in fact trained to move back and forth between inbound and outbound with each call. One industry where using blended agents has been very successful is the collections industry. In the process of making outbound calls to collect money, the agents will leave voice-mail messages asking the customer to call back and speak to them directly for the purpose of settling the account. Obviously, it is important that the agent be able to take the call and retrieve the earlier record when the person calls in.

If you intend to train your TSRs as universal agents, it is best to have some consistency between the inbound and outbound programs that they are working on, so that you can leverage the training to support both applications. Otherwise you may find that you are sacrificing too much in the way of conversion for the sake of increased efficiency of call handling. Universal agent strategies will typically increase the call-handling efficiency, resulting in lower costs per inbound call. However, they also will probably result in a lower average conversion rate versus what you can achieve in a fully dedicated outbound environment. This generally results in a higher cost per order on the outbound side. If you decide to give universal agents a try you will need to test carefully, to see which of these factors has a greater impact with respect to your bottom line.

When using universal agents, good arguments can be made for training on either inbound or outbound first. It depends a lot on what the needs of the program are at the moment. If you need more inbound support, you start there. If outbound is the pressing issue, you start there.

It's important to remember that training starts with recruitment, and it is far easier to recruit inbound reps than outbound. For instance, if your company runs two ads, one for inbound help at $8 an hour and another for outbound help at $9 an hour, you will probably get 10 responses to the inbound ad for every one you get for the outbound ad. So if you are in a real recruiting crunch that may force your hand to train on inbound first. We know of one universal agent telecenter that is operated by a regional phone company that trains on outbound first, and then overcomes the recruiting problem by using the services of a temp agency to supply TSRs.

On the other hand, if you recruit for outbound sales help, you will attract people who are comfortable with making outbound sales calls, which are more intrusive and assertive in nature than inbound calls. Outbound-trained sales reps will experience little difficulty in transitioning to inbound calling as long as they can make equal money handling inbound versus outbound.

It is difficult to take an inbound person who is not generally proactive on the phone and try to transition that person to outbound calls. So, if you are recruiting for universal agents and starting them out on inbound, you should be very clear in the hiring process that ultimately they will be expected to make outbound calls as well. Remember, building an outbound mentality in an inbound environment starts with recruiting, hiring, and proper communication about what is to be expected on the job.

Interactive Voice Response Unit (IVRU) Technology

IVRUs have become so prevalent in today's inbound telecenters that there are now some companies that use them exclusively. Of course, companies that use totally automated systems are generally more interested in cost savings than with the quality of the customer experience.

It's good to understand the difference between auto-attendants and IVRUs. Auto-attendants are call-answering machines that allow each caller to route the call to the correct person without the intervention of a switchboard operator.

IVRUs on the other hand are fully interactive computer systems. They will allow you not only to reach the person within the organization that you would like to speak to, but they will also gather or disseminate information and/or allow you to review the status of your account, or even take an order, all without the intervention of a live operator.

IVRUs are truly amazing in what they can do. However, you do need to approach their use with one eye on the cost-savings opportunity and the other eye on the reality of the customer experience.

You have to be careful that you do not put in too many menus or too many options within each menu. You need to watch the reports closely. If you are losing calls because there are too many menus or options, your reports will tell you exactly where this is happening.

You should always list your most popular menu selection as option 1. Explanation of the options must be clear enough that people will not be tempted to select the wrong option because it sounds close to the one they want.

The point here is to be very careful when setting up the programming logic for an IVRU. We highly recommend that you trap some of the ANIs (automatic number identification which identifies the called-from number) or records of the people that called into the system, and call them back a week later. You can ask them what they thought of the experience and whether they left the transaction with a sense of satisfaction. This can be a real eye-opener.

When to Use IVRUs

Customers really like this technology when they have the sense that they are in control. They like it when they can see what the system really says about their account status without having the bias of a customer service rep filtering the information. They like the sense of privacy. They like getting quick access to what they want to know or do without having to wait for a live operator to become available. Companies like this technology when it allows them to hold a caller on the line until a live operator is available during busy peak-response periods. They also like the cost savings that can accrue when the customer is able to complete a purchase or information gathering transaction without the involvement of a live operator. IVRUs generally cost 50 percent less than routing the calls through live agents.

These systems are efficient because they can gather some preliminary information from the callers and speed up the overall process by routing the call to the correct specialist along with all the account information.

Basically, if the cost savings outweighs the conversion lift that you get with live operators, then using IVRUs is the way to go.

When Not to Use IVRUs

Don't expect an IVRU to do a good job of cross-selling or upselling. If your program is conversion sensitive, you better make sure that you are getting the proper ROI (return on investment). You should have live operators take those calls that must be handled with an outbound sales mentality.

As with everything else in direct marketing, you should think about who your typical customer is before settling on this technology. For instance, senior citizens may have much less tolerance for interacting with the IVRU than would younger, more technology-savvy customers. Seniors may also become more easily confused with the menu options and have a higher tendency to hang up rather than deal with complex choices. They may also have a harder time pressing the correct keys and getting the receiver back to their ear in time to hear the next set of options if they are using a phone that has the keys built into the handset rather than the base unit.

Should You Always Provide a Live Operator Opt-Out?

If you are running a sales program that doesn't require a cross-sell or an upsell, and you don't give the customers an opt-out to a live operator, your only risk is lost revenue. On the other hand, if you are running a sensitive application such as a member-save program and people are calling in to cancel a service that they may feel they didn't even order in the first place, you can have a major legal problem if you don't offer a live agent opt-out. This can be particularly troubling if every time customers call back they wind up in a loop and get no satisfaction. If that happens, the next call you get may be from the customer's state attorney general's office. We highly recommend that you always provide a live agent opt-out to all IVRU applications.

What Problems Should You Watch Out for When Using IVRUs?

We're sure that many of our readers have had the experience of getting stuck in an endless loop within an IVRU. Getting stuck in a loop is like getting on a highway off-ramp with no exit. You just go round and round. The only way out is to hang up and try again. The solution to the loop problem is to test every conceivable path to make sure that there are no loops.

Another problem revolves around the fact that there is no guarantee that the customer will press the correct number. Most IVRU systems are programmed so that if a customer presses a number that is not a valid option, then the original menu is replayed. Similarly, many systems are programmed so that if the customer doesn't make any selection within a specified amount of time, the system will automatically move to a default option, either the original opening menu or a live agent. You can generally program the system to wait for whatever number of seconds you feel is appropriate before automatically moving to the default. You can also set a limit to the absolute amount of time that the customer is allowed to stay in the IVRU without being automatically transferred to a live operator.

Remember that there are still a lot of rotary phones in service, and IVRUs won't work with rotary phones. This is another reason to make sure that you default to a live agent if the customer doesn't press a number within the specified time allotted.

Capacity to answer calls is an issue just as it is in regular live agent programs. IVRU capacity is measured in the number of ports and phone lines that are connected to the system. A port is like an agent in that you can only have one call per port at any given time. Each port will need to have access to a separate phone line if all the ports are active simultaneously. If you have more calls than available ports and lines, your callers will either get a busy signal or be placed on hold.

A Final Word on IVRUs

The most important thing to remember about using IVRU technology is that you should view it from the "customer experience" perspective first, and then consider the cost savings.

Computer Telephony Integration (CTI)

Simply stated, CTI, or computer telephony integration, is the linking of the computer and the telephone so that the voice and data portions of the communication come together and speak to one another.

Years ago an agency such as DialAmerica might have had many different companies all using one popular and easy-to-remember phone number. Each client whose calls were using that line would be assigned a unique extension number that they would print after the phone number in all their advertising. When the calls came in the operator would ask the caller for the desired extension. The TSR would then select the extension number from a menu and get the correct order screen on the terminal.

CTI has changed everything. In today's environment every program has (or should have) its own 800 number, and when a call comes in, it has a DNIS (dialed number identification service) attached to it. The ACD (automated call distributor) looks at the incoming call and decides which rep to send it to based on who is qualified to handle the call, and who has been waiting the longest for a call. However, it may first need to talk to the data side and ask to have the correct screen sent to the rep terminal, because that is where the voice is going. At the same time the ACD may review the caller's ANI (automatic number identification) and reach into a mainframe database, either on-site or thousands of miles away, to retrieve the customer's account and purchase history, so that the screen comes up with specific caller information.

Even though the technology would permit it, most companies will not use the ANI to answer the phone by using the customer's name in the greeting. Callers tend to find it very disconcerting when the TSR knows who they are before they've had the chance to introduce themselves. A major financial services company first tested this tactic in 1987. It was an absolute disaster. Callers were hanging up right and left because they said that they felt like it was "Big Brother" on the other end of the line.

CTI can also be used with IVRU technology to allow customers to interact with their own purchase history.

We are now at the point where CTI will not only allow the TSR access to the data side of the communication, but also the caller can have simultaneous visual access to the same data over the Internet.

Convergence has become a major technology theme as we begin the new century, and this is nowhere more evident than in the linking of phones and computers through computer telephony integration. Very soon consumers will be using multifunctional wireless devices that will do everything from opening the garage door to calling long distance for free over the Internet, and CTI will be at the heart of all this technology.

Inbound and the Internet

Of course, it's very tempting to make bold statements about where the relationship between inbound telemarketing and the Internet is going. However, it's important to remember that sometimes the hype can be bigger than the reality. As we begin the twenty-first century, a majority of the American public is still not using the Internet on a regular basis. Of those that are using it, there is still only a small percentage who are actually going to a website's order page to make a purchase. We've heard recent reports by seminar speakers that seem to indicate that as many as two-thirds of those would-be buyers are abandoning the transaction midway through, because they have unresolved questions or have changed their mind. Herein lies the great opportunity for telemarketing and the Internet. Live agents can help Internet users by answering their questions and giving them confidence that they are making the right decisions.

There is one thing about this relationship that we are very certain about, and that is that the technology is racing ahead faster than the consumer education required to fully utilize it. That will create an ongoing need for live agent support to satisfy the consumer's desire to participate fully in this global phenomenon we call the Internet.

Another point to remember is that the Internet and telemarketing are both essentially telecommunications-based services, and because of that we believe that their futures are inextricably woven together.

So the question really becomes: How will we communicate in the future? Will it be via the coax cable that services our television set? (Probably yes.) Will the TV become truly interactive like our PCs, and just switch from mode to mode to either watch a program, surf the Net, play a video game, view our E-mail, or answer a phone call? (Probably yes.) Will we communicate via radio waves from a satellite to a wireless device that can do all sorts of things besides act as a voice-only telephone? (Definitely yes.) Will we still be dependent upon the copper wire pair that has so faithfully served us with land-line telephone access for the last hundred years? (Probably not.)

One inbound-Internet application that has definitely arrived is the connect-to or call-me technology. Customers are clicking on a "live operator" button on a website, which is sending a message to a customer contact center that says that the person wants to communicate either via a Web chat session over the Internet or via a live voice or both. The limitation for simultaneous voice and data communication is related to whether or not the customer has sufficient bandwidth in their Internet connection or the presence of multiple phone lines in their home. Industry experts report that only a small minority of households in the United States are wired for multiple lines. However, bandwidth and modem speeds are expected to increase dramatically over the next few years.

Another emerging Internet-related technology that will have a major impact on telemarketing is VOIP (voice over internet protocol). This holds the promise of providing free long distance phone calls for a low monthly ISP access fee. Customers using VOIP will use their computers to call regular direct-dial numbers for customer service or tech support, or to place an order, all at no charge, rather than using a toll-free 800 number. The cost of a phone call has certainly plunged over the last several years, owing primarily to fierce competition among the service providers. The advent of VOIP coupled with advertising-supported free Internet access may drive the last remaining costs out of the telecommunications equation.

One final point about the Internet and call-center technology is that consumers now have yet another pathway with which to communicate to your company. This will expand both the marketing opportunities, and the actual number of customer contacts you will have to deal with. Your organization may be accustomed to receiving a million contacts a year via voice, mail, or fax. The Internet provides the customer with another path, and it's a pretty darn cheap and easy one to use, so you may find that with the same customer base, you are experiencing an explosion of customer contacts as people become more comfortable with E-mail, Web chat, and website interactions. You will need to be prepared to respond to this increased demand.

Unfortunately, according to industry experts, a majority (more than 60 percent) of all American companies take five days or longer to respond to an E-mail or Web chat request for assistance. Clearly, this is a very poor level of service. The risk is that in a global economy with so much competition you may only get one chance to earn a customer's loyalty.

The standard for responding to E-mail from customers should be 24 hours or less, and you should respond to call-me buttons for a live-voice or Web-chat request immediately, just as you would for an inbound phone call.

There are still a lot of undecided issues out there as to where all of this technology is really going. One thing is for sure, though—the Internet is here *now*, and people are using it to communicate with each other in faster and cheaper ways than ever before. As a telemarketer, you can either try to stay on the cutting edge, or try to catch up later.

Summary

- Always consider technology issues before putting your inbound marketing plan together.
- The "80 percent in 20 seconds" rule is a good rule of thumb for initially estimating a proper service level when you have no other experience.
- Abandoned calls do not necessarily represent lost revenue, as a person may call back at a later time and reach a live agent. The

abandonment rate is never as high as the ACD reports indicate because some callers will always call back.

- Whether to place your inbound program in a shared, semi-dedicated, or dedicated environment is one of the most important decisions you will make. Try to be as realistic as possible when deciding how much focus your program really needs. You could add a lot of unnecessary expense if you opt for a fully dedicated environment when you don't need it. On the other hand, you may lose sales if you settle for too little focus when you really need it.

- Disasters happen every day. You need to prepare for them by acquiring as much redundancy in your systems as you can reasonably afford.

- Retention is the secret to profitability, and training is the secret to retention. Successful training starts with recruiting the best-qualified people for the job.

- Let candidates know early in the hiring process if you are trying to build a staff of universal agents who are trained to handle both inbound and outbound calls. It may be easier to first train the reps on the outbound applications and then move to inbound ones rather than vice versa.

- Always provide a live agent opt-out of your IVRU. Test the programming thoroughly for unintended loops before you allow live callers into the system. There is nothing worse than having callers fall into a black hole within the IVRU.

- CTI sometimes appears more complex than it really is. It is simply the joining of the voice and data portions of a telephone communication, so that TSRs and callers can communicate more effectively with each other and the computer systems supporting the call.

- The Internet will ultimately change everything we know about telemarketing. Inbound call centers are already busily making the transition from handling inbound phone calls only to being able to respond to E-mail, Web chat requests, and call-me buttons on websites. They are fast becoming full-service customer contact centers. As the Internet and E-commerce grow in the twenty-first century, so will inbound telemarketing grow to handle the additional customer-driven activity associated with it.

6

Fulfillment

The Road to Success or the Bane of Direct Marketers

For years direct marketers have known that the performance of their fulfillment system can make all the difference between success and failure in any campaign. It's an area that never takes a rest and the decisions made are crucial to the success of any direct marketing product or program.

So, what are the key fulfillment areas that impact the success of your program?

1. Transmittal of orders from your telemarketer to your fulfillment center
2. Promptness of shipping
3. Source key integrity
4. Credit and collection
5. Bad debts
6. Returns
7. Reporting system
8. Accuracy of information
9. Customer service

Each of the above fulfillment components impacts the others, as well as your back-end results. Review each of them and you'll notice the position each one has within the fulfillment process, and how one impacts the other. Your fulfillment operation may be excellent in most areas, but it only takes one weak link to disrupt the entire operation, and negatively impact your business.

As we mentioned in chapter 2, there are four critical areas in a telemarketing campaign that are under the control of the client marketer. These are the offer, the product, the list universe, and fulfillment.

Let's take a closer look at each of the key areas in the fulfillment function with an eye toward pointing out good practices and potential mistakes.

Order Transmission

Transmitting the orders from your telemarketer to your fulfillment center is the first order of business in the fulfillment process. In outbound telemarketing you may not have the luxury of having your fulfillment center receive your customer orders directly, as is usually the case for direct mail or media promotions. Outbound telemarketing usually requires that this extra step (order transmittals from the telecenter to the fulfillment center) be executed perfectly by both your telemarketing and fulfillment organizations. The better this is executed, the lower your returns and bad debts.

If the order received by your telemarketing organization is recorded and processed properly, you have eliminated a number of potential customer service problems that would have developed had there been an initial order transmission problem. The most important of these is the delayed shipment of the product. Delayed shipment should be defined as any delay, no matter how brief, that is greater than 24 hours after the scheduled shipment date.

Source Key Integrity/Accuracy of Information

Delays usually happen for technical reasons, but transmission problems are not limited to delays. We know of one case where the source key was incorrect, and the wrong product was subsequently shipped. In this case, the product was very similar to the product with the correct code and the back end held up. The company handled it properly and offered to ship the correct product to each customer. Most of the customers accepted this solution, even though they had forgotten what they had originally ordered. It's a confirmation of one of the axioms of telemarketing:

Memory is fleeting and the longer it takes you to ship the product, the higher your returns—which in telemarketing are higher to begin with than other direct-response marketing areas, including direct mail and alternative media.

Generally speaking, the longer it takes you to ship, the more unopened returns you receive.

Remember that maintaining the accuracy of the data is vital. If you can't read and/or rely on the data, you can't make the right decision. The whole premise of direct marketing is based on the principle of using today's data to predict tomorrow's behavior.

Prompt Shipment of the Product

The most important aspect of the fulfillment function is timely shipment. If your order is processed and shipped quickly and accurately, it will impact your P&L positively by increasing payments and decreasing returns. The faster the customer receives your product, the greater your profit.

Nothing is more frustrating to customers than not receiving a product to which they have been looking forward. Moreover, nothing is more damaging to your revenue (and credibility) than a customer not receiving that product.

The customer cannot affect the shipment; the company *can*. It's surprising how many direct marketers take their fulfillment operations for granted. Dick Benson, a well-respected industry expert and member of the Direct Marketing Hall of Fame, has said repeatedly, "You should visit your fulfillment organization or division at least once a month to head off any problems, and to let them know you are watching them closely." Taking care of all the component parts of the fulfillment system should be a top priority in your organization.

Returns and bad debts are critical factors in all direct-response programs, but in outbound telemarketing there's typically an increase in returns, and a decrease in bad debts. Your product's real cost plays an important part in the analysis.

The Relationship Between Returns and Bad Debt

The back-end relationship of outbound telemarketing orders is a bit more difficult to predict than that of orders generated by other media. However, it would not be unreasonable to project a 50 percent increase in returns, and a 50 percent decrease in bad debt versus direct mail results. The logic behind this assumption is based on the fact that the customer has not seen the product or a promotional brochure of any kind, and is therefore far more likely to make a return than a direct mail customer who has at least seen a picture of it.

Credit and Collection

Credit and collection is a vague description for one of the more intricate processes in direct marketing. It involves the setting of the criteria for extending credit and executing the most effective method of collecting from those who passed through the output selection screens but still became collection opportunities.

Incredible as it may seem, every one of your bad debtors is a collection opportunity. The techniques used to convert a collection *opportunity* to a collection *success* vary from organization to organization.

Once a potential customer passes your credit screens and performs outside of your expectations, the process of actually turning this collection opportunity into cash begins. This should be an extremely creative and intense process. Let's review the normal procedure for collecting from your customers who are less than prompt with their payment(s).

The Collection Series

Every direct marketing organization or their fulfillment house has a collection series. Most have been tested time and again and the process is ongoing. Most are effective, and if you don't have an effective series of your own, then you should use what is tested and available from your fulfillment house.

Most collection series contain six efforts, but they should include as many efforts as your P&L projections show are profitable. In plain language, you mail until the amount you collect from an effort is less than the cost of the effort. There's little difference between telemarketing and direct mail collection techniques.

An effective collection series presents a strong collection opportunity. Realizing that the objective of any collection series is to take advantage of every collection opportunity available, the key to maximizing profits lies in identifying and testing new efforts, techniques, and methods on a continuing basis.

Let's take a look at a typical collection series and probably one of the strongest fourth efforts available. The *first effort* is a bill and, for those who feel relationship marketing is important, a thank-you note with another offer (usually a buckslip) to include with the payment.

The *second effort* is a bill with a reminder that the account is past due. If the customer already paid the previous invoice, he or she should disregard this notice.

The *third effort* is a critical effort and should not look like the previous two bills. A different color envelope is essential. The language should be firm yet leave an opening in case the customer's payment has crossed in the mail. Remember, at this point you still have a potentially good customer with whom you would like to do business in the future.

The most crucial is the *fourth effort*, as there are diminishing returns on all subsequent efforts. Figure 6.1 shows one of the most effective fourth efforts ever written. It's currently in use as a control for a number of direct marketing organizations. It arrives as a personalized letter in a white envelope.

The reason this effort works is because it informs the person that we have absolutely identified him. We know where he lives, that he did indeed place an order, and that we are serious about collecting the amount due.

Many years ago, we added a line to a similar letter and the results improved considerably. The line was: "What do you and this letter have in common? You're both in the red." Of course, the letter was printed in red ink.

Date

Mr. John Doe
Address
City, State, Zip

Dear Mr. Doe:

Despite our repeated requests, the facts remain the same:

1. You ordered (*product name*) from us and it was shipped to you at the above
   address on (*date*).
2. We billed you for (*product name*) on numerous occasions. These repeated
   reminders have been ignored by you.
3. If payment is not received promptly, further efforts to collect this unpaid sum will
   be made by the collection office.

Prompt payment will protect your credit rating.

Please pay this obligation today!

Sincerely,

(*Name*)
Credit Manager

Figure 6.1 Fourth Collection Effort

It worked quite well. The problem was the number of customer complaints that surfaced in response to this letter. The owner of the company decided it was best not to include it in the collection series.

Earlier in this section we mentioned that the first effort often includes a thank-you note as part of a relationship-building strategy. The first-effort welcome letter shown in Figure 6.2 has been thoroughly tested and should be a good starting point for anyone wishing to build an effective billing series.

Date

Dear Mr(s). _____ ,

Thank you for speaking with us on the telephone recently. You'll be pleased to know
we have processed your order, and you should be receiving _____
(product name) shortly.

Once you receive _____ (your product), you have a full 30-day trial
period to use it. You'll discover _____ (some outstanding product
feature or benefit).

You may now send in payment in the envelope we've provided, or you may wait until
the end of your 30-day trial period. Either way, simply return the top portion of this
order confirmation, along with the total amount due and your account will be paid in
full. Please make a check or money order payable to (company name), or you may
pay by credit card by filling out the information above.

Sincerely,

Customer Service Manager

P.S. You'll also be receiving your free gift shortly. If you have any questions, please
call us toll free at 1-800-xxx-xxxx and ask for extension xx, from 8:00 A.M. until 8:00
P.M. EST Monday–Friday.

Figure 6.2 First-Effort/Welcome/Thank-You Letter

Using a Collection Agency

Turning your slow payers over to an outside organization is the last step
in the collection process. It effectively ends the "collection opportunity"
designation and begins the final recovery stage.

Most of the top collection service agencies will be able to provide
billing and payment processing as well as offering a multilingual customer service phone capability with English-, French-, and Spanish-
speaking operators.

One of the most important issues in using an outside collection organization is their compliance with postal regulations and government regulatory agencies. They must comply with the Fair Debt Collection Practices Act (FDCPA), and all other applicable federal and state laws and statutes.

Collection organizations work in myriad ways, but the usual method of compensation is a negotiated remit rate to the client. Receiving something is better than nothing. The key is to be very sure that the account being collected is truly a bad debt, and not the result of a customer service problem.

Returns and What They Really Mean

Figure 6.3 shows two examples that illustrate the importance of the product-cost and the returns–bad debt relationship.

The first example is for a collectible with an actual product cost of $6.50 and a selling price of $35. Bad debts for all direct mail orders averaged 16 percent. Returns on the mail-sold orders averaged 18 percent. A return including shipping, handling, refurbishing, and restocking costs approximately $4.50. In this situation, based on the value of the product, a return *positively* impacts the bottom line, because the cost to restock a return is less than the cost to manufacture a new unit.

The second example, a juvenile continuity book series, ships two books a month with a selling price of $4.79 each, and an actual cost per book of 59 cents. The total cost of goods for each two-book shipment is

Example 1: Collectible Product		Example 2: Juvenile Book Continuity	
Selling Price	$35.00	Selling Price	$9.58
Cost of Goods	$6.50	Cost of Goods	$1.18
Cost to Restock Returns	$4.50	Cost to Restock Returns	$4.50

Media	Returns	Bad Debt	Media	Returns	Bad Debt
Mail	18%	16%	Mail	15%	15%
Phone	24%	8%	Phone	22%	8%

Net Impact of Processing Return = + $2.00   Net Impact of Processing Return = $3.32

Figure 6.3 Returns–Bad Debt Relationship

$1.18. Bad debts and returns each averaged 15 percent on mail-sold orders. A return costs $4.50 to process back into inventory. In this situation, based on the value of the product, a return *negatively* impacts the bottom line. In fact, from a purely financial standpoint you might prefer that a customer would go to bad debt, rather than return the product. Of course, processing a return does take the customer out of the collection process, which will save some money in printing and postage—not an insignificant issue these days.

Now let's look at these two examples from a telemarketing standpoint. The collectible product from the first example would have approximately 24 percent returns and 8 percent bad debt on outbound telemarketing sold orders. As we mentioned earlier, in most telemarketing situations returns increase 50 percent versus direct mail or media, and bad debt decreases by 50 percent, a positive P&L change. In this case, you're receiving $6.50 back and it's costing you $4.50.

Returns for the juvenile continuity book series in the second example increase to 22 percent, and bad debts decrease to 8 percent with telemarketing sold orders—a negative P&L change. You're receiving $1.18 back, but it's costing you $4.50 to receive the return, a loss of $3.32.

Cost of the product is definitely an important consideration when planning any telemarketing or direct response campaign.

Returns usually are a significant influence on your final P&L projections; but how do returns impact future promotions to those customers? What does it mean when a customer returns one, two, three, or more products to you? How should it be viewed? What are your options? These are critical questions.

Promoting New Offers to Returners

Remember that the use of an outside collection organization does not necessarily remove the customer's name from your house file. You may wish to eliminate those customers from future promotions, and your selection process may do that automatically. However, it does become an interesting test opportunity.

A number of direct marketing organizations select "bad debt" segments as part of an ongoing test program. The issue is intriguing. If the customer, who is now a bad debt, has been a long-term, loyal customer with numerous on-time payments, how should he or she be handled?

What happens if the customer is a member of your video club, book club, and music club and is in the collection process for only one of the clubs? If either of these situations exist, the customer requires a voice contact and an immediate resolution of the issue.

Customers who, while in the collection process, order another product through telemarketing, media, direct mail, etc., should be sent a letter informing them of their status and clearly stating that if they send a check for the full amount in advance, the product will be shipped to them promptly.

One return by itself is not generally a predictor of future purchasing behavior for telemarketing or any of the other direct marketing channels. Two or more returns can become a significant predictor for all channels, particularly when the customer has returned more products than he has kept. Customers who return more products/shipments than they keep are classified as frequent rejecters and in many organizations they become "do-not-promotes." These do-not-promotes can become a significant portion of your file. One of the issues in telemarketing is that because telemarketing incurs higher returns, frequent rejecters should always be eliminated from your outbound calling lists prior to initiating each new campaign.

The frequent-rejecters segment does offer an opportunity for future sales, but the opportunity is based on reestablishing communication with the customer. Many companies, including one of the top TV home-shopping channels, have found ways to turn frequent rejecters into future good customers. If a customer tends to return more products than is deemed reasonable, the company sends them a letter asking them to consider their future purchases more carefully. Other companies have tackled this problem by becoming more refined in their mailing list selection and merge-purge process.

Many companies send out a confirmation letter whenever they receive a return. If the "returner" is a customer in good standing, the confirmation is an excellent opportunity to include a new offer.

If the product is part of a continuity program it's often less expensive to reinstate a previous customer than it is to acquire a new customer. Telemarketing is the best method available for reinstatement. The response rates for reinstatement programs can more than justify the cost and as mentioned previously, it's less costly than acquiring a new member.

Surveys About Returns and Bad Debts

One of the most important considerations in a customer service program is effective communication with *all* customers. Figure 6.4 is a survey format used to determine the reason for product returns. It is sent with a cover letter explaining why the customer is receiving the survey. The letter states that the survey is part a customer service policy to communicate with customers who have stopped participating in the program. The example uses a book program offer, but you can adapt it to your specific needs.

When research is utilized to determine your customer's reasons for canceling or returning a product it's important to get the customer to be specific about the reason for the action. Furthermore, you can be much more direct to a person who has already made a return than you can with a customer who is still in the collection process.

The key questions to ask bad-debt customers are:

Are you currently receiving new product shipments from
_____ ?

□ Yes   □ No

If "No": Why not? _____

_____

The reason for this question is that, in many cases, they do not know they are part of your collection procedure. Many believe they have a customer service problem. Some, because of database problems, may even be receiving additional shipments for this or other programs. Asking why the bill has not been paid may alienate a good customer who simply has a customer service problem or mixup.

Research can provide you with some definitive answers to your cancellation, return, and collection questions, but it must be undertaken carefully.

As with many areas of direct marketing, there is a time sensitivity to surveying returners for information on why they have returned the product. If you wait more than a few weeks, most will have forgotten the real reasons behind their decision. They will simply offer excuses and justifications fearing that you won't honor their return.

Survey

Please answer all questions completely and accurately.

1. Overall, did the _____ program meet your expectations?
   ☐ Yes   ☐ No

   If no, why do you feel this way? _____
   _____

2. Why did you order _____ program? _____
   _____

3. Approximately how many shipments did you receive prior to canceling your
   membership in _____?
   ☐ 1   ☐ 2   ☐ 3   ☐ 4   ☐ 5   ☐ 6

4. Why did you decide to return this particular _____
   program/shipment? _____
   _____

6. How would you rate the service you received from _____?
   ☐ Excellent   ☐ Good   ☐ Fair   ☐ Poor

   If fair or poor, why do you feel that way? _____
   _____

7. Please check the appropriate box below that expresses your feelings about each
   of the following areas as they pertain to _____ program.

	Excellent	Very Good	Good	Fair	Poor
Value for the money	☐	☐	☐	☐	☐
Quality of books	☐	☐	☐	☐	☐
Appropriateness of books for child's reading level	☐	☐	☐	☐	☐
Timeliness of shipments	☐	☐	☐	☐	☐

Figure 6.4 Example Mail-Back Survey to Customers Who Returned a Shipment from a
Children's Book Program

	Excellent	Very Good	Good	Fair	Poor
Accuracy of bills	☐	☐	☐	☐	☐
Clarity of bills	☐	☐	☐	☐	☐
Amount of bills	☐	☐	☐	☐	☐
Durability of books	☐	☐	☐	☐	☐
Overall satisfaction with nonbook items (posters, cassettes, and stickers)	☐	☐	☐	☐	☐

8. What particularly did you find appealing about _____?

_____

9. What did you find unappealing about _____?

_____

10. Why did you recently discontinue your participation in _____?

_____

11. Are you currently a member of any other "at-home" reading programs?

    ☐ Yes   ☐ No

    If yes, which at-home reading programs do you participate in? _____

_____

12. Would you recommend _____ to a friend?

    ☐ Yes   ☐ No

Classification Data

Are you: ☐ Male   ☐ Female

Is your child: ☐ Male   ☐ Female

What is the age of your child?

☐ Under 2 years of age   ☐ 2 years old   ☐ 3 years old   ☐ 4 years old

☐ 5 years old   ☐ 6 years old   ☐ 7 years old   ☐ 8 years old

Your education: ☐ High school graduate   ☐ Graduated college

☐ Attended college   ☐ Postgraduate work

Is the area you live in: ☐ Rural   ☐ Urban   ☐ Suburban

Figure 6.4 (Continued)

Outbound telemarketing can sometimes be used to gather this information; however, you will not be able to ask as many questions, and the answers will carry the bias or influence of the questioner as well as the person who is providing the answers. It is therefore recommended that you eliminate most or all of the open-ended questions when you are conducting the survey over the phone. Figure 6.5 shows an example of a suitable survey to use when following up with continuity club returners over the phone.

Hello, Mr(s). _____ . This is _____ calling from DialAmerica Marketing with a brief market research survey for xxxxx. How are you this evening?

That's fine, Mr(s). _____ . The reason for my call is that we are conducting a brief survey to help us better serve our xxxxx members. There are only five questions, so it will only take a minute. OK?

1. Great. Our records indicate that we had contacted you by phone last (July) about joining our xxxxx *club*. Do you recall receiving our phone call Mr(s). _____ ?

    _____ Yes   _____ No

2. Fine, do you recall receiving your membership card, and welcome letter in the mail?

    _____ Yes _____ No, Well, maybe we have the wrong address. Are you at _____ (address)?
    _____ Yes   _____ No

Great. Now I'd like to describe the xxxxx *club* to you and then ask if that matches your recollection of how the club was described to you over the phone. Here's how it works; in the same package with your gift, you would also receive _____ for $$$$$ plus shipping and handling. If you decided to keep it, we would have activated your account. Then about once a month we'd have sent you a new unit to examine for _____ days. Any additional

---

Figure 6.5 Phone Survey to Returners

Reporting Systems

Back-end (fulfillment) reporting systems will vary depending upon whether you use an in-house operation or an agency. Everyone has their own way to track the data and report the results. Regardless of how the system is set up, you will need to get timely reports on a list-by-list, and cumulative, basis that show you:

- *Shipments*—in units and dollar value
- *Payments received*—in units, dollar value, and as a percentage of the total
- *Bad-debt (open)*—in units, dollar value, and as a percentage of total shipments
- *Returns*—in units, dollar value, and as a percentage of total shipments

---

units you decided to purchase would have been at the regular low price of just $$$$$ plus shipping and handling. To the best of your recollection, was this how the xxxxx club was described to you?

3. _____ Yes   _____ No   Comments _____

Fine. Now our records indicate that you returned our shipment. Can you tell me the reason why?

4. _____ Can't afford/too expensive   _____ Already has similar products
   _____ Not interested   _____ Slow delivery
   _____ Changed mind   _____ Received wrong product
   _____ Never agreed to join   _____ Other

5. Fine. One last question Mr(s). _____ . If your circumstances change, would you consider purchasing other products from us in the future?
   _____ Yes   _____ No

Thank you for your time, Mr(s). _____ . We really appreciate your help, and if xxxxx can be of any service in the future, please let us know.

Figure 6.5 (Continued)

We've seen some pretty confusing back-end reporting formats over the years, and you may have to fight your way through half a dozen reports to get these few key pieces of information. However, there are five key elements on which all of the back-end portions of the P&L stand. Figure 6.6 shows an example format that gives you everything you need for a one-shot.

Don't be in a hurry to read the back-end fulfillment results. It can often take four, six, or eight months, or even a year, to get a full reading on the back end. This is particularly true of continuities. In fact, we know of certain subscription marketing campaigns that have taken up to three years to read accurately, because the renewal's pattern in years three and beyond was so different from the front-end acquisition and second-year conversion patterns.

There is usually no mistake more dangerous to the profitability of a direct marketing campaign than to misread the back end and roll out a loser. In fact, we've seen this mistake end careers and shut down entire business divisions. Please take your time and be careful. If you are not 100 percent sure about what is really happening, it's time to call in a consultant, and work hard at conducting confirming retests.

List Key Code	Units Shipped	Dollars Shipped	Units Paid	Dollars Paid	Paid %
A1	250	$10,000.00	140	$ 5,600.00	56.0%
A2	300	$12,000.00	190	$ 7,600.00	63.3%
A3	200	$ 8,000.00	160	$ 6,400.00	80.0%
A4	100	$ 4,000.00	75	$ 3,000.00	75.0%
A5	150	$ 6,000.00	80	$ 3,200.00	53.3%
Total	1,000	$40,000.00	645	$25,800.00	64.5%

List Key Code	Units Returned	Dollars Returned	Returned	Units Open	Dollars Open	Open %
A1	90	$ 3,600.00	36.0%	20	$ 800.00	8.0%
A2	70	$ 2,800.00	23.3%	40	$1,600.00	13.3%
A3	35	$ 1,400.00	17.5%	5	$ 200.00	2.5%
A4	20	$ 800.00	20.0%	5	$ 200.00	5.0%
A5	45	$ 1,800.00	30.0%	25	$1,000.00	16.7%
Total	260	$10,400.00	26.0%	95	$3,800.00	9.5%

Figure 6.6 Example Format for a Reporting System

Customer Service

Incorporating a great customer service operation into the mix is the last ingredient needed for an outstanding fulfillment process. Of course, we are not trying to say that it is the last thing you should consider. On the contrary, great customer service is what this book is all about. Every customer service caller should be happier when they hang up the phone than they were when they picked it up, regardless of their reason for placing the call.

What do customers expect when they call for service?

- They expect you to answer the call promptly, but as we mentioned in the last chapter, they typically are more willing to interact with a VRU prior to speaking with a live operator. If they are calling with a problem, putting them on hold for six and a half minutes is not going to make them any happier.
- They expect to be treated with courtesy and respect.
- They expect that the customer service agent will understand them when they speak. That may require a multilingual agent. They also expect to be able to understand the agent.
- They expect that the agent will have access to their full customer history including all previous purchases, billing, and account transactions, and phone calls. This is particularly true when they are calling a second time for the same problem.
- They expect that the agent or the agent's superior will have the responsibility and the authority to solve the problem and/or give valid and accurate advice.
- If you are selling a technical product, they will expect that the agent or someone that they can be transferred to will be able to offer at least limited tech support. Sometimes this is not the case, as live tech support is very expensive. At a minimum they will expect that the customer service agent can refer them to a non–toll-free number for live tech support. Alternatively, they may ask for a website or E-mail address for on-line support.
- They expect prompt fulfillment of whatever action the agent promised as a result of the phone call. It is not at all helpful to your reputation to tell your customers that you will send out the replacement or adjust your records in two to four weeks. This is

particularly true if the customer has to call back a month later to complain again that you didn't even make *that* deadline.

Fulfillment is where the money is made or lost. There are a tremendous number of details to keep track of. Good luck. Remember, if you get in trouble, call a consultant. They've seen it all and can usually size up a problem, and offer a solution, within a very short period of time.

Summary

- Fulfillment, billing and collections, and customer service are where money is made or lost in most direct marketing campaigns.
- We are rapidly approaching a world where electronic transmission of data can make instantaneous fulfillment of orders a reality, which will have a positive impact on profitability for most campaigns.
- One back-end rule of thumb for making a prediction about outbound telemarketing results versus direct mail results is to increase the direct mail return rate by 50 percent and reduce the direct mail bad debt rate by 50 percent.
- A good, professionally written collection effort can make a huge difference in program profitability. The fourth effort is usually the most important letter in the series.
- Be careful when promoting new offers to previous returners. Consider not including premiums, or requiring more of a commitment to purchase, prior to shipping more products to someone who has returned a previous purchase. Surveying returners can be an excellent strategy for uncovering the hidden flaws in your marketing plan.
- Take your time in reading back-end results. Many companies take six months or more to read back-end results before planning their rollout.
- Always alert your inbound customer service department when running an outbound campaign through another call center. Provide them with copies of the scripts and give them a chance to monitor calls so they will be confident about what the outbound TSRs are telling the customers.

7

The Rollout

One of the beautiful things about telemarketing is that it presents corporations and other organizations with a quick read on both new products and those that have already proved successful through other marketing channels. The results of this quick read can be reviewed on a daily basis, and because of this, the risk and/or potential can be assessed almost immediately. Moreover, you, the telemarketing professional, can make changes on the fly to improve the program as you go.

The risk involved in testing telemarketing is minimal when you are working with an agency on a per-inquiry basis. Your only risk is the cost of the lists. If you decide to call your house file, the list cost is almost nonexistent.

Included in this section are test programs and the resulting rollout results, which you should find quite edifying if you are contemplating a telemarketing test in the not too distant future. You'll also find that there is a correlation between your direct mail results and your telemarketing results. A program that works in the mail should work even better on the phones.

Confirm the Test; Then Roll Out

There's no doubt that a successful test provides great excitement in direct marketing organizations, for if the original business plan was comprehensive, then the full potential of the program should immediately be recognized by management at the time the initial test results are received. Shown in Figure 7.1 are the actual results of a successful test followed by the rollout results.

Approximately 400 orders from each of the three lists in the figure were tracked for back-end performance.

As is true in all telemarketing, you must always wait for back-end performance results to determine the final outcome of your test. This usually takes at least six months for any type of bill-me offer. It can sometimes even take longer when you are working with continuities or subscriptions.

Figure 7.2 shows the final test report.

We tracked the results of the telemarketing test through eight shipments. When you add the paid cancels, returns, and bad debts together, the results are very appealing. In the case of the Girl Students List, you still have 46.7 percent of the initial starters paying and staying. For the Compiled Family List and the Girls' Birthday Club, the percentage retained is 43.3 percent and 46.6 percent, respectively. This was a successful test. As such, it warranted a much larger confirming retest.

It was apparent from the initial test that this program was a keeper and the confirming retest was planned to be comprehensive and con-

Test Results	Telemarketing Response Rate
Girl Students, Grade 4	17.6%
Compiled Family List, Household Income 30K+, Girls Age 10	14.5%
Birthday Club, Girls Age 8–12	18.6%

Figure 7.1 Preteen Girls Continuity Book Series

	Orders	Paid Cancel	Returns	Bad Debts	Cost per Starter
Girl Students	402	7.1%	27.4%	19.8%	$8.57
Compiled Family List	394	21.6%	23.4%	11.7%	$8.62
Girl's Birthday Club	414	7.3%	27.7%	18.4%	$8.72

Figure 7.2 Preteen Girls Continuity Book Series Test Report

clusive. With the goal of implementing a year-round telemarketing campaign, the following lists were selected for the confirming retest.

- Girl Students, grades 4, 5, and 6
- Compiled Family List, $30K+, girls age 10, 11, and 12
- Girls' Birthday Club, ages 8–12
- Preteen Magazine, 3 mo. hot line subscribers
- Preteen Girls Magazine subscriber list

The additional lists selected for the confirming retest were for the most part the logical extensions of the initial test list selection. They included additional age and grade selections from successful test lists. In addition, the test was expanded to include two subscriber lists of preteen magazines. On occasion, compiled lists with specific demographic selections can provide a very responsive universe for telemarketing. The results were measured through 12 months and 10 shipments; the statistics are an average of all shipments. It's not unusual in continuity programs for the initial bad debt figures on the first shipment to be in the range of 15 percent. The same is true for returns. The second through eighth shipments will generally show consecutively fewer bad debts and returns. This is especially true after the critical third and fourth shipments.

The confirming retest produced the results shown in Figure 7.3.

There's still one critical computation that will tell us whether our program warrants a full-blown rollout. That computation is the paid

	Orders	Paid Cancel	Returns	Bad Debts	Cost per Starter
Girl Students Grade 4	41,071	5.2%	28.2%	20.6%	$8.72
Girl Students Grade 5	54,473	14.5%	25.0%	21.3%	$8.74
Girl Students Grade 6	63,830	4.9%	28.2%	20.6%	$8.78
Family List Girls Age 10	976	23.2%	23.4%	25.0%	$8.75
Family List Girls Age 11	994	23.3%	25.0%	12.5%	$8.72
Family List Girls Age 12	807	23.4%	24.9%	12.7%	$8.78
Girls' Birthday Club	609	6.5%	26.6%	20.3%	$8.76
Preteen Mag 3 mo hot line	2,467	6.0%	26.6%	20.4%	$8.84
Preteen Mag Response	1,229	2.2%	28.8%	19.2%	$9.71

Figure 7.3 Preteen Girls Continuity Retest

shipments per starter. It's computed by taking the number of paid shipments and dividing by the number of starters; including those who returned the intro shipment, became bad debts, or were paid cancels. In the case of this program, the paid shipments per starter were 3.2. At $9.97 plus $3.95 shipping and handling per shipment, or $13.92, the revenue per starter was $44.54. The actual cost of goods per shipment was less than $3. This number should put a smile on even the most reserved direct marketers.

We always recommend that you do a confirming retest before making a commitment for a full-blown rollout. We also recommend that you never do a rollout to list more than 10 times the original test quantity.

Wait for the Back-End Results

The next program we'll analyze is an adult needlecrafts program where the average age of the program participant is over 50. As you review the results, you'll notice that the number of bad debts is significantly lower than those listed for the previous preteen program. The reason, based on a market research study we did to verify our suspicions, is that older customers have a different, more responsible view of their financial obligations than younger customers. Older respondents generally feel that it is unethical to keep a product without paying for it, while younger respondents often do not. In fact, approximately 18 percent of our respondents under age 35 were more interested in receiving the free premiums than they were in keeping the product. We often refer to this younger group as premium bandits, and we factor these realities into our financial projections.

The final test results are shown in Figure 7.4.

Test Results	Telemarketing Response Rate
Needlecraft Catalog Buyers A, 6 mo expires	17.5%
Crochet Magazine B, 3 mo hot line, active subscribers	22.6%
Crochet Magazine C, 3 mo hot line subscribers	19.5%

Figure 7.4 Adult Needlecrafts Continuity Final Test Results

	Orders	Paid Cancel	Returns	Bad Debts	Cost per Starter
Needlecraft Catalog A	414	19.7%	28.2%	13.5%	$9.31
Crochet Magazine B	422	18.7%	28.2%	13.5%	$9.63
Crochet Magazine C	403	15.6%	25.0%	12.2%	$12.60

Figure 7.5 Final Test Report

Once again, approximately 400 orders from each list were tracked for back-end performance. The final test report is shown in Figure 7.5.

The results of the telemarketing test in Figure 7.5 are also shown through eight shipments. When you add the paid cancels, returns, and bad debts together, the result is once again very appealing.

The most attractive part of this program is that it had 6.2 paid shipments per starter! There are two reasons for this. The first is that the program is a very specific needlecraft, and the second is that the program appealed to an older demographic group that feels generally more obliged to pay bills on time. The rollout verified the results of the test. However, given the fact that the average take was more than six shipments per starter, it took a long time to read that number accurately. Remember: Always wait for the back-end results before you commit to a full-blown rollout.

Picking Winners and Losers

The ultimate purpose of all this testing and retesting is to be able to pick out the winning combination of offers and lists, and then roll out in force to make some really big money. To illustrate the point, let's take a look at a juvenile continuity book series that appealed to those same young mothers we previously referred to as premium bandits.

This program included a rollout of 53 lists with one million total names and generated more than 50,000 orders from a six-month telemarketing effort. We tested a variety of offers with different premiums (including posters and flashcards), but the winning combination turned out to be an introductory package that contained one free book as a premium plus two additional books for a 14-day preview. The preview books cost $4.79 each plus shipping and handling. If the customer purchased the first two books, he or she would receive additional two-book shipments about once a month. There was no minimum number of books to buy. This rollout was a huge success.

Listed in Figure 7.6 are the initial test results, followed by the rollout numbers.

Once again, approximately 400 orders from each list were tracked for back-end performance. Figure 7.7 illustrates what the final back-end test report showed.

As you can see, the test lists appeared to be successful. Figure 7.8 shows the 10 top-performing lists from the rollout. Three of our test lists made it into the top 10 and quite interestingly had identical conversions on the rollout. Who says the rollout results are always lower than the test!

As you can see, there's a wide disparity in response rate for these lists. It's important to understand that when you use a telemarketing agency that bases your PI on the response rate, the higher the response rate the lower your PI. When you use an hourly billed telemarketing organization you have the same issue, but it's in a slightly different guise. Your cost per order would be computed by dividing the number of orders generated per hour into your hourly charge. The basic difference is that hourly telemarketers get paid their hourly charge whether they perform

Test Results	Telemarketing Response Rate
Children's Magazine A, active subs	15.4%
Baby Magazine B, 6 month hot line	17.1%
Young Family Magazine C, 30 day hot line	18.1%
Compiled Young Family List D, $30K+, children age 0–2	13.7%

Figure 7.6 Juvenile Book Continuity Initial Test Results

	Orders	Paid Cancel	Returns	Bad Debts	Cost per Starter
Children's Magazine A	412	2.8%	26.6%	12.7%	$10.23
Baby Magazine B	385	9.4%	26.5%	8.9%	$9.49
Young Family Magazine C	428	9.3%	24.8%	15.2%	$8.87
Compiled Young Family D	432	2.4%	22.3%	16.5%	$8.94

Figure 7.7 Juvenile Book Continuity Back-End Test Results

	Telemarketing Response Rate
Children's Magazine A, active subs	15.4%
Baby Magazine B, 6 month hot line	17.1%
Young Family Magazine C, 30 day hot line	18.1%
Children's Magazine E, 3 month hot line	10.4%
Children's Magazine E, expires	9.9%
Children's Magazine F, 3 month hot line	17.9%
Cosmetics Buyers G, 3 month hot line	25.7%
Young Family Catalog Buyers H	23.8%
Fun Park Attendees I	13.4%
Catalog J, 3 month hot-line mail order buyers	18.6%

Figure 7.8 Juvenile Book Continuity Rollout Results

	Orders	Paid Cancel	Returns	Bad Debts	Cost per Starter
Children's Magazine A	505	2.8%	26.2%	13.1%	$10.23
Baby Magazine B	2,134	15.7%	23.6%	7.3%	$8.91
Young Family Magazine C	880	7.4%	22.1%	9.0%	$9.01
Child's Mag E, 3 month hot line	642	21.0%	17.6%	12.9%	$9.46
Child's Mag E, expires	285	9.5%	22.0%	16.9%	$9.74
Child's Mag F, 3 month hot line	982	13.8%	22.0%	12.2%	$9.86
Cosmetics G, 3 month hot line	147	1.4%	26.6%	13.9%	$10.25
Young Family Catalog H	697	4.5%	26.6%	12.7%	$9.78
Fun Park Attendees I	205	4.5%	22.1%	14.7%	$10.05
Catalog J, 3 month hot line	347	1.8%	24.7%	16.5%	$9.49

Figure 7.9 Juvenile Book Continuity Back-End Results

up to your expectations or not, while the PI organization has made a commitment to you based on actual test results and must meet their objectives to make a profit. There are many very reputable telemarketing organizations in both categories, and you should be aware of the differences, as your ongoing telemarketing programs depend on careful monitoring of daily, weekly, and monthly results. Figure 7.9 shows a sampling of the back-end results from the rollout.

As you look at the results from these three tests, it's extremely important to realize that there are a number of additional factors in the equation. From the number of paid cancels to the number of returns that require postage refunds, refurbishing (if possible), restocking, and more, it's an equation that varies with the product. Remember that it's sometimes cheaper to absorb a bad debt than to accept a return.

The Relationship Between Telemarketing and Direct Mail Response Rates

In chapter 1 we mentioned that one technique for estimating telemarketing response is to multiply the direct mail response by a factor of 4 to 10. There is one caveat to this rule and that is that the higher multiples (7 through 10) seem to work best when the mail response is between 0.5 percent and 2.0 percent. If you are getting 4 percent, 5 percent, or 6 percent in the mail, you are obviously not going to get 40 percent, 50 percent, or 60 percent on the phone. The higher the direct mail response, the lower the multiplier you should use when you are using direct mail results to estimate potential telemarketing results.

Figure 7.10 shows three lists with their results from the juvenile direct mail and telemarketing efforts. As you can see, there's a definite relationship between the direct mail response rate and the telemarketing response rate.

The relationship rule of thumb from this comparison is that the telemarketing response rate for these lists ranged between four and six times the direct mail response rate. The multiplier was at the lower end of the rule-of-thumb range because the direct mail results were on the high range to begin with. There will, however, always be exceptions and they can be based on price, offer, premium, and other differences.

List	Direct Mail % Response	Telemarketing % Response
Young Family Magazine, active subscribers	3.0	18.1
Compiled Young Families, children age 0–2	2.8	13.7
Catalog Buyers, infant/toddler 6 month hot line	2.0	12.9

Figure 7.10 Juvenile Mail-Phone Response Comparison

List	Direct Mail % Response	Telemarketing % Response
Girls Magazine, Active Subscribers Age 8–12	2.8	18.2
DRTV Contest Entrants, Girls Age 8–12	4.0	17.0
Girl Toy Buyers	4.0	20.4

Figure 7.11 Preteen Mail-Phone Response Comparison

Figure 7.11 is another comparison from the preteen program.

Once again there is a definite front-end response relationship between telemarketing and direct mail, but is there a back-end relationship?

The back-end relationship is a bit more difficult to predict, and inconsistency of fulfillment can change everything. However, as we have mentioned previously, a good rule of thumb is to project a 50 percent increase in returns and a 50 percent decrease in bad debt.

Developing an Overall Contact Management Strategy

Developing an overall contact management strategy for a successful product promotion is essential to maximizing the revenue potential of your telemarketing program.

Telemarketing must be planned in such a way that it enhances what you are doing in your other media (direct mail, space ads, and other media). (We covered many of these issues in the first few sections of chapter 3. You may want to go back and review some of that material if you have any questions remaining on this topic.)

Assuming that you have completed your first successful rollout, and the test results were confirmed, what should your goals be? It's essential that the goals be realistic, achievable, and within the framework of the overall organization.

It's important, unless you have a seasonal product line, to keep the flow of telemarketing orders on an even schedule. Not only does this allow you the opportunity to keep your trained telephone sales reps working on your program, but you also avoid stressing your fulfillment operations.

Keeping the trained reps on your program on a continuing basis is an important part of the telemarketing equation. If you discontinue your program for even a brief period, the TSRs that have been calling successfully for you will be switched to other programs. It will require a new training period for new reps to get your program back to its previous level of productivity, and your order flow will require time to build to its previous level. A better plan is to run a minimum program in slow periods to hold onto your best reps.

The List Universe Is Your "Circle of Life"

In telemarketing as in all direct response marketing, the list is your "circle of life." There have been many instances in which telemarketing tests were successful but when the rollout was planned, a list universe large enough to meet projections did not exist. Planning for potential rollout opportunities should always be part of the initial marketing strategy.

As Dick Benson, direct marketing consultant extraordinaire and member of the Direct Marketing Hall of Fame, says, "Lists are the most important part of your promotion." Without a doubt, lists are the most important part of your telemarketing test and the subsequent rollout.

Telemarketing also presents another dilemma, and that is the requirement of having a phone number for each potential new customer you call. Telematching should provide you with a net match of 50 percent to 55 percent of the gross list. Fortunately, in many cases, compiled lists with specific demographic selections and telephone numbers either already in place or easily appended are very often a large enough universe all by themselves. The programs reviewed earlier in this chapter are examples of campaigns that required compiled lists to achieve a large rollout status. But those compiled lists often performed as well as the smaller direct mail buyer lists.

There is always the chance that many of the secondary lists you've selected for your confirming retest will not work, in which case you will most likely end up with a small ongoing program with a limited calling universe and limited potential. It's not the worst thing that could happen. Failure to test telemarketing is the worst thing!

Summary

- The point of testing is to pick out winners and losers and then roll out aggressively with the winning combination to maximize profits.
- One of the worst mistakes you can make is to roll out an apparently successful test without waiting for the back-end results to be fully revealed.
- It can cost more to process a return than to absorb a bad debt.
- There is a predictable relationship between front-end direct mail response rates and outbound telemarketing conversions on a list-by-list basis. The multiplier can be anywhere between 4 and 10.
- Outbound telemarketing plans should be coordinated with other media. List fatigue can become a problem if you are too aggressive in your contact management strategy.

8

Business Versus
Consumer Telemarketing

In this chapter we will explore the similarities and differences in consumer telemarketing projects versus business-to-business from the following perspectives:

- Lists
- Selling strategies
- Contact rate realities
- Products that sell well over the phone
- List penetration limits
- Scripting
- Training

Within the context of these seven criteria we will explore the similarities and differences of consumer versus business telemarketing. We will also expose some common myths and share some great trade secrets for solving problems.

Predictive dialers have had a major impact on narrowing the differences between business and consumer telemarketing. We are now able to call both consumers at home and business prospects at their offices using the same sales force during the daytime shift. Prior to this innovation, we generally were required to limit consumer calling to the nighttime/weekend hours because we just couldn't get enough contact to make most consumer projects profitable. Given the fact that there are vastly more consumers than businesses, DialAmerica, like many other out-bound agencies, was continually faced with the problem of having unused capacity during the day and scarcity at night. With the help of predictive dialers, we are now able to call many consumer programs efficiently during the day. Projects that involve calling parents of preschool children and/or senior citizens are particularly productive during the day. This simple fact has allowed us to share the fixed costs of the operation over a larger calling base, thus driving down the costs on every project.

The opportunity to do more daytime calling has led to a more stable rep sales force. There has always been a fundamental difference in the personality profile between day and night reps. There are usually many more college students, aged 18 to 21, on the night shift. Day reps tend to be more mature (older) on average and, for many, telemarketing is their only job. By comparison, many night reps often have other full- or part-time employment. Many of the day reps are housewives with children in school; they appreciate the flexible part-time hours that allow them to be home in the afternoon when their children come home from school. A great many of these homemakers are highly intelligent college graduates. Many gave up careers to have a family and are not yet ready for a full-time 9-to-5 job. On the other hand, night reps are more likely to be working in telemarketing as a second job to supplement their income. (In fact, this is how one of the coauthors started with DialAmerica in 1982.) Night reps are more likely to leave telemarketing once they have achieved their short-term income goals, or if their circumstances change in their primary daytime job. Consequently, it is not unusual to have a higher turnover rate on the night shift than the day shift. Reducing turnover is an ongoing challenge for all telecenters. Increasing the call volume during the daytime hours, thus employing a greater number of daytime reps, has been beneficial in the effort to maintain staff consistency.

Perhaps someday we will be able to call business-to-business programs at night by calling into other countries in Europe, Asia, and Africa from here in the United States using instantaneous voice recognition and translation technology to help us bridge the language and culture gap. That will be a tremendous development. We can't wait!

The Hardest Part Is Always the List

As we have mentioned numerous times, the best lists to start your testing with are usually the most recent multibuyer segments of your house file. These are the prospects that already have an established relationship with your company. Hopefully, that relationship has been built upon trust and mutual respect. These are enormous assets when you must take customers from an unexpected interruption in whatever they were doing through the telemarketing procedure (introduction, gain attention, make offer, close, sales continuation, final close, confirmation, and pleasant termination) within the space of four to six minutes.

Outside lists are readily available from list brokers for both business and consumer applications. Some of them may perform as well as (and sometimes even outperform) your house file. Some of the best business lists come from trade magazine (Bureau of Publications; BPA) circulation files. However, keep in mind that there is always more risk in testing outside lists, because a list that performs well on the front end can be a disaster on the back end. Moreover, responsiveness will change over time, so you should always be careful with large rollouts to outside lists.

When considering outside lists, whether businesses or consumers, there are essentially two types, response and compiled. A *response list* is one in which the prospects have all responded to an offer for some product or service. A *compiled list* is one in which the prospects all have some geographic, demographic, or psychographic component in common. A response list can either be a current customer (house file) or an outside list.

Typical consumer list sources would be magazine subscribers, new birth lists, recent moves, book/video/music buyers, etc. Typical business list sources would be trade magazine subscribers, buyers of business products from companies serving the same market with noncompetitive products, and compiled lists.

Many of the business trade magazines are free to eligible readers who happen to work in the particular field. These free publications are called *controlled-circulation magazines*. The revenues are generated from selling advertising space and list rentals. One of the reasons that these controlled-circulation magazine lists work so well is that they constantly are updated to satisfy the BPA for eligibility and recency of interest in the topic covered by the magazine. This audit gives advertisers confidence that their ads are reaching the right audience. Another reason for controlled-circulation magazines' success with telemarketing is that readers frequently are asked to fill out an extensive survey, which qualifies them for eligibility for the free subscription. The survey's questions ask for detailed information about the company, as well as the reader's position and purchasing responsibilities. A final reason for their effectiveness is that many of these BPA audits are actually done over the phone, which indicates a high degree of telemarketing accessibility and responsiveness.

Compiled lists are created from directories such as the yellow pages or from market research.

A hot-line source is one in which the names are newly added to the list (less than three months old). Hot-line names frequently outperform all others for both business and consumer applications. Once again this shows the relative importance of using recency as an indicator of future response.

Clearly the accuracy of the data, particularly the names and phone numbers, is critical to success for both business and consumer telemarketing.

Selling Strategy

In general, the sales psychology for consumer selling is more emotional in nature than business-to-business selling ("Your child will do better in school!" "These books are fun to read!" "I know you'll really enjoy the recipes!"). The sales psychology for business selling is based more on logic and financial gain ("You'll save your company time/money." "You'll advance your career." "You'll stay in full compliance with the law"). This difference, along with the more complex language/jargon/acronyms, indicates a slower rate of delivery for business selling. The prospect needs more time to think about and consider each of the features and benefits that would be part of the decision to examine or purchase a more expensive professional-use product. Consider the two presentations shown in Figures 8.1 and 8.2.

30-Day Preview @ $29.95 with Premium

Introduction: Hello, Mr(s). _____ . This is _____
calling for Xxxxx. Can you hear me OK?

Gain attention: I'm sure you're busy, so I'll be brief. I'm calling to thank you for purchasing _____ , and to let you know that we're sending you a gift
just for agreeing to examine Xxxxx's *Xxxxx* for a full 30 days.

Offer: Xxxxx is the fun, easy way for your child to build language, reading, and
social skills that are so necessary for success in school. Your child will learn faster
and retain more by making learning fun. And everything is specially geared to your
child's age and stage of development.

Now, Mr(s). _____ , if you like it and decide to keep it, it's just
$29.95 plus shipping and handling. That's a $15 savings off the regular price, which
will be charged right to your credit card. Otherwise return it within 30 days.

Figure 8.1 Consumer Offer: Children's Educational Software (Ages 5–9)

One of the fascinating points about each of the presentations presented in Figures 8.1 and 8.2 is that the products are very similar (children's educational software), and the customer could easily be the exact
same person, as the business application in this case is a parent of a child
who is being taught at home as opposed to a regular classroom setting.

The consumer project was mostly called at night, and the business
(home-schooling) project was largely called during the day. The first
thing you will notice is that there is a great deal more dialogue in the
business script. This has to do with the more logic/feature/benefit-based
selling proposition as opposed to the more emotional approach in the
consumer script. Let's look at each section of the script separately:

Introduction

The consumer script moves as quickly as possible into the gain-attention
section where there is immediate mention of the premium (gift). The
business script uses the more professional confidence-building line, "I'm
calling for the *Educational Publishing Division of* . . ."

30-Day Preview @ $69.95 with Premium

Introduction: Hello, Mr(s). _____ ? This is _____ and I'm calling for the Educational Publishing Division of Xxxxx. How are you today/tonight? Can you hear me OK?

Gain attention (Qualify Prospect): Great! Thanks for taking my call. I'll be brief. I'm sure you recognize Xxxxx as the world's foremost publisher of classroom textbooks, but we also publish supplementary teaching materials for families such as yours, with children in home schooling. . . . and the reason for my call is that we'd like to send you and your child . . . a free Xxxxx just for previewing one of our computer-based multimedia home-schooling programs for 30 days, absolutely risk-free. But, first, may I ask what grade-level material are you currently using with your child for social studies?

Offer: That's great, Mr(s). _____ , because your gift is a beautiful full-color atlas packed with hundreds of maps, charts, and graphs. And it's yours to keep, free, just for previewing our . . .

        (Grades 2–3) . . . Product A . . .   (Grades 4–5) . . . Product B . . . .
        (Grades 6–7) . . . Product C . . .   (Grades 8+) . . . Product D . . . .

This is a comprehensive computer-based multimedia teaching program, specially designed for children working in social studies in grade levels _____ (x through y). It includes a CD-ROM packed with hundreds of maps, charts, graphs, lessons, and student activities designed to support your regular home-schooling curriculum. In addition to the CD-ROM you also get a teachers' guide packed with individual preplanned lessons and reproducible student activity sheets, plus a binder to hold it all in. It's really too much to describe over the phone, and that's why we send it out for 30 days risk-free.

    Now this program would normally cost considerably more in a classroom setting because of the need for multiple copies for each child, but we've now made it available in single-unit packages specifically for the home-school market, and if you like it as much as we think you will, it's just $69.95 plus shipping and handling. And if you use a credit card, we can bill that in three easy installments.

Figure 8.2 Business Offer: Computer-Based Multimedia Supplementary Teaching Program for Home Teachers

Gain Attention

The consumer script acknowledges the fact that the call is an interruption of the person's private time. It tries to establish quick rapport by mentioning the product previously purchased, and immediately mentions the gift and the risk-free nature of the offer. The business script also acknowledges the interruption of the call but then immediately moves to establish the credibility of the call as a business contact by leveraging the reputation of the client. Here again the business script mentions the premium and the risk-free nature of the offer, but also goes a step further in qualifying the customer for eligibility before moving on to the offer. In both cases the ultimate purpose of the gain-attention section is to break the customers out of whatever chain of thought they were in prior to the phone call and prepare them to listen attentively to the offer.

Offer

This is the section with the greatest difference in strategy. The word count for the offer section in the consumer script is 93. The word count for the offer section of the business script is 252. The consumer offer uses emotional ideas such as "fun, easy way . . . to build . . . skills," "success in school," "learn faster," "retain more," and "making learning fun." The business offer uses fact-based language such as "comprehensive computer-based multimedia teaching program," "packed with hundreds of maps, charts, graphs, [etc.]," "teacher's guide," "preplanned lessons," and "reproducible student activity sheets." The fundamental point here is that even though the products are similar, and the customer may in fact be the exact same person, it required two completely different selling strategies to be successful.

Contact Rate

There are some very significant differences in the outbound contact rate between business and consumer calling. This is not the case with inbound telemarketing, since in that case the customer calls you and you don't need to deal with phone screeners and assistants. Contact rate is usually measured in leads used per hour (LUPH). A used lead is any contact that results in a final disposition of the record (refusals, duplicates, ineligibles, wrong numbers, disconnects)—in other words, any record that will not remain in the callable inventory for a future call attempt on the project in process.

When you call someone at home you have a 50/50 chance that the person who answered the phone is a person you can sell to, particularly in any program where you can sell to any eligible adult in the household. A major exception would be any list where there is an incidence of teenagers in the household. In most households, teenagers are the first to answer the phone.

Author's Note

I started at DialAmerica in the magazine renewal division in the summer of 1982. Whenever I called for one of the teen magazines I could always count on having the reader (usually a teenage girl) answer the phone by the second ring. I would say my name, Richard Simms, mention the purpose of my call, and ask to speak to the parent. Inevitably, the phone would bounce on the floor as I heard running, giggling, and "Mom, Mom, Mom." A few moments later the teen's mother would pick up the phone and breathlessly ask, "Is this really Richard Simmons?" Well, of course in the early 1980s Richard Simmons was the king of daytime TV with his hugely popular exercise program. I would laugh a little and explain who I was and why I was calling. Needless to say, I had the customer's attention. I could usually count on a sale. After all, how could mom explain to her daughter that she said no to Richard Simmons?

—Richard Simms

When you call someone at his or her business the contact rate is generally 50 percent or less of what you might expect if you were to call the same person at home. This is because in the business setting the person who answers the phone may be a corporate receptionist who will transfer your call to a phone screener. This screener will want more information before passing your call on to the prospect. You may spend several minutes or more on the phone (on hold) only to discover that the prospect is "not available at this time."

Listed below are some general guidelines regarding the contact rate for a few generalized markets. These numbers are for a hypothetical project using a predictive dialer with an average call length of about two to four minutes on the consumer side and three to seven minutes on the business side. They are for a basic bill-me offer where the customer does not need to leave the phone to go get a credit card to secure the order. There are always exceptions, and it is not unusual to see numbers for programs running outside these averages.

Consumer Leads Used per Hour	*Business-to-Business Leads Used per Hour*
Daytime: 10–20 LUPH	Daytime General Business: 8–15 LUPH
Nighttime: 15–25 LUPH	Daytime Schools and Libraries: 8–12 LUPH
	Daytime Teachers in Class: 4–6 LUPH
	Daytime Day-Care Administrators: 8–12 LUPH
	Daytime Construction Owners/ Managers: 7–10 LUPH
	Daytime Transportation Managers: 8–12 LUPH
	Daytime Hospital Administrators: 6–8 LUPH
	Daytime Doctor's Office Managers: 8–13 LUPH
	Daytime Doctors in-between Patients: 0.5–1 LUPH

As you can see, there is more consistency in consumer contact rates than in business contact rates. Again the basic reason is that people in certain types of jobs may be harder to reach because they either have an effective phone screener (presidents of companies), or they spend a lot of time away from their desk out on the job site (construction managers), or they are hard to reach on the phone during certain times of the day (teachers in the classroom).

A good rule of thumb would be to estimate 10 leads used per hour for most business-to-business campaigns where the prospect has some sort of desk job, and 20 leads used per hour for most consumer campaigns where the call is for a reasonably short bill-me type offer. If your campaign requires that all orders be secured with a credit card, you can expect the LUPH rate to drop by 20 to 30 percent or more. The reason for this is that you will have to wait while the customer gets his or her card. You can always expect more questions when they return.

Keep in mind that you may need to call certain business markets outside the normal nine-to-five workday to have the best contact. Two examples would be construction managers and schoolteachers/principals. In both cases we would recommend that you start calling as early as 7:00 A.M. local time, and, as you move across the time zones, keep the local contact time between 7:00 A.M. and 8:00 A.M. Once you reach 8:00 A.M. in the Pacific time zone you can move back to East and call from 11:00 A.M. to 1:00 P.M. (lunch break) again across all of the time zones. Another good tactic might be to call between 5:00 P.M. and 6:00 P.M. local time, starting in the East and working across the country from a Pacific time zone call center. This is a good way to reach decision makers after the phone screeners have left for the day.

Products That Sell

Examples of products that sell successfully with outbound telemarketing include the following.

Consumer Products	*Business-to-Business Products*
Magazines, books, videos, music	Training products (books and videos)
Computer software	Regulatory compliance products
Internet service	Engineering/scientific reference products
Cable/satellite TV	
Fund-raising	Career development products
Bank cards	Computer software
Credit card enhancements	Consumable supplies
Insurance	Gas and electric utility service
Financial products	Financial products and services

Consumer Products	*Business-to-Business Products*
Telco products and service	Insurance
Gas and electric utility service	Telco products and service
Home improvements	Seminars and conferences
Travel and vacation services	Fund-raising
Extended warranty plans	School and library educational
Supplementary classroom	products
teaching materials	Checks and business forms
(sold to teachers at home)	

This is obviously not a complete list, but it does give you an idea of the range of products that an agency might sell over the phone. Publishing products of all sorts have always been a natural for telemarketing—on both the consumer and business sides. Financial services, telco, home improvements, fund-raising, and travel have all been huge categories for successful telemarketing. Now, with the deregulation of gas and electric utilities, we can expect to see the same kind of growth in telemarketing for these industries that we saw occur with telecommunications when AT&T was split up and long distance service was deregulated.

As a final thought on whether a product or service might be suitable for outbound telemarketing, particularly in an agency setting, you should consider the following points.

- Are there any highly targeted lists available? (Remember, it always starts with the list.)
- Is the product conceptually simple enough that it could be reasonably described in 25 to 50 words, so that someone who knows little about it before the call might be expected to become at least curious within the context of a four- to six-minute conversation?
- Can an order be consummated over the phone (telesales), or will live contact be needed to finalize the deal?
- Once you acquire the customer, is there anything else you can offer him or her? We've seen a lot of projects ultimately fail because the order-acquisition cost on a first-time buyer transaction is so high that the company is lucky to break even. In

fact many direct marketers actually *plan* to lose money on the initial sale. The intent is to maximize the response and size of the customer file. Their marketing plan is grounded in the belief that they can go back to these customers two more times within the next 12 months and offer additional products at higher margins and lower order-acquisition costs.

- If you can sell it in the mail, you should be able to make it work on the phone.
- Successful consumer campaigns usually have product price points under $100. Business price points are usually between $100 and $1,000.

List Penetration

The concept of list-penetration limits recognizes the fact that there will always be some people who are impossible to contact regardless of how many times you attempt to call them. In general your best contact will occur on the first dialed attempt through the lead base; you will be reaching all of the easiest contacts in the first pass. However, if there are a lot of wrong numbers and disconnected phones in the lead base, you may actually make more presentations once you've cleaned the list with the first attempt by eliminating the nonworking numbers. The contact rate also will decline after six or more previous attempts. DialAmerica generally presets its predictive dialers to make eight attempts at each record. After that, the remaining names go into a maximum-attempts file. The marketing team reviews each list segment for overall productivity and list penetration to that point. Based on that review they may decide to return the remaining leads to the callable lead inventory for another eight attempts (if this is a high-performing list segment) or delete them altogether (if the remaining names are judged to be unproductive for continued calling). In most instances, eight attempts marks the point at which the productivity takes a significant downward turn, which means that it is no longer profitable to continue the calling.

There is a significant difference in the list-penetration expectations for consumer versus business calling. One of the reasons for this is that in the business environment, even if your call results in no contact, you still may have actually spoken to one or more people who asked about the nature of the call. There is a limit to the number of times you can speak to these intermediary people before they begin to feel that the calls are overly aggressive. If you reach that point, they will begin to complain (usually to the person you are trying to reach). Once that happens you have lost any opportunity to find your prospect/customer in a positive frame of mind when you do finally get through.

The last thing you want to be doing at the end of a promotion is to be calling through the entire remaining lead base several days in a row. That is almost certain to generate complaints. We would highly recommend that you rest the leads at the end of a business-to-business promotion, and never call the same names two days in a row, or more than twice in a week.

"No contact" calls in the consumer environment, on the other hand, are more likely to result in a simple "not home" or "not available," without the rep being forced to reveal his or her identity or the purpose of the call. We don't generally recommend leaving messages on answering machines unless you are involved in a debt-collection campaign. These are the normal list-penetration goals that DialAmerica uses for most programs.

> Consumer List-Penetration Goal: 80 percent to 85 percent
> Business-to-Business List-Penetration Goal: 50 percent to
>   65 percent

These penetration goals only apply to programs that are otherwise achieving the budgeted productivity targets. If the productivity/revenue is below expectations, calling usually is terminated before these goals are met. This is a decision that should be made jointly by the agency/call center and the client/marketing managers.

Scripting

There are fundamental differences between business and consumer scripts. Getting to the decision maker is considerably more difficult in a business setting, since you may need to get past a phone screener (secretary/assistant). The best strategy is simply to continue to ask to speak with the prospect while revealing as little information as possible about the exact nature of the call. You want to avoid making the presentation to anyone other than the decision maker. If the prospect is not available, simply offer to call back. We do not generally recommend leaving voice-mail messages. After all, you don't want the customer to make up his mind even before you speak to him. This is particularly true in an agency environment, where the use of high-speed predictive dialers and flexible work schedules means that the next contact attempt probably will be made by a different sales rep.

Another element of business calling is that the name on the lead may not be the right person to speak to. Many of those listed are likely to have changed jobs, which means that a new person is now responsible for the purchase decision of the product or service you would like to offer. In fact, we've had many programs over the years where we've found it best to ignore the name listed on the lead and simply ask to speak to the person in charge of the specific area ("May I please speak to whomever is in charge of safety training for your facility?"). Certain industries and positions have more stability than others. Presidents typically have more job stability than department managers. Schools and libraries are more likely to stay in the same locations than restaurants. Clearly, the best situation is the one in which the name on the lead is accurate. However, you should always be prepared in business-to-business programs to seek out the right person.

Business products are often priced higher than consumer products, and this is another reason why the offer section for the business product script is usually longer than the one for the consumer product script. In general, the higher the price point, the more you will need to describe the product to establish a proper perceived value in the mind of the customer. Business scripts are also more likely to use industry-specific jargon and acronyms.

Let's look at two outbound scripts section by section, one a consumer children's book continuity and the other a business reference book continuity.

The Introduction

Consumer Script Hello, Mr(s). _____ , this is _____ calling from DialAmerica Marketing for the Xxxxxxxxx Children's Book

Club. Can you hear me OK? (If normal response, continue. If strong, i.e., very busy, just eating, etc., respond with: I'm sorry for the interruption, it's just a courtesy call. I'll call back at a more convenient time, OK? Thanks, and good day/evening.)

Business Script Good morning/afternoon, I need to speak to _____ (name on lead) or the person responsible for employee safety compliance, and who would that be? (If not available: Update name/phone on record.)

    Hello, Mr(s). _____ . This is _____ calling on behalf of Xxxxxxxxx Publishing. How are you today? Can you hear me OK?

    Great! We're a leading publisher of information on safety regulations. Are you the person responsible for purchasing safety compliance materials for your company? (If no: To whom would I need to speak?)

Right away you can see that there is a difference in length between the two scripts. The business script opens with a *preintroduction* designed to get past the receptionist and other phone screeners. The business script also includes an early qualifier as to the nature of the person's job responsibilities.

The Gain Attention

Consumer Script Great, thanks for taking my call, Mr(s). _____ . I'll be brief. I'm calling to let you know that your child is entitled to receive two special gifts just for previewing the first two books of our new Xxxxxxxxx Children's Book Club. But first, our records indicate that your child is between the ages of two and eight. Is that correct?

Business Script Great, thanks for taking my call, Mr(s). _____ . I'll be brief.

    I'm calling today because we'd like to send, as a gift, a free PC diskette containing a complete set of valuable safety compliance forms, documents, and policies. The disk is yours to keep, as our gift, just for examining our new Employee Safety Compliance Service for a 30-day risk-free preview.

As noted in chapter 4, the gain-attention section is the most important part of most scripts. This holds true for both business and consumer applications. One of the differences is that the consumer script will usually qualify the customer at the end of the gain-attention section, whereas the business script has already done that in the introduction. Both scripts start out by recognizing the inherent inconvenience of the call, which has interrupted the prospect's day, and then move immediately to mention the premium, since this is our best hope of capturing the customer's attention as we move to the offer section.

The Offer

Consumer Script That's great Mr(s). _____ , because our gift to you includes a colorful wall poster, plus a delightful storybook titled, Xxxxxxxxx. These gifts are yours to keep just for agreeing to preview two additional books for 14 days.

Each hardcover book contains a beautifully illustrated story that uses simple sentences and rhymes to help your child learn to read. And every book stresses important family values, such as helping, sharing, and love. All are exclusive titles, not available in any store. If you like the preview books, they're just $4.89 each plus shipping, handling, and sales tax, if any. And if you choose to continue, you will receive two new books about once every six weeks, always on a 14-day approval, and at the same low price. However, if you are not completely satisfied with the two preview books, just return them and owe nothing.

Business Script Mr(s). _____ , this sturdy three-ring binder reference is written in easy-to-understand language and is updated throughout the year with new laws and regulations that affect your business. It provides ready-to-use training materials for your safety meetings, including read-from-the-script topics. It's a complete, cost-effective, system of interlinked project safety observation reports that can help you organize and manage on-site safety inspections. There are even individual employee safety handouts and self-evaluation report forms. In all there are 29 different reports and forms. It all comes in a heavy-duty case with complete instructions that explain when and how to use each form, as well as how the forms link together to create a complete project safety record.

It really is too much to describe on the phone, and that's why we'd like you to take a look at it for 30 days and see firsthand how it will benefit you. Now, normally a comprehensive service like this with continuous quarterly updates would cost $1,000 or more from a safety consultant, but if you like it as much as we believe you will, the basic reference is just $149 plus delivery. And then if you continue, the quarterly updates are $59.95 each.

The business script uses more dialogue to describe the complex nature of this more expensive continuity product. You can easily see the major difference in selling strategy between the two scripts. The consumer script's emotional approach uses words such as "helping, sharing, and love," and concepts such as "family values" and "learn to read." The business script is full of fact-based features, benefits, and logic.

The Close

Consumer Script And remember, no matter what you decide, be sure to keep Xxxxxxx and the wall poster as our gift, OK?

Business Script But for right now, we'd just like you to take a look at it for 30 days, share it with your staff, and see firsthand how this will benefit your organization. Remember, no matter what you decide, the PC diskette with the safety compliance forms is yours to keep as our gift. OK?

In both cases the close ends with a mention of the premium and a strong "OK?" However, even here, you can see the longer dialogue in the business script with the appeal to "share it with your staff, and see firsthand how this will benefit your organization."

The Sales Continuation

Consumer Script I understand your reluctance, Mr(s). _____, and that's why we're not asking you to make a decision over the phone.

We think you'll agree, though, that learning to read is a vital part of a child's early development. And the Xxxxxxxxxx are very popular and effective teachers for a child such as yours.

So, just take a look at the program, and then decide if you want to continue. Remember, the gifts are yours to keep, OK?

Business Script I understand what you're saying, Mr(s). _____. But keep in mind by saying yes now, you're only agreeing to "examine" this valuable manual . . . (Choose one or more.)

- and the *Wall Street Journal* reports that OSHA violations have doubled in the last year and tripled since 1993.
- and even paperwork errors and honest mistakes can result in big fines of up to $100,000 or more.
- and with new federal mandates, the odds are high that sooner or later, your company will be hit with an OSHA safety audit.

. . . if you use just one tip from this practical manual, it will pay for itself. So Mr(s). _____ , take the full 30 days, look it over, see how it will benefit you, and then decide. OK?

Both the business and consumer scripts use the same trade-secret formula for sales-continuation selling, namely, agree, change subject, sell benefits, and close. Once again, the business script has more options for benefit selling and is based more on business logic as a strategy.

Please note that several states now have telemarketing laws that make it illegal to offer a second effort once the customer says no. You will need to be extremely careful in this area.

The Confirmation

Consumer Script (word-for-word): That's great, Mr(s). _____. May I have your first name please? And your child's name? And his/her birth date? Thank you. Now, I show your address as _____. Is that correct? Do I need an apartment number? Is this the address to which your bills are sent?

Fine, just so we're clear, in the same package with your gift, you'll also receive two additional books to preview for 14 days. If you like them, or any others in the program, they're just $4.99 each, plus shipping, handling, and sales tax, if any. The bill is attached to the box, so simply make out one check or money order for the price listed on the invoice. After you buy the first set of two books, other two-book sets will follow, about every six weeks at the same price and on the same examination basis. Of course you only buy the books you enjoy, and your only obligation is to take the time to open the package when it arrives, examine the books with your child, and then make your purchasing decision within 14 days, so we'll know whether to send you the next set or not. Is this commitment OK with you, Mr(s). _____? Great, then I'll go ahead and get the books right out to you. They should arrive in four to six weeks. Do you have any questions?

By the way, be sure to look for the book *Xxxxxxx*. It's a fun tour through the *Xxxxxxx*. Thanks for your interest. I'm sure your child is really going to enjoy these new *Xxxxxxxxxxx* books.

Business Script Great. Mr(s). _____, may I have your first name please? And I show your full address as _____ (no P.O. boxes—must have regular street address). Is that correct? And can you give me your complete company name and job title?

Great, just so it's clear, a copy of *Xxxxxxxxxx* will be shipped from our warehouse 48 hours after the order is received, along with your free gift. Preview the manual for 30 days, and when you decide to purchase it, the cost is $149 plus shipping and handling ($6.50) and sales tax, if any. And then the supplements keep you updated year-round for $69 each plus shipping and handling.

Do you understand and accept our offer? Great! Now, for our records, what is the exact nature of your business? Do you have a fax number where we can reach you?

Thank you, and we're sure you'll find the information to be very valuable.

Finally, we have an example where the dialogue is longer in the consumer script than the business script. The reason for this is that with a continuity offer, it is really important that the customer understand that there is a stream of shipments that will continue until either all of the units have been shipped, or the customer cancels out of the program. There is considerably less revenue associated with the consumer offer ($9.98 intro versus $149 for the business intro). Break-even on the consumer continuity will not occur until the customer has kept and paid for approximately 2.5 shipments. The business continuity may only need one additional shipment to reach the break-even point. Accordingly, we have not only described the continuity process in greater detail in the consumer script, we have also incorporated more commitment-building dialogue, such as assuring customers that their children will really enjoy the books.

The Final Close

Consumer Script Thank you for your time. If you should need it, our customer service number is 800-XXX-XXXX. Have a good evening/day. Good-bye.

Business Script Thank you for your time. If Xxxxx Publishing can be of any help in the future, please call us. (Give out customer service phone number only on demand.)

In both cases, the purpose of the final close is to end the conversation on a positive note, regardless of whether or not the customer has placed an order. One interesting difference is that we generally do not offer a customer service phone number in the business script, since we are not wanting to drive calls into the inbound center until we have had time to process the order. The reason that we include it in the consumer script is so that we can stay in compliance with the Telephone Consumer Protection Act of 1991 (TCPA) and Telephone Sales Rule, which specify that we must state the company's address or phone number on every call. The TCPA and Telephone Sales Rule only cover consumer calling, not business-to-business.

From the inbound perspective, scripting is usually closely tied to the screen that the TSR is working from. In fact there will probably not be the same kind of tightly scripted dialogue that is common in outbound campaigns. Most inbound reps are simply taught to work their way through the screens and fill in the blanks as they go. Of course, keep in mind that inbound selling is still very conversion sensitive, and there may be definite scripting connected with the transitions and details of upselling. However, there really isn't much difference in approach when you consider business versus consumer calls. The major difference between business and consumer inbound scripting lies in the fact that business callers tend to ask more questions about the product or service and terms and conditions. Hence, business-call fact sheets are usually longer and more detailed. They are designed to assist the TSR in properly answering all of the possible questions that may come up.

Training

There is some truth to the generalization that reps/branches tend to be good at either consumer selling or business selling, but not both. The reason for this has to do with their personality and their style of phone communication.

Training was covered in some depth in chapter 4. The only point that we would like to make here is that there needs to be a greater emphasis on teaching how to get past the phone screener and reach the decision maker in outbound business-to-business programs. The best advice we can offer is that no matter what you say, you should always finish the sentence with "So may I speak with Mr(s). _____ , please?" Another point to emphasize for outbound business-to-business reps is to help them develop the skill of finding the right person when the name on the lead is no longer there or has other responsibilities.

The technical nature of some of the business products and services may lead to longer training sessions. This is certainly the case with inbound projects. Inbound business-to-business training periods usually take 30 percent to 50 percent longer than consumer training periods. This is primarily due to the greater length and complexity of the support materials and the commonly asked questions. Remember that it is not always necessary for the reps to understand completely the technical details of the product or service being offered. DialAmerica has sold millions of highly technical reference products simply by teaching its part-time sales reps how to recognize and pronounce the buzzwords and industry jargon. As we've proved time and again, if the reps can pronounce the words properly, the customers will supply the understanding.

We would like to reemphasize that regardless of how difficult or complex the product or service is, there is tremendous value in getting outbound reps on the phones for at least an hour on the very first day— even if it means that you must limit the first day's training to the primary offer and return to the training room on a subsequent day to train reps on the balance of the products.

By comparison, we believe that before you put your inbound reps on the phone you should invest enough training in them to give you reasonable confidence that they will not be lost if the customer asks an unforeseen question. This may certainly mean that they may need several days of classroom training before they handle their first call.

As you can see, there are plenty of similarities and differences between consumer and business telemarketing. Listed below is a recap of the more important points to remember.

Summary

- Modern predictive dialers allow us to call consumer programs (particularly those targeted to parents of young children and retired senior citizens) during daytime hours.
- Good list segmentation is vital to the success of both business and consumer telemarketing. Business lists tend to have more detailed information available in the record (e.g., Standard Industrial Classification [SIC] codes, job titles, company size). Order the list with phone numbers attached, if possible. Watch out for business-to-business semi-duplicate listings.
- Consumer selling strategies tend to be more emotional in nature. Business selling strategies are usually more logical. Business contact rates tend to be about 30 to 50 percent of consumer contact rates.
- Most consumer offers have product price points under 100 dollars. Most business price points that involve selling a product on the initial outbound phone call are between 100 and 1,000 dollars.
- Business products costing more than 1,000 dollars require a multistep, multichannel approach such as an intro lead-generating call, followed by literature fulfillment through fax/E-mail/postal mail, followed by a higher-level qualifying call, followed by a live meeting.
- A reasonable list penetration goal for consumer programs is 85 percent. A good penetration goal for business programs is 65 percent.

- The basic structure of a well-written business script is the same as a well-written consumer script. However, there is more dialogue in a business script, and the selling strategy is quite different.
- Product training takes longer and is more important in business programs because of the stronger emphasis on a logic-based selling strategy.
- Aggressive list testing is equally important to both business and consumer calling projects.
- If your direct marketing efforts are successful in the mail, test the addition of an outbound telemarketing follow-up call. Programs that work in the mail almost always work even better on the phone.

9

Business and Consumer Markets and Offers

In this chapter we will explore a series of actual outbound case studies, both business and consumer.

Business Market Segments That Love to Buy by Phone

Listed in Figure 9.1 is a sampling of 50 business market segments that traditionally have been both easily accessible by phone and highly responsive to outbound telemarketing. The response rates are actual conversions for programs that one or both authors have worked on over the years.

Please keep in mind that these response rates are a function of many other factors beyond the list (notably, whether or not there was a previous business relationship [house list as opposed to outside list], the product, the price, and the terms and conditions of the offer). We have included the response rates simply to add some credibility to the list and also to give you some insight into the wide range of possibilities available for business-to-business outbound telemarketing. It would certainly be unfair to draw any conclusions about one market segment being more or less responsive to telemarketing than any other on the list. In fact, it's hard to imagine a business market segment that has not been the target of successful outbound telemarketing at some point or another. There

Market	Response*	Market	Response*
Ambulance Company Administrators	15.0%	Library Administrators	22.1%
Architects	6.8%	Maintenance Engineers	26.1%
Attorneys	30.3%	Mechanical Engineers	25.8%
Banking Executives	59.5%	Mental Health Administrators	20.8%
Church Pastors	18.2%	MIS Computer Managers	25.6%
Civil Engineers	26.5%	Nursing Home Administrators	17.0%
College Librarians	16.5%	Optometrists	39.3%
Commercial Building Owners	25.8%	Payroll Managers	33.5%
Computer Programmers	23.7%	Petroleum Engineers	24.6%
Construction Executives	9.7%	Police Department Administrators	16.0%
Corporate Controllers	13.8%	Public Relations Managers	27.5%
Credit Managers	15.2%	Public School Librarians	23.7%
Customer Service Managers	14.9%	Purchasing Managers	21.9%
Day-Care Center Directors	23.9%	Railroad Safety Managers	7.5%
Elementary Grade Teachers	35.0%	Real Estate Agents	13.5%
Environmental Managers	9.3%	Clergy	10.1%
Fire Department Administrators	8.0%	School Principals	35.1%
Hospital Administrators	19.0%	Small Boat Marina Managers	6.5%
Human Resource Managers	16.5%	Stock Brokers	20.0%
HVAC Engineers	24.3%	Telecommunications Managers	26.8%
Industrial Engineers	28.7%	Training Managers	6.0%
Industrial Safety Managers	18.7%	Unix System Administrators	15.5%
Insurance Agents	14.6%	Various Small Retailers	5.0%
Interior Designers	6.3%	Video Retailers	95.1%
Jewelry Retailers	53.0%	Yellow Pages Advertisers	17.7%

*Response = orders divided by total leads used, which includes TPs, dupes, and ineligibles

Figure 9.1 Accessible and Responsive Businesses

are even programs that are designed to call physicians at their office and get them on the phone in between patients. Think of the last time you were actually able to speak to your doctor on the phone when you were the one who placed the call. By the way, calling doctors at their office does require a good amount of patience. Waiting on hold for 15 minutes or more just to find out if the doctor will eventually come to the phone is not unrealistic. It certainly requires a special TSR to deal with this type of program.

Consumer Market Segments That Love to Buy by Phone

The consumer market is obviously much larger than the business-to-business market, and that holds true for the individual segments contained therein. In the previous section we saw how the business market was segmented primarily by profession and job responsibility. Consumer market segments tend to align themselves around previous purchase history and lifestyle issues such as hobbies, family structure, religious beliefs, and other personal interests.

The table shown in Figure 9.2 represents a sampling of 50 consumer market segments where the authors have had considerable success with outbound telemarketing.

The response rates shown in Figures 9.1 and 9.2 are actual results, but you should not try to make any comparisons between the segments, as the conversions are a function of many other factors beyond the list.

Here is a good short list of issues that you should consider when you are trying to decide whether a particular market segment is a viable target for testing telemarketing.

1. Are there good lists available? (It always starts with the lists.)
2. Is my product/service positioned to appeal to a highly targeted market segment, or is the appeal so broad that anyone can use it? (Universal-appeal products usually don't work well with a highly targeted one-to-one media such as outbound telemarketing. They will usually only work with broad-based response media such as DRTV, FSIs, and space advertising.)
3. What hours of the day can I expect my prospect to be available by phone? (Daytime/Nighttime? Can I/Should I call this business before 9:00 A.M. and/or after 5:00 P.M. local time? Will weekend calling be profitable?) (Parents with preschool children and senior citizens have traditionally been good targets for daytime residential calling.)
4. Does my business prospect have a desk job, a walking-around job, or an out-of-the-office job? (What is a reasonable estimate for contact potential?)
5. Will I need to get past a phone screener? (How will I do that?)

Market	Response*	Market	Response*
Apparel Buyers	18.7%	Health Book Buyers	12.5%
Association Members	15.1%	History Book Buyers	16.8%
Automobile Club Members	32.5%	Hunting and Fishing Enthusiasts	39.2%
Buyers of Food by Catalogue	13.0%	Hunting-Book Buyers	37.6%
Cable TV Subscribers	90.4%	Investment Newsletter Subscribers	10.4%
Charitable Contributors	16.5%	Magazine Subscribers	19.6%
Children's Book Buyers	16.2%	Military History Video Buyers	21.4%
Children's Continuity Actives	27.6%	Music Club Buyers	13.5%
Children's Software Buyers	36.1%	Music Video Buyers	8.0%
Christian Music Buyers	15.1%	Mutual Fund Customers	2.0%
Cigar Smokers	27.2%	Mystery-Book Buyers	18.4%
Classroom Teachers at Home	23.6%	Nature Video Buyers	19.8%
Collectible-Coin Buyers	8.0%	Newspaper Subscribers	16.1%
Computer Game Players	29.8%	Nonprofit Foundation Supporters	7.0%
Computer Owners	21.0%	Porcelain Plate Collectors	20.0%
Consumer Banking Customers	12.5%	Residential Telephone Customers	8.0%
Cookbook Buyers	22.4%	Residential Utility Customers	85.0%
Craft Book Buyers	15.9%	Romance Book Buyers	31.3%
Credit Card Holders	4.0%	Sports Memorabilia Buyers	9.5%
DRTV Nature Video Buyers	15.0%	Stamp Collectors	10.9%
Encyclopedia Owners	15.1%	Stock Market Investors	21.3%
Families w/Children 0–6 Months	10.0%	Toy Collectors	13.0%
"For Sale by Owner" Home Sellers	5.0%	Tree Ornament Collectors	16.0%
Gardening Enthusiasts	19.5%	University Students	7.5%
Gourmet Coffee Buyers	7.0%	Western Book Buyers	21.3%

*Response = orders divided by total leads used, which includes TPs, dupes, and ineligibles

Figure 9.2 Accessible and Responsive Consumers

A good rule of thumb is that if your program works in the mail, it should work even better on the phone. If it doesn't work in the mail, you will want to have a good idea why not before you take the program onto the phones. However, there are many programs that work only on the phone and *not* in the mail, so this should not discourage you from testing telemarketing. A live telemarketing sales rep can very often solve a problem that a passive mailpiece is helpless to overcome.

Offers That Work on the Phone

Listed in a side-by-side format throughout this chapter are actual telemarketing case studies that will illustrate a variety of consumer and business-to-business offer structures that have proved consistently successful for companies in a wide variety of industries. Please note once again we have taken steps to protect the confidentiality of the clients and products to which these studies relate. In some cases we have combined several similar projects, in others we have provided average numbers across a group of nearly identical campaigns. In all cases we maintained the essential integrity of the core data, which illustrate the point under discussion.

Analysis of Figure 9.3 Ship-till-forbid continuity clubs historically have been among the most profitable offer structures available to both consumer and business-to-business marketers. This type of offer structure is a natural for telemarketing. It is not unusual to see response rates of 12 percent to 20 percent on outside lists. We have seen conversions as high as 30 percent on certain highly targeted lists. The reason these offers work so well is that they usually combine a low introductory shipment price with a risk-free trial and an attractive premium, which helps mitigate any perceived risk the customer might feel about an offer that is presented sight-unseen over the phone. The key to profitability in these programs lies in the number of shipments that each of the customers will take on average before canceling out of the program. Break-even on consumer continuities is usually somewhere between 2.25 and 2.75 shipments per starter.

As you can see, business continuities often can support much higher price points on the introductory shipment. However, they too usually take at least two shipments to break even. In both cases it is very important to do everything possible to maximize the number of starters at the lowest cost-per-order attainable, while minimizing the percentage of returns on the first introductory shipment.

The following cookbook example will illustrate the incredible profit potential for continuity selling. Suppose you were to buy a 400-page cookbook, containing 1,000 individual recipes, at retail for approximately $40. Your cost would amount to about 4 cents per recipe. Now suppose those same recipes were individually printed on separate cards,

Consumer Case Study		Business Case Study	
Video Continuity Sales to House File Lists—In this campaign we called a house list of magazine subscribers and offered them an introductory package to a video continuity. The first shipment was offered at a discount price of $9.95. Future shipments were billed at $19.95. A video slipcase was offered as a premium with the second shipment. Both the U.S. and Canadian markets were called.		Computer Reference Manual with "Continuity" Update Service for MIS System Administrators—In this campaign we called an outside magazine subscriber list of network system administrators and offered them a 30-day preview of a new binder reference manual on Xxxx. A PC disk containing shell scripts and utilities was used as a premium. The intro cost was $95.95 plus shipping and handling. Customers would then receive updates for $44.50 plus shipping and handling about every other month on a ship-till-forbid continuity basis.	
Names Received	309,000		
Names with Phone Numbers	165,000		
% with Phone Number	53%		
Orders	22,160	Names Received	6,000
		Names with Phone Numbers	5,826
Total Leads Used	140,250	% with Phone Number	99.8%
Response %	15.8%	Orders	587
U.S. Market	14%		
Canadian Market	26%	Total Leads Used	3,787
		Response %	15.5%

Figure 9.3 Ship-Till-Forbid Continuity Club Offers

came with a ring binder, and were sold in packets of 20 via direct marketing. The intro offer might be to get one pack (20 recipes), plus a ring binder, a set of category divider cards (so you can sort the recipes by type as you add to your collection, and put them in the binder), plus a bonus set of cooking technique cards—*all for free*! Your only commitment would be to agree to examine a second set of 20 recipes risk-free for 10 days. This second set would be priced at $4.99 plus $4.95 shipping and handling. If you decide to keep and pay for that set, two additional

A Note About the Canadian Market

As you can see in Figure 9.3, we had a much higher response in the Canadian market for the same offer. This is regularly the case. A good rule of thumb would be to take the U.S. response and multiply it by 150 percent as a working first assumption for what will happen in the Canadian market if all other variables are the same.

sets would automatically arrive, approximately once a month, at the same low price ($4.99 + $4.99 = $9.98 plus $4.95 S/H = $14.93 total), on the same risk-free examination basis. In all there would be 25 shipments of 40 recipes (two packs of 20 each). The average cost per recipe goes from 4 cents to 35 cents. Here are the numbers.

Shipment	Shipment Revenue	Cumulative Revenue
Intro	$4.99 + $4.95 = $9.94	$ 9.94
2nd	$9.98 + $4.95 = $14.93	$ 24.87
3rd	$9.98 + $4.95 = $14.93	$ 39.80
4th	$9.98 + $4.95 = $14.93	$ 54.73
10th	$9.98 + $4.95 = $14.93	$144.31
20th	$9.98 + $4.95 = $14.93	$293.61
24th	$9.98 + $4.95 = $14.93	$353.33

The beauty of continuities is that they set up an ongoing revenue stream that will continue until the customer either completes the series or cancels out early.

Analysis of Figure 9.4 Outbound telemarketing is an excellent choice for reinstating good cancels from negative-option clubs. However, unlike ship-till-forbid continuities, it is not usually used for bringing on new starters from outside lists. The reason for this lies in the fact that part of the appeal of the introductory offer is for the customer to select his own first title(s) from what is usually a long list of possibilities. An outbound telemarketer would get completely bogged down in the process of trying to describe each of the titles. Stamp-sheet offers with an inbound

Consumer Case Study

Negative-Option Book Club Reinstatement—In this campaign we called "good cancels" from a house file of a consumer negative-option book club and offered to reinstate their club membership over the phone. This club offers best selling genre novels. Customers who accepted this offer would have no further commitment beyond the next book but would again begin receiving negative-option notices for upcoming selections. We price-tested two "welcome back" offers as follows:

1. The first book at $1.99 + S/H
2. The first book at $4.99 + S/H

Names Received	14,124
Names with Phone Numbers	8,259
% with Phone Number	58%
Orders	1,285
Total Leads Used	6,987
Response %	18.4%
$1.99 Offer	19.6%
$4.99 Offer	16.8%

Business Case Study

Professional Interest Negative-Option Book Club Reinstatement—In this campaign we called "good cancels" from two different "engineering interest" negative-option book clubs and offered to reinstate their club membership over the phone. One club was for mechanical engineers, and the other was for civil engineers. Customers were allowed to pick their next book from a list of five possible titles. We tested two offers as noted below:

1. Civil Engineers: Choice of next title for $2.97, plus a $10 discount coupon for a future purchase.
2. Mechanical Engineers: Choice of next title for $4.97, plus a $10 discount coupon for a future purchase.

Names Received	9,500
Names with Phone Numbers	6,700
% with Phone Number	70%
Orders	650
Total Leads Used	4,480
Response %	14.5%
Civil Engineers	16.6%
Mechanical Engineers	12.5%

Figure 9.4 Negative-Option Annuals and Clubs

800-number response option are a much better way to accomplish this task. Using an 800 number on an offer such as this can lift your response dramatically.

As was the case in the continuity example, profitability occurs only after the customer has received and paid for several shipments. A good rule of thumb for estimating the average shipments per starter on these reinstated orders would be to use the same number that is used when estimating the persistence or average take of new starters.

Price testing was an essential part of both of these projects. It is always a good idea to test price. It is amazing how a seemingly small change in the intro price can make a large difference in overall profitability. In general you will find that price has an effect on both the front and back end, and believe it or not, the effect is usually larger on the back end, than the front end. The reason for this is that they only *hear* the price on the phone, but they actually *see* the price in print on the back end. So be sure to wait for the full results over time before making any final decisions about what your control offer should be.

Analysis of Figure 9.5 We discussed in the earlier case how ship-till-forbid continuities are among the most profitable offer structures. Load-up promotions are easily recognized as the most profitable part of continuity selling.

The concept is simple. You call people who have received, and paid for, several shipments. You offer to deliver the remaining units in one complete shipment, while allowing the customer to continue to pay on the same monthly basis. As an additional incentive the buyer will be saving the shipping and handling charges for future shipments, which can add up to a significant amount of money over the course of time. This allows your customer to have the satisfaction of having access to the complete set or series without having to wait for delivery over the next year or two. This is a very important issue, since the motivation to build and own a collection is at least as important to the continuity customer as the desire to own the intellectual content contained therein. Let's face it, a cookbook that is missing 80 percent of the recipes is not nearly as useful as one that contains them all.

The order-acquisition cost for a load-up order is usually very low because of the high response rates. Overall profitability usually soars because you are also driving up the average shipments per starter by turning 30 percent to 50 percent of your remaining customers into completers. Furthermore, customers who decline the load-up stay in the

Consumer Case Study

Book Continuity Load-Up—For this promotion we called active continuity subscribers and offered them the opportunity to examine the remaining books in the set in one complete (load-up) shipment. The full continuity consists of 18 volumes. The books cost $15.99 each. We called customers who had received anywhere from six to eleven volumes. The exact offer customers received depended upon how many books they already had. The customer would pay in five regular monthly installments as noted below. A sports book was used as a premium. Shipping and handling was free, which amounted to a 15 percent discount. Customers who declined the load-up offer stayed in the regular monthly continuity.

Load-Up	Monthly Bill	Price to Subscriber
7 Books	$22.38	$111.93
8 Books	$25.58	$127.92
9 Books	$28.78	$143.91
10 Books	$31.98	$159.90
11 Books	$35.18	$175.89
12 Books	$38.38	$191.88

Names Received	7,725
Names with Phone Numbers	4,450
% with Phone Number	58%
Orders	1,440
Total Leads Used	3,829
Response %	37.6%

Business Case Study

Day-Care Continuity Load-Up—For this promotion we called day-care center teachers who were active continuity subscribers, and offered them the opportunity to examine the remaining units in the series in one complete (load-up) shipment. The full continuity consists of 24 units. The regular cost is $12.95 each. We called customers who had already received anywhere from three to seven units. The exact offer the customer received depended upon how many units they already had. The customer would continue to pay on the same regular monthly basis as before. Shipping and handling were free, which amounted to an 18 percent discount. Customers who declined the load-up offer stayed in the regular monthly continuity.

Load-Up	Monthly Bill	Price to Subscriber
Units 4–24	$12.99	$272.79
Units 5–24	$12.99	$259.80
Units 6–24	$12.99	$246.81
Units 7–24	$12.99	$233.82
Units 8–24	$12.99	$220.83

Names Received	12,375
Names with Phone Numbers	10,750
% with Phone Number	86%
Orders	3,440
Total Leads Used	6,880
Response %	50.0%

Figure 9.5 Ship-Till-Forbid Continuity Load-Ups

continuity and continue to receive shipments monthly. They don't cancel out on the phone. There really is no downside to this promotion.

Analysis of Figure 9.6 Here we see a consumer case in which both inbound and outbound telemarketing have a role to play. The original order was taken via an inbound 800 number from a DRTV commercial.

Consumer Case Study		Business Case Study	
Music One-Shot—In this campaign we called house customers who had responded to a DRTV commercial. They purchased a one-shot music set with a credit card. We called and tried to cross-sell another one-shot set of music products with similar music tastes at a cost of $39.95. The credit card numbers were on the client's file. Therefore, we asked the customers to charge the purchase on the same card they used to buy the first one-shot set. (85 percent of the people did use the credit card option, the balance of the orders were processed as bill-me.) The customers' satisfaction was guaranteed, and they had the option of returning the product risk-free.		One-shot to Engineers at Work—In this campaign we called a wide variety of lists, including house-file book buyers, compiled lists of engineers, controlled-circulation magazine subscribers, and an outside list of engineering book buyers from the following professions: mechanical engineering, civil engineering, petroleum engineering, industrial and maintenance engineering, HVAC engineering, and general engineering. We offered them an engineering reference book priced at $97.50 plus shipping and handling for a 15-day examination. An engineering formulas pocket guide was used as a premium.	
		Names Received	24,000
		Names with Phone Numbers	20,500
		% with Phone Number	85.4%
Names Received	28,110		
Names with Phone Numbers	19,480	Orders	3,405
% with Phone Number	67%		
		Total Leads Used	13,303
Orders	1,870	Response %	25.6%
Total Leads Used	15,580		
Response %	12%		

Figure 9.6 One-Shots

We then called those customers back to add additional revenue and value to the relationship. One-shot offers have traditionally been the simplest format to use in outbound telemarketing. They have been successful across all markets. Product fulfillment, billing, and collections are all vastly less complex for one-shots than for continuity or negative-option club promotions. However, the downside is that the profitability rests entirely on the revenues generated by one shipment. Hence, the average order value usually needs to be higher for a one-shot offer than for a continuity intro. This is true for both the business and consumer markets. Consumer one-shots usually won't work with outbound telemarketing at costs under $25 to $30. Business one-shots usually need to start at $70 to $90 to work in an outbound promotion. This is particularly true in a bill-me payment environment.

Another interesting rule of thumb is that if you have a product that can be sold to both the business and consumer markets via outbound telemarketing, you often will see a higher response rate from the business segment compared to the consumer segment, all other factors being equal. The likely cause for this variance is better list targeting available from many business lists, along with the fact that there is somewhat less price sensitivity in the business market because the customer's company often pays for the product, rather than the customer himself.

Analysis of Figure 9.7 Successful cross-selling is usually the key to building and maintaining a long-term, mutually profitable relationship with customers. Outbound telemarketing is a terrific media choice for this task given the often high response rates. In fact, many good direct marketing companies will actually have a preset strategy for scheduling an optimum mix of mail and phone contact to generate as many orders as possible during first year of the relationship from each new customer they acquire.

We will take a closer look at the credit card versus bill-me issue a little later in this chapter. However, it is interesting to note that even though this is a cross-sell to existing customers, 95 percent of the orders are bill-me, even with aggressive scripting and offers designed to maximize the percentage of credit card–secured orders.

Given a choice of list sources and potential test possibilities, we recommend that you start with a house-file cross-sell or reinstatement cam-

Consumer Case Study		Business Case Study	
CD-ROM—Cross-Sell to House Lists— In this campaign we called at home a house list of customers who had previously purchased a children's software product. We offered customers a 60-day trial of a different children's software product. Customers were asked for their credit card number over the phone. If they refused to give the credit card number, they were sent an invoice for the product instead. The price point was $29.99.		One-Shot Book and Video Set Sold to Health-Care Professionals—In this campaign we called a house list of individuals who had purchased training materials in the past, and offered them a preview of a 20-minute video and companion hardcover reference book relating to critical-care nursing. The cost was $68.95 plus shipping and handling. A pocket reference on health assessment was used as a free premium.	
		Names Received	21,881
Names Received	24,362	Names with Phone Numbers	19,950
Names with Phone Numbers	20,075	% with Phone Number	91%
% with Phone Number	82%		
		Orders	1,879
Total Orders	6,093		
Bill Me	5,783	Total Leads Used	10,497
Credit Card	310	Response %	17.9%
Total Leads Used	16,739		
Response %	36.4%		
Credit Card Sales	5.3%		

Figure 9.7 Cross-Sell Promotions to House-File Names

paign as a first test for outbound telemarketing, as these programs have the highest potential for success.

Analysis of Figure 9.8 Upgrade selling is somewhat unique to computer software marketing. It leverages the advantages of conducting a cross-sell campaign to your best house customers, with the recognition and loyalty that customers develop for a frequently used (and well-liked)

Consumer Case Study

PC Utility Software Upgrade to Previous Customers—In this campaign we called existing customers who had previously purchased a utility software product, and offered them a three-product bundle containing an upgrade version of the software product they already owned. The other products in the bundle were also utility products. The price for the bundle was $65.50. The offer included a free premium of a Windows tutorial CD-ROM. The individual products could be ordered as one-shots at $25.95.

Names Received	16,282
Names with Phone Numbers	10,811
% with Phone Number	66%
Customers Sold	1,011
Primary Bundle	596
Alternate Only	415
Total Leads Used	9,190
Response %	11%

Business Case Study

Computer Software Upgrade Offer to Buyers of Previous Versions—In this campaign we called a wide variety of business computer users that had purchased a previous version of this popular software product, and offered them an upgrade version at a more than 60 percent discount. The primary offer was for a deluxe version at $100 (regular price = $300). We offered a hardware accessory priced at $30 as an add-on upsell, and there was also a downsell offer for less expensive versions of the program at $50. All orders included $6.50 shipping and handling. All orders were secured with a credit card. There was no bill-me option.

Names Received	143,000
Names with Phone Numbers	131,417
% with Phone Number	91.9%
Total Orders	7,602
Deluxe Version w/Upsell	547
Deluxe Version Only	4,718
Std Version Downsell	2,336
Total Leads Used	85,416
Response %	8.9%

Figure 9.8 Selling Upgrades to Current Customers

product. These campaigns can be very successful as long as the product developers continue to do a good job of incorporating significant new features and benefits into each new version. The response rates will fall once the product hits the mature stage, at which point product improvements lessen.

Analysis of Figure 9.9 Offering one or more free trial issues with an invoice as an introduction to a regular subscription is a classic approach to gaining new subscribers in the magazine business. If customers want to continue the subscription, they can pay the invoice. Otherwise they can cancel and owe nothing. This model works in both the consumer and

Consumer Case Study		**Business Case Study**	
Consumer Magazine Subscription—New-Customer Acquisition—In this campaign we called outside lists of consumers at home. We offered 12 issues of a digest-sized magazine at $17.95, or 6 issues at $9.95. A soft-cover booklet was used as a premium. The first issue was sent out on a free-trial basis. Customers could cancel by writing *cancel* on the invoice.		Reference Subscription Service Offered to Parochial Secondary, University, and Research Libraries—In this campaign we called public and private libraries from an outside compiled list to offer them a 10-day preview of a new reference subscription service. Each volume in the series covered a different section of a related topic. Participating libraries would automatically receive 12 brand-new titles over the course of the year. The cost for a one-year 12-book subscription was $255.25 plus shipping and handling. The offer included an atlas as a premium.	
Names Received	28,875		
Names with Phone Numbers	15,525		
% with Phone Number	54%		
		Names Received	3,520
Orders	2,101	% with Phone Numbers	100.0%
12 Issues (2 yr)	1,365		
6 Issues (1 yr)	736		
		Orders—Libraries Sold	625
Total Leads Used	12,656		
Response %	16.6%	Total Leads Used	2,056
		Response %	30.4%

Figure 9.9 Selling New Subscriptions

business markets. Of course magazines are not the only products that can be marketed using subscription offers.

The last two case studies offer only a small glimpse of what can be accomplished with outbound telemarketing as it relates to generating first-time customers for subscription and membership (club) offers. It is important to note that both the business and consumer cases rely heavily on a risk-free trial/10-day preview offer. Herein lies the central leverage point for profitability and success. An unconditional satisfaction guarantee is an absolute requirement whenever you are going to be calling outside lists. Under these circumstances, there is truth to the statement that "the selling doesn't really start until the customer has the product in his hands." Ultimately, it will be the quality and value of the product along with the efficiency of the fulfillment that will determine whether these types of programs can succeed over the long run.

As an additional note, we have done a number of tests in which we compared subscription offers versus continuity offers for the same product. The continuity is the consistent winner on the front end, because you are not asking the customer to pay for a full year of service in advance. However, the subscription format does guarantee that customers will stay in the service for at least 6 to 12 shipments depending upon frequency of delivery, and seems to be the offer format of choice when the series contains newly created material each month, or when the service is totally open-ended (such as with a magazine). Hence, it may be worth testing to determine which format works best for you.

Analysis of Figure 9.10 When it comes to subscription renewals and club, continuity, or membership reinstatements, outbound telemarketing is almost always at the heart of the media mix. These calls can be placed almost anywhere in the renewal cycle, and they will be successful. One strategy involves adding a call at the end of the direct mail series as a final effort. Another approach might be to insert the call right at termination, or perhaps two or three months after cancel. Each program has different dynamics and testing is the only real way to determine which approach is best for your situation. Renewal/reinstate programs are about as close as you can get to a sure thing in outbound telemarketing.

Analysis of Figure 9.11 One often-asked question is "What is the most expensive product that can be sold by phone?" Of course the answer is

Consumer Case Study

Newsletter Subscription Renewal—In this campaign we called customers at home whose subscription had expired, and asked them to renew. The renewal rates were as follows: 1-year = $125, 2-year = $199, 6-month = $69. A choice close between the 1-year and 2-year offers was used as the primary offer close. The short-term, 6-month, offer was used as a downsell.

Names Received	15,550
Names with Phone Numbers	7,307
% with Phone Number	47%
Total Orders	646
1-Year Renewals @ $125	483
2-Year Renewals @ $199	121
6-Month Renewals @ $69	42
Total Leads Used	6,211
Response %	10.4%

Business Case Study

Stock Market Reference Book Renewal Subscription—In this campaign we called brokerage professionals who had recently canceled or failed to renew their subscriptions to a stock market financial reference service that would regularly cost $129.95 per annual subscription, and offered to renew their subscriptions at a discounted price of $89.95.

Names Received	10,500
Names with Phone Numbers	5,974
% with Phone Number	56.9%
Orders	836
Total Leads Used	4,182
Response %	20.0%

Figure 9.10 Renewals and Reinstatements

that there really is no upper limit to what can be done. However, if you ask the question in a slightly different way, by adding the words "in a service bureau setting" to the end of that question, you can get a vastly different answer.

Keep in mind that service bureaus work in a very different way than an in-house sales force. The in-house operation will probably hire well-paid, full-time sales reps. These reps will be trained for weeks, even months in some cases, before they make the first call. Their telemarketing sales strategy will certainly involve relationship marketing and account-based marketing.

Consumer Case Study		Business Case Study	
Lead Qualification for a Public Utility—In this campaign we called existing residential customers for a gas and electric utility and qualified them for interest in a new service that was under consideration. There were eight simple questions. The purpose of this lead qualification survey was to help the utility identify its best prospects for this new type of service.		Qualify leads for a Business Computer Product—In this campaign we called outside lists of computer systems managers. We asked four qualifying questions. The first two were about their type of business. The third inquired about their time frame for purchasing this type of software, and the fourth asked if they wanted a sales representative to contact them in the future.	
Names Received	2,000	Names Received	56,250
Names with Phone Numbers	2,000	Names with Phone Numbers	54,000
% with Phone Number	100%	% with Phone Number	96%
Qualified Leads	1,050	Qualified Leads	9,050
Total Leads Used	1,462	Total Leads Used	36,200
Response %	72%	Response %	25%

Figure 9.11 Lead Qualification/Generation

Relationship marketing recognizes the fact that in most cases there will be a relatively long sales cycle, and that developing a good one-to-one relationship between the buyer and the sales rep is essential to the sale. Account-based marketing also recognizes the fact that an ongoing series of contacts will be required to close the deal, and that it is very important that accurate notes about all the previous contacts be available to the sales rep each time he or she makes a call.

Account-based marketing and relationship marketing are more difficult to do in an agency setting. The sales reps will be moving from campaign to campaign, client to client. Many of them are part-time permanent employees. There is no easy way to ensure that the same person will make each follow-up call. Most of the agency promotions are designed to secure a yes-or-no answer on the very first call. As you can see, developing an actual relationship in such an environment is a real challenge. Similarly, many of the high-speed predictive dialers that are used in today's telemarketing centers have a fixed record length that doesn't allow much freedom to insert notes into the record that would be available in future calls.

In our view, the practical limit for the consumer price point on an outbound telemarketing order is about $100 in a service bureau setting. The business-to-business limit is probably in the range of about $500 to $1,000. Of course, we are quite sure that there are many exceptions to this. However, we believe that they are the exceptions rather than the rule. Obviously, these limits do not apply to inbound 800-number applications.

Given the boundaries of what can be done with an outbound call in a service bureau setting, lead generation/qualification is the practical solution. Believe it or not, the most important issue to consider when managing these programs is not "What is the conversion percentage?" Rather, it is "How can I ensure that all of the qualified leads are being promptly followed up, and do I have sufficient systems in place to monitor what actually happens after the lead is turned over to the house sales force?"

The biggest challenge you will face is ensuring that there is a balance between the telemarketer's ability to generate leads and the sales force's capacity to follow up on them promptly. There's nothing in life that gets cold quite as quick as a "qualified" lead.

Lead generation/qualification can be an excellent in-house outbound application if the number of calls is small and there is an opportunity to build a bond of trust between the telemarketers and the sales force. A service bureau is best when the call volume is large, or if you prefer to outsource the management of the telemarketing operation so you can focus on other responsibilities. Our case studies clearly show that the response rates can be excellent if you have the right list, offer, and qualifying criteria.

Of course inbound telemarketing is the response media of choice whenever you are using space ads, card decks, direct mail, TV, or radio to generate a lead. The reasons for this are the same as for outbound, namely, telemarketing provides a live interactive qualifying exchange between the prospect and the TSR. It also allows you to process the lead very quickly and accomplish the follow-up in the shortest amount of time possible. In fact, with hot voice and data transfer we can now transfer the qualified prospect call from an agency TSR directly to an in-house sales rep so that the order can be completed on the initial call without the customer hanging up. This application is particularly effective for home equity loans and insurance programs, where you need a licensed broker to complete the deal.

Analysis of Figure 9.12 Market research survey work on average yields the highest conversion percentages of any outbound telemarketing application. The reason is simple. You are not asking anyone to make a purchase or even to qualify themselves for future purchase consideration of a product.

Consumer Case Study

Cable TV Guide Survey—In this campaign we called cable TV subscribers and conducted a market research survey as part of an effort to better understand the customers' TV-viewing interests and also to increase the circulation of a new cable television program guide. Customers who participated in the survey were offered a free subscription to the guide.

Names Received	33,000
Names with Phone Numbers	16,500
% with Phone Number	50%
Completed Surveys	10,084
Total Leads Used	13,200
Response %	76%

Business Case Study

Survey to Banking Professionals at Work—In this campaign we called current subscribers to a controlled-circulation magazine servicing the banking industry and conducted a requalification survey to satisfy the BPA requirements. We were permitted to speak with the prospect's secretary or assistant.

Names Received	4,770
Names with Phone Numbers	4,650
% with Phone Number	97.5%
Completed Surveys	2,500
Total Leads Used	4,170
Response %	60%

Figure 9.12 Market Research Surveys

Outbound telemarketing is the basic staple in the arsenal of market researchers. Our general guidelines would include the following.

1. Keep the survey as short as possible.
2. Offer a premium if you believe your respondents may run out of energy before you reach the end.
3. When you get near the end, mention that there are only a few questions left.
4. Test the survey out on your coworkers to make sure that it can be delivered the way you intended and that the answers are valid.
5. Hire a professional to help you design, compile, and analyze the results.

We believe that most readers will find some parallel between their own business and one or more of the above referenced case studies. The response rates shown represent good middle-of-the-road targets for these types of campaigns. Hopefully, you will now have some good ideas and insights into how telemarketing can fit into your business plans in new and better ways.

Summary

- When testing outbound telemarketing on a project that doesn't work in the mail, plan to spend a good deal of time monitoring calls during the first days and weeks of the campaign. You may not only turn an otherwise hopeless situation into a success, you may also uncover the real reason for the mail failure.
- Continuity club offers are among the most profitable in all of direct marketing because they not only have high initial response rates and low order acquisition costs, but also set up an ongoing revenue stream.
- The Canadian market often outperforms your U.S. market segment by 50 percent for the same offer sold.
- Direct mail has more sensitivity to price than outbound telemarketing on the front-end. People are more affected by price when they see it in print than when they hear it on the phone.

It's good to test price when using outbound telemarketing, but wait for the final back-end results before making any rollout decisions. Just because customers say "yes" to a price on the phone doesn't mean the product will pass the price/value comparison once they actually have it in their hands.

- Continuity load up offers are the best, most profitable offer structures in the direct marketer's arsenal.
- Sophisticated direct marketers occasionally run a one-shot promotion to first-time buyers on a break-even basis to acquire them as prospects for future cross-sell campaigns, which operate on higher profit margins.
- Outbound telemarketing programs that rely heavily on relationship- or account-based marketing are often more difficult to execute in an agency setting. Such programs sometimes only work in an in-house environment.
- Immediate follow-up is the key to success in lead qualification campaigns. Many programs now use hot transfer strategies so interested prospects can be immediately passed on from outbound TSRs to waiting sales executives for further qualification, and in some cases order processing, without the prospect hanging up the phone.

10

Working with an Agency or a Consultant

There are many advantages to working with a knowledgeable consultant. Most importantly, a good consultant can help you shorten the learning curve of the telemarketing organization you are working with—whether that is an in-house or outsource operation—thereby shortening the time it takes to launch a telemarketing test and the subsequent rollout. Consultants with significant telemarketing experience bring a wealth of knowledge to the telemarketing equation. They are familiar with the various telemarketing organizations, the costs, and the key players and clients of each organization. Consultants definitely can help you select the right telemarketing agency partner. They can provide you with the experience necessary to give your program a reasonable chance of success. Of course, there are never any guarantees. Some products work very well on the phone and some do not. A successful direct mail program is not a guarantee of success on the phone. Sometimes a consultant's instincts will tell him or her that something is worth a test, even if the other data point to failure.

Consultants generally have significant and varied experience and are able to help you create offers that may provide you with a strong chance of success. They may be able to negotiate favorable PI (per-item or per-inquiry) commission arrangements with telemarketing agencies, which may reduce your test costs by ensuring that you only pay for orders received.

The Advantages of Having a Good Consultant

In 1992, there was a continuity craft program that was a huge telemarketing success. However, it did not work at all when tested via mail or other media. The only profitable channel was telemarketing. The reasons for this were many but the high phone response rate and limited (but very targeted) list universe available were the most critical issues. If the marketers involved had given up on this product after the failure of the direct mail campaign, they never would have realized how successful this program would prove to be on the phone. A knowledgeable consultant could make all the difference in ensuring that you don't miss an opportunity like this.

There are few disadvantages; the only one of consequence is that retaining a consultant increases your cost. In most cases, however, the incremental increase in costs will be more than offset by additional profits gained through the consultant's efforts. Of course, you will need to look for a consultant who will fit in with the other people on your staff. You don't want to have your staff sabotage the effort because the consultant was brought in from the outside.

The Advantages and Disadvantages of Working with an Outside Telemarketing Agency

Here are some of the major *advantages* of working with an outside agency.

- The telemarketing infrastructure is already in place, so the initial startup costs will be much less than if you are either starting up or expanding an in-house operation.
- An agency should be able to provide you with an experienced account-management and promotion-planning executive who

---

Guideline for Testing More Than One Agency

If *one* of the agencies knows that it is in a test situation, *all* of the agencies should know.

---

can help you avoid many common errors and hidden flaws in your marketing plan.

- Most likely the agency will be able to provide a core group of professional TSRs with experience in programs similar to yours.
- If you are working on a PI basis, the agency will be sharing some of the financial risk for testing.
- You can test more than one agency and create competition within the groups to maximize the results and enhance the level of service that you (the client) receive.
- Agencies sometimes can be successful with projects that would fail in an in-house setting. We know of many companies that have their in-house units focus on inbound customer sales and support while at the same time outsourcing outbound sales promotions to a qualified agency.

Here are some of the major *disadvantages* of working with an agency.

- You may experience a feeling of loss of control because the people making and managing the calls are not your employees. Even if you station some staff members on site, you can't have them listen to every call. However, remember that you do have control over the script, and you can insist on close script adherence. Keep in mind that those agency people are all answerable to you, and you maintain the right to pull the plug if you are not happy.
- It's more difficult to monitor calls when you have to schedule sessions in advance rather than just walking down the hall to see what is going on.

Selecting the Best Agency to Be Your Telemarketing Partner

There are many considerations in the selection of a telemarketing partner. *Partner* should definitely be the operative word for your telemarketing agency and/or consultant relationship, because if these people are not your partners, your results will reflect it.

A true partnership with a telemarketer is reflected in many ways by the telemarketing organization you select. Here are just a few of them.

1. Excitement at the opportunity you present. This is paramount and anything less is cause for concern. If they are not genuinely excited, there is probably something wrong.
2. A thorough communications and reporting system.
3. A complete listening ability and concern for your account.
4. Constant attention to your programs and a willingness to create new test scripts, test new offers and products, etc.
5. Ability to monitor calls at any prearranged time.
6. Willingness to test at a reasonable cost.
7. A knowledgeable and experienced account executive/manager/representative dedicated to your programs.
8. Ability to meet client goals and objectives on schedule.
9. An ongoing telemarketing sales training program in which TSRs continually improve performance and stay abreast of new techniques.

The word *partner* may seem an overly emphatic term for the agency you select to conduct your telemarketing programs. However, make no mistake about the relationship. If the agency is not your partner, you have little chance of success. Your telemarketing agency must be willing to learn about your business, products, marketing efforts, fulfillment systems and procedures, and the staff they will be working with at your company. Nothing should be left to chance.

Selecting your telemarketing organization requires some diligent detective work by you and your staff. The first question, which everyone considers, is "Why don't we do it in-house?" This is probably the easiest of all the questions to answer. Setting up an in-house telemarketing capability when you begin testing telemarketing is extremely expensive. It requires hiring a knowledgeable telemarketing manager and telemarketing sales reps. Then there's the purchase of the equipment, space, telephone service, etc. It all adds up, and you haven't made even one phone call or sale. Finally, are you prepared to close down the operation if it does not live up to your goals and objectives, or are you prepared to expand your operation if the test is successful? Clearly, you will need to complete a thorough financial analysis regardless of whether you do it in-house or through an agency. A knowledgeable consultant can be very helpful in completing this initial review.

Let's say that you've made the decision to test telemarketing. You have done the analysis and determined that there's no reason to develop an in-house telemarketing unit. Here's what you need to know as you interview and select your telemarketing test partner(s).

1. You need to know who the agency's clients are, especially clients with similar products who have been clients for a significant period of time. It's important also that you speak with some of the agency's current clients about their assessment of the agency's strengths and weaknesses.

2. How long has the company been in business? The majority of telemarketing agencies stay in business only a few years or less. Longevity means the company has been successful and is therefore likely to have better training and a more knowledgeable staff.

3. Is the company large enough to handle your needs? Does it have enough capacity, TSRs, and phone lines to meet your goals on schedule?

4. How do the TSRs sound when you hear them on the phone or meet them on a branch visit? Are they good communicators? Do they have sufficient background to handle your program?

5. Does the agency have sufficient technology to meet your program needs with respect to telecommunications, data processing, engineering, and programming?

6. Will the agency be able to provide seamless order processing into your existing fulfillment systems?

7. What will it cost? Will you pay per hour, per talk-minute, or on a PI basis? What about hidden costs? What does the company charge for program set-up, TSR training, computer programming, scriptwriting, consulting, customized reporting, telephone-number appending, welcome letter or other fulfillment, and billing and collection services?

8. Where is the agency's call center? Will you be able to tour it? Is it relatively close for training purposes? Is this at all important? (We know of many clients that have never visited a telecenter even once, yet their programs are very successful.)

9. Do you like and trust the people who will be working on your program? Is there one person in charge (an account executive) who really understands your business, who will be your main contact and be fully responsible for everything that happens? This last criterion is probably the most important one of all. The value of a talented and trusted account executive/manager/representative can't be overestimated.

Some Applications Should Be Done In-House

There are some applications that should be done in-house.

Small inbound and outbound lead-qualification programs often are best done in-house. This is particularly true when you feel that the TSRs need constant ongoing contact with the sales force that is following up on the leads. The most frequent reason that telemarketing lead-qualification programs fail is that there ultimately develops an imbalance between the telemarketer's ability to generate leads and the sales force's ability to follow up promptly and turn the leads into orders. When the "hot" leads get "cold," the sales force loses confidence in the quality. One way to overcome this problem is to have the sales force spend some time remote monitoring the calls and developing a relationship of trust with the telemarketers.

Most small–call volume campaigns are candidates for in-house handling. The danger for them in an agency setting, where they are competing against much larger programs for the attention and loyalty of the staff, is that they won't get the attention they need to be successful.

However, we must note that there are some small specialized agencies that are designed to handle programs with volumes as low as a few hundred calls a week.

Programs that require account-based and relationship marketing can be a poor match for an agency that does not have the capability to access the previous contact history on the TSR's terminal. Account-based marketing recognizes the fact that it will usually take more than one contact to secure an order. It is also necessary to save the notes from all previous contacts and make them available to the TSR on future contacts. Not all outbound calling systems can do this. Relationship marketing recognizes that a relationship and bond of trust must be built between the buyer and seller before the order can be secured. This usually requires a series of contacts over time between the same TSR and the prospective customer. Many outbound predictive dialers have a hard time sending future calls to the same TSR who made the last contact.

Very complex programs that require extensive technical training (particularly if the technical details are constantly changing) are probably best done in-house.

What Does It Cost to Use an Outside Agency?

There are a number of cost factors to consider when deciding whether or not to hire an outside firm.

Hourly Rate

The most common outbound service bureau billing arrangement is to bill on an hourly basis. There may also be additional start-up fees, programming fees, training fees, consulting fees, script-writing fees, and monthly minimums. Hourly rates often run from $27 to $35 per hour, with an hour defined as one person working on the phone for one hour of time. Basically, you get what you pay for. If you squeeze your agency for a low hourly rate, they may put their lowest paid TSRs on your program. That may not make the most sense from a quality and productivity standpoint. Beware of agencies that quote very low hourly rates; they may be on the rocks and just trying for anything that will keep the doors open.

Cost per Sale

This is also known as performance-based pricing, or working on a PI (per-item or per-inquiry) basis. Of course from the agency perspective, this format always entails the risk that the project will not make sufficient money if the productivity falls below expectations. However, it does have considerable advantages to the client company, since it is the only formula that guarantees a fixed order-acquisition cost. PI rates are a function of the contact and response rates. They are essentially a commission, *but they are not calculated as a percentage of the order value*. A promotion for a $100 product might have the same PI as a promotion for a $50 product, if the contact and response rates are the same for both programs. Telemarketing is basically a high-volume, low-margin business. Agencies that work on a PI basis are motivated to make the PIs as low as possible to maximize the number of lists that work, thereby maximizing the potential call volume of the program. There are often no additional charges or fees when programs are run on a PI basis.

Cost per Call

Another less common arrangement would be to bill on a cost-per-completed-call basis. This formula is sometimes used when the purpose of the call is to present an advertising message (political campaign calls) or to gather market research. Once again, there may be other additional charges or fees. The costs will depend directly on the length of the call and the accessibility of the prospects.

Cost per Minute

This is the most common billing strategy for inbound service. Computers track the actual talk time generated for each inbound program, and the total number of billable minutes is billed at a rate that is generally somewhat less than $1 per minute. Once again, there may be additional charges or fees. Many inbound service bureaus have a monthly minimum, which makes it prohibitively expensive to run small-volume programs. Monthly minimums can run in the tens of thousands of dollars. Please note: an agency that bills at a higher cost per minute but with no other charges or fees is very often a more economical choice than one that has a lower per-minute rate but a whole menu of à la carte fees.

Regardless of which of the compensation formulas you and your agency are using, the profitability of your program still comes down to how much it costs to acquire the order. It's easy to compute your cost per order with an hourly charge. Just divide the cost per hour by the average number of orders you receive per hour and you'll have your answer. If you're paying $30 per hour per rep, and you're receiving an average two orders per hour per rep, your cost per order is $15. If you're paying $34 per hour, your cost per order is $17, a 13.3 percent increase over the $30 per-hour charge. Small differences in the hourly amount make significant differences on your bottom line.

The second most popular mode of compensating your telemarketing agency is the per-order method. Simply stated, this is a commission on orders generated. As we noted above, the industry refers to this as performance-based pricing. It's also known as working on a PI. There are no computations required to calculate cost per order since that is essentially what the PI is.

Cost-per-call strategies are most often used in promotions where there are no orders, so the cost-per-order issues are generally irrelevant. However, if you had to, you could add up the full telemarketing costs and divide that number by the quantity of orders or surveys.

Once again, if you are paying on a cost-per-talk-minute basis, and you want to calculate your total cost per order, you simply add up your costs and then divide that number by the total number of orders.

What Should You Get for Your Money?

There's no doubt that you should get the undivided attention of the agency you select to be your telemarketing partner. The question is what does the term "undivided attention" really mean? To anyone interested in achieving success in telemarketing, the following areas are critical.

First, the agency must respond promptly to all your requests no matter how unimportant those requests may seem.

The agency must meet the preapproved schedules agreed to prior to the start of your program. No changes should be made without your approval.

Your orders should be confirmed and transmitted to your fulfillment house on schedule. Delays impact back-end performance significantly.

Your agency should understand and have the capability to segment lists with key codes, perform telematch in-house or outside (hopefully without cost to you), and regularly provide detailed reports of the results.

In short, you should have unlimited access to your account rep and the details of your program. There should be plenty of backup support if your primary contact is unavailable. Remember that it's your program and you are ultimately responsible for its successes and failures. The better your communication with the telemanagement staff, and the better your understanding of the current telemarketing situation, the better your chances of success.

Ten Tips for Turning Yourself into the World's Greatest Agency Account Executive/Telemarketing Project Manager

1. Always answer your phone if you are at your desk. It might be your client, the marketing director, or your boss. You should value his or her time over your own. If your boss is talking to you in your office and the phone rings, tell him or her that you'd like to answer the call because it might be a client. Check to see if he or she values the clients as much as you do. It can give you an interesting insight into your boss's psyche and the organization as a whole. Check your voice mail regularly—even at night and on weekends. Everyone will be impressed if your return message starts out by having the machine announce that the following call was received at 10:52 P.M. on Saturday. Not only that but you have bounced the ball back into the original caller's court. It's now up to that person to get around to you on Monday morning instead of the other way around.

2. Return all calls ASAP. Set a goal to return 75 percent of your calls within 15 minutes of the time you receive them. Return 90 percent within an hour. Return 100 percent of all calls by the end of each day. (An after-hours voice-mail message back

to the caller counts and can actually be worth extra points under certain circumstances.)

3. Always know how your program is doing. Review the stats every day on every program. This includes everything about the program including

   - How many total sales you have, how close you are to your sale's goal, when you expect to hit the goal (and whether or not you have enough leads to support the calling and hit the sale's goal)
   - What percentage of the sales are primary offers as opposed to upsells and cross-sells
   - What the primary refusal reasons are—and why—and what you think can be done to turn some of them into sales
   - Which list segments are best and which are worst, and what you think can be done about it
   - How the new script is working, what the numbers show, and what your next step should be

   Don't ever be put in the position where you have to check the numbers. Clients/marketers/bosses expect you to know the numbers cold, and they will lose confidence in your ability to manage their programs if you have to check. Remember that you are their eyes and ears. They can't watch the program every minute. They are counting on you (and paying you and your company) to do that for them. Don't let them down!

4. Take every call about your service, or about a problem with a transaction, that you can. This call may be your next big client, or it may alert you to a fatal flaw in the promotion that just started. If there *is* a flaw, everyone expects you to be the person to find it.

5. Develop a responsible attitude. If it has anything to do with your program, you are responsible for any and all problems, even if you had nothing to do with causing them. That way people will believe you can fix whatever goes wrong. They will also give you much of the credit when things go right. Moreover, your coworkers will appreciate that you don't blame them for foul-ups. They will work harder than ever to do the best work possible on your programs. If you have a choice

between communicating with someone over the phone or in person, go for the live visit.

6. Lead TSR training sessions whenever you can. Interact with the telecenter managers, staff, and reps as much as you can. Make as many demo calls in front of the reps and managers as possible. The TSRs will be impressed if they see that you are not overwhelmed with phone fright. Remote monitor as much as you can. Be positive when dealing with people in the telecenter. Keep it fun. Try to organize exclusive sales promotions with gifts and prizes for your programs. Remember that in an agency setting you are competing for the attention and loyalty of the staff against every other program that is running alongside yours. Your goal is to make sure that your client's programs always have the highest visibility—even if they are surrounded by other much larger programs.

7. Speak to clients/marketers at least once a week on the phone (every day if you are launching a new project or test). Meet with clients/marketers at least three times a year (four times a year is better). Get to know as many people in the client company as possible.

8. Make friends with every consultant you can meet. Show them that you and your company are the best in the business.

9. Good script writing is critical to the success of any program. Don't just pull an old script out of the drawer and change the names. Take a little time to think about who will be on the other end of the phone. Ask yourself what will make them want to say yes to the offer.

10. Write your goals down on paper, and post them on your wall. Several years ago an Ivy League school conducted a survey of business school graduates. The survey revealed that those graduates who had consistently written their goals down on paper were earning considerably more money and had positions with much more responsibility and influence than those who hadn't bothered to write down their goals at all.

What Does It Cost to Hire a Consultant?

A consultant usually is compensated in one of three ways—either by a one-time payment, an ongoing retainer, or on a per-order basis as a commission. What you pay for is a factor of what you have contracted for. If you hire a top strategic planner to spend a few days troubleshooting and preparing marketing plans with your key executives, you may pay that person $1,000 or more per day for his or her expertise.

On the other hand, you might hire an expert to help manage the day-to-day telemarketing operations. This person might devote 5 to 50 hours per month to your program. You will either pay a monthly retainer or a commission on the orders generated. This may add to the marketing costs but typically will be much less costly than actually hiring a professional of this caliber and putting him on staff. There is a wide range for what a consultant might reasonably charge you. It's up to you and the consultant to decide what is fair. The question of course is whether or not the added expense results in a more successful program and increases the profitability of your efforts.

What Should You Get for Your Consulting Fee?

Some of the services that consultants can provide are:

- Creating strategic marketing plans that leverage the value of all the assets and expand the marketing opportunities into new and untried media
- Finding and securing new lists for testing
- Turning underperforming assets such as lists and excess inventory into revenue generators
- Rewriting the billing-and-collection series to improve payments and reduce returns and bad debt
- Helping to establish new relationships with telemarketing and fulfillment agencies
- Analyzing prior results to uncover hidden costs and unrealized revenue opportunities

- Setting up new and more meaningful reporting structures that actually reveal what is going on with the programs
- Networking with other clients for joint venture opportunities
- Managing day-to-day telemarketing programs, including ordering lists, writing scripts, remote monitoring, TSR training, etc.

Maintaining Control and Communicating with Your Telemarketing Agency

Working with a telemarketing agency can be easy—or it can be one of your most stressful responsibilities. Important aspects of your partnership with a telemarketing agency include trust, communication, and the amount of information shared. Clearly, the secret is to identify the agency that matches all of your needs and then develop a detailed communication process to keep you informed.

Loss of control is the most frequently cited reason for the decision to conduct in-house telemarketing. The secret to overcoming this negative is to stay in touch with a few trusted people who can act as your eyes and ears.

What type of communication should you receive, and how frequently should you receive it? Here are some good guidelines.

Information/Report	*Timeliness*
Dates of receipt of lists— your telemarketing agency should provide you with a periodic update when they receive new lists for your program	As new lists are received
Merge/purge/telematch results	When completed by key code
Results for test program	Next day
Results for ongoing program	Once or twice a week
Final reports that are truly insightful and analytical	At the end of the campaign

But what details should be included in the reports and communication you receive?

First and foremost you need to know when your lists arrive at the telemarketing agency. You also need a proposed schedule of important dates in your program.

The merge/purge/telematch date is critical; if there are delays in this process your telemarketing start date will also be delayed. In almost all cases, a problem here results from a list delivery snag and not a problem at the agency. No matter what the reason is for a delay, you need to resolve it immediately; in many agencies, if you miss the merge/purge/telematch schedule, your test will be delayed until the next scheduled merge/purge/telematch run is completed.

Probably the most important information you will require is the results of your initial test by list key. Essentially, these are your flash counts. They provide you with the information you need to make changes and alterations to your campaign. You'll be able to determine the response rate by list to determine which lists are performing at an acceptable level and which are not. At this point it is important that you don't make decisions too quickly. Generally speaking, performance improves as the reps become familiar with your program and can anticipate the questions of the customers. The first hard look should be at the beginning of the second full week of your test. The telemarketing agency and/or your consultant should be able to make script changes and recommend offer changes that may improve your test program significantly.

Summary

- Hiring a good consultant can be a great decision when your company doesn't have direct marketers with telemarketing experience on staff.
- Even if your company has an in-house telemarketing operation up and running, or is planning to build one, testing an outside agency can bring experience and creativity to the task that would otherwise be unavailable.
- The major disadvantage of working with an outside agency is the loss of absolute control. Moreover, it may require more planning and effort to monitor calls.

- When selecting an outside agency, always look for one that can demonstrate prior success at what you need. It is not inappropriate to use the same agency as your competitor does, as long as the agency can isolate your project into a separate call center and provide an account management team that is not involved with your competitor's programs. However, the most important criterion is to find an agency where your key contact will be someone who understands your business.
- Never select an agency simply because it has the lowest hourly rate; you get what you pay for.
- Performance-based pricing is popular because it offers a fixed front-end order acquisition cost versus a variable cost in an hourly billed environment.
- One indicator of how well you will be served by a potential agency partner is how promptly it responds to you during the selection process. If it doesn't impress you with how quickly it returns your calls before you sign on the dotted line, you probably won't be happy with how long it takes to respond to future emergencies.
- The most important tips for becoming a world-class telemarketing account manager are to always answer the phone when it rings, and always try to return every call as soon as you receive a message.
- Base your relationship with telemarketing partners on communication and respect.
- Even in situations where campaigns have run successfully for years, it is important to schedule brainstorming review sessions at least once a week.

11

Quality Assurance and Compliance Guidelines

"Customer satisfaction is your best competitive advantage"

Noreen Kaminski

The authors are greatly indebted to Noreen Kaminski, DialAmerica's vice president of quality assurance, for her invaluable assistance in supplying much of the material in this chapter. We also want to thank her and DialAmerica for allowing us to borrow heavily from several of their internal resource manuals, including *Driving Quality Within an Organization, The DialAmerica Compliance & Information Manual,* and *The DialAmerica Code of Ethics.*

Our goal in writing this chapter is not only to share with you the importance of respecting the laws, regulations, and commonsense guidelines that impact our industry, but also to introduce you to a whole new concept of quality management, which we call quality enhancement.

Quality Control, Quality Assurance, and Quality Enhancement

Years ago, most telemarketing organizations approached the issue of managing quality by attempting to maintain control over what TSRs said to the customers. Scripts were carefully written and reps were expected to read large portions of them word for word. Managers would listen to calls with this standard in mind and watch for any signs of higher-than-expected cancellation rates or customer complaints coming in after the fact. Clients/marketers were concerned about any slight deviation from the scripted dialogue. *Quality control* was mostly an attempt to verify that the TSRs were using the script correctly. The whole quality-control process was designed to employ a series of strict standards that would define expectations and control behavior. Consistency of phone calls was the main criterion.

Obviously, your first priority is always to implement the necessary controls in order to ensure that you are in full compliance with the relevant legislative requirements. As such, the main objective of any quality-control strategy is to try to catch someone doing something wrong and correct it. Unfortunately, within this context, quality-control management is mostly viewed as a negative process by everyone involved, particularly the TSRs.

More recently, however, a new concept of quality management has emerged. It is known as *quality assurance.* The main objective is now to ensure that people are doing the *right* thing, rather than trying to catch them doing the *wrong* thing. Quality assurance looks for and rewards positive TSR behavior in an effort to ensure the consistency of quality phone calls. Call consistency is one of the trademarks of call quality. TSR bonus plans are now tied into this effort. Low cancel rates and absence of complaints are rewarded with money and recognition. Today, maintaining quality assurance is the standard quality-management approach for many telemarketing organizations.

However, maintaining quality assurance is no longer the highest level of quality management. Once all of the controls are in place, and you are assured that all of the obvious quality problems have been corrected, you can turn your attention to an even higher level of quality management, one that Noreen Kaminski, DialAmerica's vice president of quality assurance, refers to as *quality enhancement.*

Quality enhancement takes quality management to a whole new level. It changes the focus, from controlling and assuring what the TSR is saying to listening to the customer and monitoring reactions to what is being said. The objective becomes to look for ways to make recommendations for program improvements that will enhance quality, deliver better customer satisfaction, and increase productivity and profitability for the clients/marketers.

When you take the step from quality control and assurance to quality *enhancement*, your quality-management personnel become active partners with the telecenter staff. The goal is to identify not only areas that need improvement (quality control) and areas of excellent behavior (quality assurance), but also to *enhance* the business by giving something back in the way of ideas and recommendations to both the telecenter staff and the marketing teams for the purpose of making the overall program better.

Recognizing the importance of this issue, many telemarketing organizations, including DialAmerica, have now set up independent quality-assurance teams with separate management reporting structures outside the normal telecenter management chain of command. These teams may report directly to the CEO, CFO, or someone else on the executive committee. The main goals of an independent quality assurance/enhancement team should be to

- Ensure that your customer's privacy is being respected
- Monitor compliance with all required laws and regulations
- Listen to what the customers are saying and develop new ways of approaching the business

Obviously, providing outstanding call quality begins with hiring the best people, providing the best training, monitoring and encouraging the best practices, and maintaining strict adherence to the highest quality standards. TSRs and staff must be knowledgeable, competent, courteous, professional, and versed in all compliance and quality standards.

Customer Satisfaction: Your Best Competitive Advantage

When you make the transition from quality control to assurance to enhancement, customer satisfaction becomes a prime objective. Every call you make or receive should ultimately be focused on the customer. The goal should always be to create customers for life. Your main strategy should be to have all callers happier when they hang up the phone than they were when they picked it up, whether they order or not.

Silent Remote Monitoring

Quality management is a continuous process. Silent remote monitoring allows managers, marketers, and clients to listen to TSR/customer conversations without being noticed by either of the parties to the call. Everyone on your quality-management team, including the director, should spend time monitoring calls on a regular basis.

Monitoring is a tool that helps ensure the quality of calls and improves individual performance. It allows clients/marketers to observe and evaluate individual calls as well as the overall performance of the program. It protects consumers from the unethical practices of unscrupulous individuals, and allows employers to supervise and regulate the quality of the work.

The major reasons to conduct ongoing and continuous call monitoring are to ensure customer satisfaction, to clearly identify training opportunities, and to measure and acknowledge superior performance.

If your quality management team is using a quality-enhancement monitoring approach, they will be considering questions such as

How does it sound?
Does it make sense?
What is the customer's reaction?
How would I feel if I had gotten that call?
How would I feel if I were making the call?

TSRs should be rated on salesmanship, ability to develop and enhance the relationship your company has with its customers, compliance with ethical and regulatory guidelines, and technical skills relating to their use of the computer terminals.

A primary objective of the quality-enhancement team is to work hand-in-hand with the telecenter managers to help them develop better reps. A second objective is to interact with the clients/marketers to help them improve the program.

The quality-management team can be useful in the initial training process for new TSRs. Participation at this level will send a strong signal to new hires that quality is important to the organization. It will also allow you to present the remote-monitoring issue in a more positive light right from the start.

All new employees should be made aware of your company's monitoring practices before they accept the job. They should be given written copies of your monitoring policies, and you should post them prominently in your telecenter. A good monitoring policy specifies why monitoring is necessary and how it will be handled. It should also mention that a review is part of the process. Reviews generally take place immediately after the call is monitored or as soon as possible thereafter.

Employee privacy with respect to personal calls is also an issue. Telecenters should have some phones that are designated for personal use. These phones should never be monitored.

New TSRs should be evaluated according to the following guidelines.

- Do they have a solid understanding of the program objectives and script?
- Are they ready to answer all of the questions?
- Are they courteous?
- Are they up to date on all the technical issues they need to know to work at the computer terminal and handle a call?
- Are there any areas where additional training is required?

Monitor Checklists. The quality-enhancement motto is "Catch us doing something good!" When you take this approach to monitor checklists it changes the whole dynamic of the process from looking for errors and problems to looking for strong performance and bestowing awards when you encounter it. Utilizing written quality-monitor checklists will ultimately lead to better overall performance.

Of course you will still have to have your eyes and ears open to detect problems and correct them. Not every checklist will be positive. We firmly believe that clients and marketers should have the right to access and utilize the monitor-checklist system, even though there will be instances where it documents failure rather than success. The important thing from the telecenter management perspective is not that a problem was uncovered, but rather that corrective action was promptly taken. Anyone can manage this business when things are running right and everyone is making money. The real test of our management skill is when we have problems, and how we (telecenter managers, account managers, marketers, and clients) work together and assume joint responsibility to solve them.

A minimum of one checklist per TSR per week should be the standard. As we mentioned earlier, monitor checklists should always be reviewed with the TSRs as soon after the call as possible. This will allow the rep to retain a reasonable memory of the call. The rep should be able to relate to the manager what he or she was thinking about during the call, as well as any perceptions he or she may have had regarding what the customer's responses really meant.

Using a written checklist system will allow you over time to build a companywide database, which you can use to measure the overall quality performance of the organization as a whole. We recommend using a simple 1-to-5 rating scale with yes-or-no options for critical issues. These forms can be fed into an optical scanner and added to a master database.

The 1-to-5 relative scale is used for items associated with sales and customer service performance. The numbers can be averaged to obtain an overall rating. Yes-or-no evaluations are used for technical issues and those that require strict compliance. Listed below are definitions that you can use in a 1-to-5 quality rating system.

5. *Outstanding:* The TSR is performing above all expectations in overall quality and productivity. This is the optimal level of expectations. (Less than 2 percent of all checklist evaluations normally fall into this elite category.)

4. *Exceeds expectations:* TSR performance is above standard expectations and is in consistent compliance with all quality standards.

3. *Meets expectations:* Overall quality and productivity comply with the program standards. (Most TSR evaluations will normally fall into this category.)

2. *Needs improvement:* Overall the TSR performance is below average. One or more areas have been deficient and require immediate improvement. (Verbal or written warnings may be issued here.)

1. *Unacceptable:* TSR performance is seriously deficient and a verbal or written warning is required. (If immediate and ongoing improvement is not seen, dismissal usually follows.)

Figures 11.1 through 11.3 are good examples of quality monitor checklists. Figure 11.1 would be used in a quality-control environment.

Figure 11.2 would be appropriate for companies that are employing quality-assurance strategies. Figure 11.3 would be a good choice for organizations that use quality enhancement.

As you can see from the figures, remote monitoring takes on a whole different approach when you are using a quality-enhancement strategy. You are focusing at least as much, if not more, attention on the customer. Customer reactions to the key issues are rated on a Yes / No / NR (no apparent reaction) basis.

Data on customer reactions is enormously valuable to clients and marketers. It can be included in the final program reports as a way of adding insight as to what was really happening on the phones. A simple refusal analysis would not provide this type of clarity. Moreover, monitor checklist comments and notes can provide many interesting ideas on how future promotions can be improved in areas ranging from list selection to scripting to offer structure.

Seven Key Concerns of Every Quality Manager

These are some of the most frequently encountered quality concern issues within a telecenter environment.

1. TSRs should always use their first and last names when identifying themselves. They should address customers as Mr. or Mrs. rather than using the customer's first name (unless they have already developed a friendly working relationship over time or are working in a consultative selling environment). If TSRs are using a stage name, it should be the same name on every call and should be noted in the TSR's human resource file.
2. Talking between calls is always a dangerous practice. TSRs run the risk of either missing a call or having the customer hear what they are saying as they pick up the phone.
3. Most outbound programs require *verbatim* confirmations. If this is your standard, make sure it is strictly adhered to.
4. TSRs should always be polite and professional when they are speaking to spouses, family members, receptionists, or phone screeners.

Selling Skills | **1-to-5 Rating Potential**

Introduction/Establish Rapport

1. TSR clearly states first and last name and client name.   Rating 1 to 5
2. TSR asks for customer's full name and address.   Rating 1 to 5
3. TSR greeting/intro encourages a sales conversation.   Rating 1 to 5
4. TSR effectively uses rapport and listening skills.   Rating 1 to 5

Explain Product/Transitions

5. TSR relays offer/service information in an effective manner.   Rating 1 to 5
6. TSR uses good judgment on sales continuations.   Rating 1 to 5
7. TSR sounds confident and well versed on offer/service.   Rating 1 to 5

Close

8. TSR closes the order assumptively.   Rating 1 to 5
9. TSR listens to customer and responds with appropriate transition. Rating 1 to 5

Customer Service Skills | **1-to-5 Rating Potential**

10. TSR addresses customer properly and in a friendly manner   Rating 1 to 5
    throughout the call.
11. TSR speaks clearly and communicates correctly.   Rating 1 to 5
12. TSR presents client positively and ends call on a positive note.   Rating 1 to 5

Compliance | **Yes / No Rating Potential**

13. TSR asks for *all mandatory* data.   Rating Yes / No
14. TSR reads compliance requirements verbatim.   Rating Yes / No
15. TSR reads confirmation verbatim.   Rating Yes / No
16. TSR reads disclosure verbatim.   Rating Yes / No
17. TSR uses mute button between calls.   Rating Yes / No

Technical Skills | **Yes / No Rating Potential**

18. TSR fully understands data entry process.   Rating Yes / No
19. TSR keys information in a timely and accurate fashion.   Rating Yes / No
20. TSR utilizes all supplemental information screens.   Rating Yes / No

Figure 11.1 Quality-Control Monitor Checklist

Selling Skills   **1-to-5 Rating Potential**

1. TSR uses a friendly, upbeat, and sincere tone   Rating 1 to 5
    that encourages a sales conversation.
2. TSR uses rapport and listening skills effectively.   Rating 1 to 5
3. TSR sounds confident and well versed on product/benefits.   Rating 1 to 5
4. TSR listens and responds appropriately using good judgment   Rating 1 to 5
    on sales continuations.

Customer Service Skills   **1-to-5 Rating Potential**

5. TSR speaks clearly and enunciates properly.   Rating 1 to 5
6. TSR uses good courtesy skills (i.e., please, thank you).   Rating 1 to 5
7. TSR presents telecenter and client in a professional   Rating 1 to 5
    and positive manner.

Compliance   **Yes / No Rating Potential**

8. TSR limits talking between calls.   Rating Yes / No
9. TSR focuses on screen so that the customer is   Rating Yes / No
    acknowledged quickly.
10. TSR addresses customers by their first and last names and   Rating Yes / No
    uses his own first and last name.
11. TSR gets OK to continue, when necessary, and exits call   Rating Yes / No
    when customer requests not to continue.
12. TSR gets permission to tape record confirmation, if applicable.   Rating Yes / No
13. TSR delivers *verbatim* confirmation.
14. TSR uses appropriate tag line or nonsale close.   Rating Yes / No

Overall Impression   **1-to-5 Rating Potential**

15. ***** Overall impression of TSR / Call *****   Rating 1 to 5

Comments:

_____

_____

_____

Figure 11.2 Quality-Assurance Monitor Checklist

Selling Skills 1-to-5 TSR Rating and Customer Reaction

	TSR Rating	Customer Reaction
1. TSR uses a friendly, upbeat, and sincere tone that encourages a sales conversation.	1 to 5	Pos. / Neg.
2. TSR uses rapport and listening skills effectively.	1 to 5	Pos. / Neg.
3. TSR sounds confident and well versed on product/benefits.	1 to 5	Pos. / Neg.
4. TSR listens and responds appropriately using good judgment on sales continuations.	1 to 5	Pos. / Neg.
5. Customer listened to presentation attentively.		Yes / No / NR
6. Customer interrupted presentation with a refusal signal.		Yes / No / NR

7. If yes, where? ❏ Intro ❏ Gain Attention ❏ Offer ❏ Close ❏ Confirmation
   ❏ Sales Continuation ❏ Upsell ❏ Cross-sell ❏ Final Close
8. Final disposition of phone call: ❏ Sale ❏ Refusal ❏ Call Back ❏ Delist

Customer Service Skills

	TSR	Customer
9. TSR speaks clearly and enunciates properly.	1 to 5	Pos. / Neg.
10. TSR uses good courtesy skills (i.e., please, thank you).	1 to 5	Pos. / Neg.
11. TSR presents telecenter and client in a professional and positive manner.	1 to 5	Pos. / Neg.
12. CUSTOMER was generally pleased to receive the call.		Yes / No / NR
13. CUSTOMER was polite and courteous in responding to TSR.		Yes / No / NR

Compliance   **Yes / No Rating Potential**

14. TSR was focused and prepared for the customer contact.	Yes / No
15. TSR uses first and last name and properly addresses customer.	Yes / No
16. TSR gets OK to continue, when necessary, and exits call properly when customer requests not to continue.	Yes / No

Overall Impression   **1-to-5 Rating Potential**

17. ***** Overall impression of TSR / Call *****   Rating 1 to 5
Note to telecenter: _____
Note to Client/Account Manager:_____

Figure 11.3 Quality-Enhancement Monitor Checklist

5. TSRs should never hang up the phone before the customer has. If the TSR hears a disconnect click on the other end of the line, he or she should ask aloud if the customer is still on the line before assuming the customer has hung up. Hanging up on a customer is a major problem. In many telemarketing organizations it is grounds for a reprimand or dismissal.

6. Proper pronunciation of names, products, and services is essential if you are going to gain the customer's attention and trust.

7. Overall phone courtesy is the standard for all calls. That means no slang or inappropriate comments. Unprofessional behavior should never be tolerated.

Taped Confirmations and Verification Audits

As we have mentioned in other sections, it is now common practice to tape-record the confirmation section of the presentation. This is done mainly to assure the clients/marketers that the TSRs are properly representing the product, offer, terms, and conditions of the transaction.

Here's how it normally works. When the customer says yes to the offer, the TSR asks for permission to record the balance of the phone call, which is the confirmation of the order. The vast majority of customers have no problem with this, and say yes immediately. The TSR then verifies the identity of the customer and restates the offer, terms, and conditions of the transaction for the sake of the recording. The customer will be asked to acknowledge acceptance of those terms and must say yes on the tape for the order to be valid. After the call has ended, the record (both voice and data) is sent to a separate staff of verifiers, who generally have no contact with the sales force. This precludes any possibility of inappropriate collusion. The verifiers retrieve each record one at a time and examine both the data and voice record. The standards are usually quite strict. If the record is incomplete or lacking in any way the verifier will attempt to call the customer back and correct the data and/or re-create a new taped record for the files. A small percentage of all the orders (usually 2 to 5 percent) will wind up being canceled at this stage.

The most frequent reason for cancellation during verification is change of mind. The balance of cancellations are usually people who truly did not understand the terms and conditions of the offer.

Verification costs money and loses front-end orders, but these are people who are much more likely to return the product anyway, so it is much less expensive to cancel the order at this stage than to send out a product, try to collect a debt that won't pay, and process a return.

One key danger signal verifiers should look for is if the customer interrupts the TSR with a refusal signal in the middle of the confirmation, which forces the TSR to go back and resell the product. Whenever you hear that happen on the tape, you should always call those customers back to live-verify.

Creating a Zero-Complaint Environment

Well, of course, if you make enough calls you will get complaints. Some are unavoidable. However, the quality standard should be that you will tolerate zero complaints. The corporate philosophy has to be that one complaint is too many. DialAmerica makes hundreds of millions of phone calls per year and enforces a zero-tolerance-for-complaints policy.

Here is a seven-point plan for establishing this type of environment.

1. Establish a written code of ethics. Make sure that everyone involved, especially the TSRs, knows and understands it.
2. Monitor every TSR using formal monitor checklists at least once a week. Review the checklists with the reps and make them partners in your efforts to improve the quality and performance of the organization.
3. Work closely with your human resource professionals to develop effective recruiting, hiring, and interviewing strategies.
4. Emphasize training and make it an ongoing process for everyone. It is amazing how often the worst complaints come in about the most experienced and presumably trustworthy TSRs.
5. Look for and listen to customer feedback when you are monitoring calls or reviewing monitor checklists.
6. Treat each customer complaint that does come in as the highest priority you have. Insist on taking those calls yourself. Send written apologies immediately acknowledging that the

TSR acted inappropriately or unprofessionally. Promise the customer that you have already taken immediate action. Send copies of your apology to the telecenter manager, his bosses and your bosses, all the way up to the executive committee. Remember, one complaint is too many. Be sure to include titles next to the names on the CC list. This looks impressive to customers and gives them a real sense that you are paying attention to their complaint. If the complaint involves behavior that could lead to termination of the TSR, it is a good idea to call the customer directly and apologize personally. This will also allow you to verify the details of the situation. Speak to the telecenter manager and have him or her deal with the rep in a fair and legal fashion. Everyone should be a little uncomfortable with the process if you are doing it correctly.

7. Include a review of the complaint file when you review telecenter management performance. Establish a telecenter award for TSRs who operate for three months, six months, or a year without a complaint. Remind everyone that the standard is zero complaints.

Dealing with irate customers over the phone is always a challenge for the unsuspecting TSR. Here are some guidelines for handling an irate customer.

- TSRs should be polite, courteous, and empathetic.
- They should properly identify themselves and their company name when asked.
- They should not discuss any legal or legislative issues relating to their call.
- They should turn irate customers over to a supervisor whenever possible.
- Supervisors should listen attentively and promise to forward any complaint on to the people within the organization who can resolve the issue.
- They should immediately notify superiors including the account-management team, who may have responsibility for maintaining the client relationship. Clients should be notified immediately of problems and complaints, particularly if a customer is threatening legal action.

Most complaints that occur during a phone call have more to do with the customer's past experience with the company being represented than they do with the call itself. If you are doing a good job of maintaining a zero-complaint mentality, you should have very few complaints specifically about the TSR or the call.

Responsible Use of Predictive Dialers

This has become a major issue within the direct marketing community. Abandonment of calls placed in the dial queue is the biggest problem. We are sure that all of our readers have had the experience of running to grab the phone before the answering machine kicks in, only to discover that there is no one on the other end of the line. Whenever this happens you can be pretty sure that there was a predictive dialer on the other end that had no one to send the call to.

The abandonment rate of predictive dialers should be set as close to zero as possible. This is the standard that most responsible telemarketers and manufacturers of predictive dialer equipment have adopted. If your company has a policy of dismissing any TSR who routinely hangs up on customers, why would you allow the predictive dialers to do it as a normal course of business? At present your customers don't know who it was that just had them racing to the phone and then hung up on them. However, that will certainly change in the future. Will it still be acceptable when every phone has Caller ID and your customers know that is was your company calling when the line went dead?

We may never get to the point where we can guarantee a zero-abandonment rate, but we certainly need to try.

Watching the dialers to monitor the abandonment rate and ensuring that all of the local calling curfews are respected is another natural responsibility for an independent quality-management team.

Setting up an independent quality-management team with a corporate reporting structure that is outside the normal chain of command of the telecenter staff is not intended to diminish or replace normal call center monitoring. On the contrary, it is intended to supplement those efforts and provide an unbiased outside view of what is happening on the phones. If the criticism is constructive and the feedback is truly valuable and insightful, then everyone, including the telecenter staff, will appreciate it.

Legislative Compliance Requirements

Keeping telecenter managers up to date on legislative requirements and ensuring that they are in compliance is a major responsibility. This should be another function for your quality-management team. It's a big job and it can be a full-time endeavor to monitor the changes, particularly at the state level, to ensure that your operation remains in compliance.

The fact that people believe that they are getting too many calls is the underlying driver behind most of the laws under consideration. Every viable telemarketer should have a law firm on retainer to deal with tele-service legislation.

If you are a client marketer that deals exclusively with outside telemarketing agencies, the law usually sees you as even more responsible for things like maintenance of Do Not Call files than your agency. This is not an issue that you can just assume is being handled properly. You need to be involved, ask questions, and definitely have your own attorneys keep you up to date.

Disclaimer

Please note that the authors are not legal experts. This book's material on legislation and compliance represents their best effort to characterize the requirements and restrictions that telemarketers must abide by. You should speak to your attorney if any of this material raises questions in your mind.

TCPA and the Telemarketing Sales Rule

These are the two main federal laws/regulations that regulate the telemarketing industry. The Telephone Consumer Protection Act of 1991 (TCPA) was the first federal law designed to regulate the actions of legitimate telemarketers. Its purpose was to strike a balance between protecting the rights of consumers while allowing legitimate business to continue to use telemarketing effectively.

Regulations to implement the TCPA were written by the FCC (Federal Communications Commission). They cover four broad issues:

- *Proper identification.* Outbound TSRs are required to reveal their identity, the identity of the company making the offer, the fact that the purpose of the call is to offer products or services for sale, and the nature of the goods or services for sale. Offers must be simple, clear, and easily understood. At some point during the call a telephone number or address must be offered that will allow the customer to recontact the company.
- *Calling hour restrictions.* No calls to private residences are permitted before 8:00 A.M. or after 9:00 P.M. (local time at the called party's location). Please note that some states have more restrictive time-of-day rules.
- *Do-not-call policies.* The TCPA requires companies to maintain a list of those people who do not wish to be contacted by phone and to develop a *written* policy implementing the requirement. These written policies must be made available to anyone upon demand.
- *Enforcement of policies.* Calling a consumer who has asked not to be called may be a violation of the TCPA and could result in civil penalties. Misrepresentation of a product or service, or the refund, repurchase, or cancellation policy are all prohibited. Misrepresenting an affiliation or an endorsement by any charitable, governmental, police, civic, or similar third-party organization is prohibited.

Although the federal statute creates an exemption for "established business relationships," the FCC requires that the do-not-call requests of existing established customers be honored. Hence, once an established customer asks not to be called, the established-business-relationship exemption ceases to apply.

Automatic dialing recorded message players (ADRMPs) are auto-dialers that play a prerecorded message to anyone who picks up the phone. There is no intervention of a live operator.

ADRMPs get special attention in the TCPA. The law prohibits calls to

- Emergency phone lines such as 911, police, fire, ambulance, hospitals, etc.
- Individual patient rooms in hospitals or nursing homes

- Cell phones, pager services, or any line where the called party is charged for the call
- Any residential phone used for commercial purposes without the prior consent of the called party

The TCPA also prohibits using ADRMPs to engage two or more lines of a multiline business simultaneously. It also bans the transmission of unsolicited advertisements to telephone facsimile machines. If the caller has an established business relationship with the intended recipient, then expressed prior consent is assumed until a do-not-fax request is received.

All ADRMP calls must begin with a clear statement of the identity of the business, individual, or other entity that is initiating the call. At some point during the call, mention must be made of a phone number or an address where the caller can be reached. This number must be separate from the one that the ADRMP is using.

Of course, there are plenty of exemptions to the ADRMP restrictions. Here is a sampling of the ones that we are aware of. However, check with your attorney before proceeding.

- Calls that are initiated for emergency purposes are exempt.
- Calls that are exempt under other provisions of the TCPA are exempt here as well.
- Calls that do not include an unsolicited advertising or marketing message are exempt.
- Here's a big one: Calls to people who have an established business relationship with the caller's company are exempt.
- And, of course, calls on behalf of tax-exempt nonprofit organizations are exempt.

Congress passed the Telemarketing and Consumer Fraud and Abuse Protection Act in 1994. Under this act the Federal Trade Commission (FTC) adopted the *Telephone Sales Rule* on December 31, 1995. Many of the provisions of the rule are similar or identical to those contained in the TCPA. However, the requirements of each are separate and may be enforced separately. Some of the Telephone Sales Rule provisions are listed below.

- Full disclosure of the cost to purchase, receive, or use the products or services being offered is required.

- Disclosure of the total quantity of goods or services that the called party must pay for or receive is also required.
- Promotions that contain a prize must have the stipulation that no purchase or payment is required to participate or win.

All offers must be clearly and honestly stated so that consumers will know the costs as well as what they will get in return. False and misleading claims are strictly prohibited.

Negative-option plans and continuity clubs generally are exempted from the restrictions relating to the disclosure of the total cost and total quantity disclosure provisions. This is because neither the seller nor the buyer knows for sure how many shipments ultimately will be shipped and purchased. Only the costs and quantities relating to the initial shipment must be fully disclosed, along with any required commitments.

The Telephone Sales Rule requires that the seller must maintain sales and promotion records for a minimum of two years.

The rule carries a number of exemptions. It is our understanding that the following businesses are exempt primarily because they are regulated by other government agencies or regulations.

- Banks, federal credit unions, federal savings and loans
- Common carriers such as long-distance telephone companies and airlines
- Nonprofit organizations
- Insurance companies, to the extent that state laws regulate their business

However, outside telemarketing agencies that are employed by these four types of entities are not exempt and must comply with the Telephone Sales Rule. Violations of the rule carry penalties that can include monetary fines, nationwide injunctions prohibiting certain conduct, and redress to injured parties.

State Laws Have Become the Single Biggest Issue

New state laws are popping up every day, and telemarketing is an easy target for any state legislator that would like to curry favor with voters by sponsoring a "Do Not Interrupt My Dinner" law.

Unlike the federal restrictions, which are generally straightforward and relatively easy to comply with, the state laws vary widely requiring such things as

- TSR registration and bonding
- Securing permission from the called party at the beginning of the call to continue with the presentation
- Immediate disconnect requirements if the called party declines to listen to the offer
- Complex do-not-call mechanisms
- Follow-up signature requirements for valid sales
- Additional disclosures if the offer includes a prize, premium, or free gift of any kind
- Cooling-off periods to cancel sales (and oral disclosure of such)
- Time-of-day calling restrictions

Time-of-day calling restrictions are probably the biggest potential problem. There have been numerous laws proposed that would outlaw any calling after 5:00 P.M., which would clearly be a disaster for any organization trying to market directly to consumers.

The good news is that most states offer plenty of exemptions. However, as this is being written, there are at least five states that currently have no exemptions to their telemarketing regulations. Clearly it is not safe to believe that what is permitted in one state will be permitted in another.

Some of the most common state-related exemptions for compliance with telemarketing regulations are as follows.

- Calling existing established customers
- Fund-raising activities
- Sales of books, magazines, or videos
- Being a telemarketer in "good standing," which may mean having a business residing in that state for three to five years, and having 75 percent of your business be otherwise exempt
- Calls from publicly traded companies
- Calls from issuers of catalogues
- Calls from otherwise supervised financial institutions or insurance companies

Do-Not-Call Requirements

This is probably the area of regulations that gets the most attention. As we pointed out in the previous sections, companies that market by phone are required to maintain a suppression file of all persons who have requested not to be called. Calling lists must be purged against this file. It is very important that all TSRs be properly trained on how to handle those requests. This is particularly true for TSRs that work in a multi-client agency setting, as they need to be very attentive to what the customer is really saying. Does the customer not want to be called by this client for this program only, or is he in fact saying he doesn't wish to be called ever again for any reason? There have been instances where customers who were suppressed from all calling have actually written in to inquire why they didn't receive a call to continue a desired service. It's a difficult problem. However, it is probably best to err on the side of too much suppression rather than too little.

The main reasons that customers ask to be placed on do-not-call lists are as follows.

1. They feel that they are receiving too many calls. (This is the most-cited reason—more than 50 percent of complainants claim this is their reason.)
2. They feel that they have received too many calls from the specific company or for the particular type of product being offered.
3. They have miscellaneous reasons, including receiving the call at a bad time or having a basic lack of interest in the product and/or company.

In addition to purging your call lists against your own suppression files, many companies also purge against the Direct Marketing Association's Telephone Preference Service (TPS). The TPS is updated monthly and has the names of several million consumers who have asked to have their names removed from as many call lists as possible.

We have included an example of a written do-not-call-policy in the appendix at the back of the book. If you have not yet established a written policy you may want to use this one as guideline. However, once again we would suggest that you have your corporate attorneys review this document to ensure that it is sufficient to meet the regulations currently in effect.

Canadian Guidelines

Canada has its own set of regulations. Fortunately, complying with U.S. federal regulations will keep you in compliance with many of the Canadian regulations. There are, however, some special circumstances that you should pay attention to. One major difference is that no calling is allowed on Canadian national holidays, some of which are different from those in the United States. Another notable difference is that Canadian law has a restriction that says that marketers shall not knowingly contact customers more frequently than once a month for the same product or service. If you are using a 13-week suppression as a basic contact strategy, this should keep you out of trouble on this score.

Busines-to-Business Is Generally Exempt

In general, U.S. federal law does not regulate business-to-business telemarketing except for the sales of nondurable office supplies. However, it is certainly prudent to honor all do-not-call requests regardless of whether the program was targeted to businesses or consumers. It is also important to remember that there are many home-based businesses and situations where business phone calls are automatically forwarded to residential numbers after business hours.

The Privacy Promise

Effective July 1, 1999, members of the Direct Marketing Association have been required as a condition of membership to abide by the four following privacy protection guidelines.

1. *Notice of list practices.* Members must provide customers with notice of their ability to opt out of name rental and information exchanges.
2. *Honor opt-out requests.* Members must honor all customer requests to opt out of name rental and information exchanges.
3. *Do-not-call suppression.* Members must accept and maintain customer requests to be placed on in-house do-not-call/mail files.
4. *Use DMA TPS and MPS suppression files to purge names from future campaigns.* Members are required to use the DMA's

Telephone Preference Service (TPS) and Mail Preference Service (MPS) files to purge out customers who have asked to be removed from call and/or mail lists.

In the case of telemarketing the TCPA requires that individuals who ask not to be called again be placed on in-house suppression files for a period of 10 years.

The opt-out notice need not be offered over the phone. It is widely recognized as being time consuming and distracting. However, notice should be given in writing in fulfillment packages, bills, and whatever other written customer-contact methods are at your disposal. The opt-out notice should be offered in the first written correspondence after the phone call with the customer.

Examples of Opt-Out Notice Language

The DMA suggests that you use an opt-out notice similar to the examples listed below.

Example 1 We make our customer information available to other companies so they may contact you about products and services that may interest you. If you do not want your name passed on to other companies for the purpose of receiving marketing offers, just tell us by contacting us at _____ , and we will be pleased to respect your wishes.

Example 2 We make portions of our customer list available to carefully screened companies that offer products and services we believe you may enjoy. If you do not want to receive those offers and/or information, please let us know by contacting us at _____ .

Adopting a Corporate Privacy Statement

We feel that every company would benefit by adopting a corporate privacy statement. Listed below are some of the main points such a statement should cover.

- Your company is committed to protecting the privacy wishes of prospects and customers.
- Your TSRs will honor all do-not-call requests.
- Your company is committed to purge do-not-calls from calling lists using in-house, state, and industry do-not-call lists.
- Your company will abide by all industry-ethics standards and governmental compliance guidelines.

Technology Puts Consumers in Control

The telephone is no longer that little black box that rings unexpectedly and brings a mystery voice into your life.

Answering machines originally were designed to capture messages from callers when there was no one available to receive the call. It didn't take long for consumers to discover that this same technology would allow them to screen calls before deciding whether or not to answer the phone. Responding to consumers' desire to be in control, the telcos introduced Caller ID units that used the ANIs of the incoming call to display the phone number of the caller. This worked fine for calls coming from residential phones but proved generally ineffective in identifying calls coming from telemarketers using predictive dialers.

Hence, we now have Privacy Manager®, a device that screens incoming calls that do not arrive with an ANI attached, and asks for caller identification before the call rings on the called party's phone.

It's not possible to know where all of this privacy-related technology will ultimately take us. However, one thing is certain: people want to know who is calling before they pick up the phone, and they will pay a good amount of money for this option. As telemarketers we must recognize this consumer desire for privacy and control. In time, many, if not all, phones will have this capability. It may be a costly and cumbersome process to deal with. This only adds to the importance of our own efforts to provide the best quality of service possible and to approach every call with the goal that the customers will be happier when they hang up the phone than they were when they picked it up, whether they order or not.

Our Biggest Challenge

Many industry experts believe that outbound telemarketing will shrink in call volume and effectiveness over time. We don't necessarily agree with this analysis. However, the risks are certainly there that privacy-management devices eventually will be used to screen out all sales calls. Furthermore, legislation ultimately may restrict the number of times per year that we are permitted to contact customers by phone. It is imperative that we have the best quality standards and best quality TSRs possible. Good communication always begins with good communicators.

Beyond our need for the best quality staffs at our telecenters, our biggest challenges are the following.

- Customers believe that they are very well informed about their legal right to privacy and are not hesitant to quote the law, whether they have the information right or not.
- Because of the large volume of calls they receive, customers have a much lower tolerance for poor-quality calls.
- Telemarketing competition is fierce and clients have more choices than ever about which organization to outsource to. Unfortunately, many of these users of telemarketing service place too much importance on acquiring call-center support at the lowest cost rather than securing the best-quality and most customer-friendly service possible.

These should be your priorities with respect to quality management.

- You should employ the highest quality of personnel to represent your company.
- You should make sure you are in compliance with all laws, regulations, and industry guidelines.
- You should be continually thinking of ways to enhance the business as a by-product of all of the good quality-assurance work you are doing.

Summary

- Your first priority in any quality management strategy is to ensure that you have all of the necessary "controls" in place to maintain compliance with all relevant government regulations. Your second priority is to *ensure* that you are doing everything possible to make each call a positive experience for the customers you are speaking to and the client or marketing interests you are representing on the phones.

Once these first two priorities are secured, you then have the opportunity to turn your attention to strategies that will actually *enhance* the quality of the telemarketing campaign.

- To be truly effective it is important to set up an independent quality-management team that is outside the normal telecenter management chain of command.
- Call-center quality always begins with recruiting the best people possible for the TSR positions. Your quality managers can play an important role in ensuring that your telecenter recruiters are meeting management's expectations in this regard.
- The people you speak to should be happier when they hang up the phone than they were when they picked it up, whether they place an order or not.
- Silent remote-monitoring should be an ongoing process. Every TSR should be monitored at least once a week.
- Formal written monitor checklists should be prepared for each TSR at least once a week. Veteran reps should be monitored as comprehensively as new reps.
- The seven deadly sins of telemarketing are
  1. Improper use of TSR or customer names
  2. Talking between calls
  3. Sloppy verification dialogue
  4. Impolite behavior with phone screeners or other family members
  5. Hanging up before the customer does
  6. Poor pronunciation for names, products, or industry jargon
  7. Use of slang or inappropriate comments
- Taping and verifying confirmations is a standard practice for ensuring quality of the order or lead generated.
- You should establish a zero-tolerance-for-complaints environment.

- You should insist on the responsible use of predictive dialers and set the abandonment rate as close to zero as you can.
- If telemarketing is a central component of your business, you should have a law firm on retainer that specializes in telemarketing issues so that you can stay informed on all legislative developments.
- It is very important that you understand your responsibilities under the TCPA and Telemarketing Sales Rule. Every company that uses outbound telemarketing, whether they do it in-house or outsource to an agency, must maintain an up-to-date do-not-call file and a written policy on how requirements are being implemented.
- State regulations are equally important and even more complex to deal with than federal regulations.
- Every company that uses telemarketing should adopt a corporate privacy promise and position it prominently in all of their written customer-contact media.

12

A Look into the Future

It's an ongoing dilemma. Which lists will work on a particular telemarketing offer? If you have a large dynamic house file that's responsive to your telemarketing offers, the issue is less critical than if your house file is small and you rely heavily on outside lists. In previous chapters we've included data on lists including response rates and back-end results. Finding lists that work has always been the most difficult part of using telemarketing (and direct marketing as a whole). But what does the future hold?

The Internet, of course, brings with it a tremendous opportunity for future list and data acquisition. It has already become an important additional marketing channel and source of names. The most interesting and challenging component of this new technology is the issue of combining the Internet, E-mail, and telemarketing, and how to use all three most effectively. The advent of Web TV and calling over the Internet in combination with E-mail may prove most effective in the sale of your products.

In the future, the list-acquisition process and the ultimate selections will become far more intriguing and complex. Future advances in the science of list modeling, segmentation, and profiling will not only give direct marketers many more targeted lists to test, but may also allow us to craft specific offers for each customer based on what we have learned about how that customer has responded in the past. We may even be able to make predictions as to the best day and time to present the offer.

A number of issues stand out when lists are evaluated for use in telemarketing programs. The first is how the company that owns the list originally acquired the names. Currently, as a general rule, names that were acquired through telemarketing generally work better than those acquired through other marketing efforts. These are people who are telemarketing responsive. Moreover, if they were acquired through telemarketing, an accurate phone number should be available. That's a definite plus.

Compiled lists can become a very appealing option for telemarketing campaigns targeted to specific demographic groups. Large database compilers may have phone numbers available as a select. You can merge these with other response lists that lack this critical piece of information and turn an otherwise unusable list into an important part of your telemarketing plan. It's an appealing option.

We know of one large list company that is building a national database of E-mail names cross-referenced with mailing addresses and phone numbers. The database is being built from hardware and software product registration cards. You will be able to take E-mail addresses from people that have visited your website and append data so that you can use the information for both direct mail and telemarketing. We see the Internet turning into the largest list-generation vehicle of all time. You should definitely save every E-mail listing you can get. It could turn into a gold mine of highly responsive prospects. With this in mind, it's more important than ever that you post an opt-out notice on every page of your website advising visitors that you are gathering this information for the purpose of staying in contact (and making future offers for products and services that you believe they will enjoy hearing about).

But what about acquiring lists? We understand your concern and realize that it isn't going to get any easier to acquire responsive lists for what we currently refer to as telemarketing. Imagine for a moment that it's the year 2010. Lists are still rented in the traditional way, except that you can now order and receive your lists on-line. With all of the segmentation possibilities available it's now a bit more complicated to make the right decisions about which response lists to select for your next marketing campaign. Let's look at a specific situation.

Your brokers have recommended a number of lists and the segments present some intriguing possibilities. Here's an example of what your brokers may present you with:

1. Multibuyers—purchased all products through traditional telemarketing.
2. Multibuyers—purchased all products except one through traditional telemarketing; purchased last product from a call through Web TV and watched a two-minute video prior to ordering.
3. Multibuyers—purchased all products through a telephone call to Web TV but never purchased any product until after receiving E-mail about it.

There may be segments of the population that require repeated reminders through E-mail, Web TV, or telephone before they are ready to purchase a product. The advertising industry uses reach, frequency, and cost per thousand to calculate the cost of acquiring a customer. The same calculations may become appropriate using a multicommunication approach. It may be that making more than one customer contact to secure an order will become the norm. Merge-purge criteria may change in that instead of just knocking out the duplicate we actually may be appending into the record data about all previous contacts.

The list issue is complex and may require a complete change of process for direct marketers with significant telemarketing programs. The sequencing of how, when, and how frequently to reach the potential consumer will become the keys to success.

There will be E-mail buyer lists, telemarketing lists, Web TV (Internet) product buyer lists, computer (Internet) buyer lists, and more. There may or may not be significant overlap between these lists requiring a very sophisticated merge-purge.

The cost of renting a list based on all of these product purchase dynamics may create some controversy within the list industry. If a list owner has the telephone number, E-mail address, street address, product purchase history, method of purchase (Web TV, Internet, telephone), and the charge card number that is required for on-line secured-site purchases, what is all that information worth on a rental basis?

Teleweb

The relationship between telemarketing and the interactive marketplace will broaden and expand during the next decade. These two disciplines most likely will become almost inseparable. As the Internet expands, telemarketers will want to include websites and E-mail in their sales initiatives. In addition, with interactive video capabilities expanding daily, telemarketers may include a video presentation as part of their sales program. This will allow the consumer to see the product prior to making a purchase decision. It may provide for increased payments and fewer returns. Wouldn't that be great!

The realization that communications opportunities will expand should provide for some unique futuristic thinking in telemarketing, entertainment, Internet, direct marketing, and television boardrooms. There's little doubt that being the first to adopt these new communication technologies will be a definite advantage.

Integrating Technologies

Integrating emerging technologies may require telemarketing organizations to form alliances with Internet and E-commerce companies as well as software companies. This alone, however, will not guarantee success. The success or failure of all these new technologies ultimately will depend on the delivery of the final product. To be successful you will still need a flawless fulfillment system with an excellent product and world-class customer service. The business news is full of stories of companies that have taken enormous volumes of orders only to discover that they could not deliver the products on time.

The Repercussions of Caller ID

There may come a time when Caller ID is part of the basic package provided by phone companies. The manufacturers are already building it in as a standard feature on their top-of-the-line phones. There's little doubt that it will have an effect on the telemarketing industry. The question is what will the ultimate impact be? Here's a quick look into the future.

Caller ID may not present the obstacle that many in the industry expect. It may result in improved response rates because by answering the phone customers will indicate their interest in the call. In turn, the telemarketing industry may find it beneficial to avoid contacting households that prefer not to be contacted. Response rates may indeed improve. The negative side may be that more names will be needed for each campaign to reach the sales objectives.

The Repercussions of Cellular Phones

We see it already. Consumers love their cell phones. Given a choice between picking up a nearby standard instrument tethered to the wall, and reaching into their pocket for a wireless portable, they are opting for the freedom to place and receive calls anywhere and anytime they want. Cell phones with wireless E-mail capabilities may in fact turn out to be a huge growth area for telemarketers—and a new part of the telemarketing equation. This presents the industry with some huge issues.

1. Cell phone users are currently paying for incoming calls. How will they feel about receiving a call from a telemarketer when they have to pay for the call? The answer may be to have those costs charged back to the caller. If so, how will this affect the profitability of outbound telemarketing? The answer certainly will revolve around the actual costs. The good news is that all telecommunications costs are coming down.

2. How will consumers react when they can receive a telemarketing call at any time and in any place? Many cell phone users leave their phones on so that they can receive calls while they are at work or traveling. How will they feel about it if you have just interrupted a meeting with their coworker or boss? Keep in mind that if the person has abandoned his or her land line this may be his or her only phone number. You may ultimately have to create a special do-not-call file of consumers who do not wish to take calls on their cell phones from telemarketers at particular times during the day, but will accept them at other times. The telcos may have to send a signal back to the telemarketer's predictive dialer alerting it to the fact that it is

attempting to reach a cell phone. As we have mentioned, many new cell phones are being manufactured with Caller ID built in. This may allow the consumer to elect not to answer the call if the place or time is inappropriate.

Unless we can overcome these challenges, outbound telemarketing as a stand-alone marketing channel may in fact cease to exist. Telemarketing as part of the technology revolution must become a dynamic consumer-friendly opportunity as telemarketers provide valuable information services along with offers for specially selected products and services targeted to the specific interests of the consumer. On the other hand, telemarketing may come to be seen in the same way that banner advertising is seen on the Internet. That is, as a positive opportunity for the consumer to be introduced to information about new and valuable products and services. With the help of pictures, videos, etc., the future can be stronger than ever.

We believe that the outlook from a telemarketer's perspective is one of great promise. There's an opportunity to establish a comprehensive and interactive contact with the prospective buyer. This may include videos, pictures, information, and any additional help the potential customer may require to negotiate the sale. It will all be available almost instantaneously through interactive communication.

The Repercussions of All-in-One Technology

The communications technology revolution may one day find you sitting in your home watching television and noticing a blinking icon indicating an incoming call. You answer the call by clicking on the icon and immediately the telemarketer introduces him or herself, and begins the presentation while you are watching a video demonstration of the product on a small window on your screen. To order you can either click on the "Order Now" icon or place the order with the assistance of the TSR. Of course you will also be able to end the sales presentation with a click or save it for viewing at another time with another click. To enter an order on the screen you might complete the order form as you now do with other on-line E-commerce sites. The cable and satellite TV industries are developing interactive formats. The forecast is that almost all cable and satellite TV providers will utilize an interactive format in the not-too-distant future. The telemarketing industry will be an important partner and contributor to the growth of this industry. Of course, the true impact of this new technology is yet to be determined.

The Repercussions of Voice-Recognition Technology and Instantaneous Language Translation

In the future, differences in language may disappear as a barrier to communication. This has some amazing consequences for telemarketing. It may become possible to operate outbound and inbound telecenters at full capacity 24 hours a day, 365 days a year. Callers speaking in English may be able to call around the globe and be understood by customers who speak different languages. The called party would hear the TSR speaking in his own natural voice but in the language of the party being called. The translation would occur instantaneously, and neither party would suspect that the other was not speaking in his or her own native language. Predictive dialers would move from time zone to time zone around the globe throughout the day. The fixed costs of telecenters would be spread out over a 24-hour day rather than the 15-hour day we have now. The costs of telemarketing would go down for everyone.

As we pointed out in previous chapters, gaining the customer's attention is usually the most important key to success in outbound telemarketing. Think about how compelling it will be to start out the conversation by saying, "Hello this is _____ calling from San Diego, California, in the United States. How are you today?" We already know of many instances where the response rates have increased by 50 percent or more for calls to outside of the borders of the lower continental United States.

However, communication is not the only issue. Understanding the native culture will be equally important. We may need to seek out first- and second-generation immigrants for TSR positions. These people's understanding of local customs and sensitivities could prove invaluable. Of course, fulfillment will still be a key issue. Delivering the product promptly and with adequate service and support will continue to be critical. Fulfillment operations may become global businesses with warehouses around the globe all connected to a central distribution network.

Offering globally recognized trademarks and branded merchandise will probably be the key to overcoming the natural reluctance of consumers to dealing with a foreign corporation.

The Repercussions of Worldwide Low Rates

As we pointed out above, global calling may become a reality because of the technological breaking down of language barriers. It may also become economically feasible from the standpoint of telecommunications costs. We have already seen a tremendous decline in the cost of calls spurred on by the fierce competition of competing long-distance providers. VOIP (voice over Internet protocol) could ultimately provide us with global access to every telephone in the world for one low monthly fee per phone line with no per-minute charges.

Technological Breakthroughs in Predictive Dialers

Predictive dialers are computers that link phone lines with TSR workstations. They use algorithms to analyze call flow and then make a prediction as to when the next TSR will be ready to receive a new call. Based on that prediction they are then programmed to dial out on as many open phone lines as is appropriate to try to secure a contact at just the right time. To maximize that opportunity, these predictive dialer computers generally have more phone lines connected to them than TSR terminals.

At present the only variable that predictive dialers generally measure is the overall call flow within the telecenter. We believe that ultimately they will be designed to take into account the complete customer contact history and thereby predict not only when the next TSR will be ready, but also which consumers are most likely to be available at the other end of the phone at that particular point in time. Ultimately they may even be able to model the customers as to their receptivity to outbound telemarketing by time of day and day of week. Let's face it. Most people will say no to any offer if it comes at an inconvenient time, such as mealtimes or children's bedtimes. These same people might be more than happy to take the call 20 minutes later.

Advances in predictive-dialer technology could greatly advance outbound telemarketing by both increasing response rates and limiting unwanted calls at inopportune times.

The Threat of the Call Explosion

We made the point earlier on in chapter 11 that much of the public's concern about outbound telemarketing revolves around the fact that consumers believe that they are receiving too many calls. This is the central issue driving much of the legislative agenda that regulates telemarketing. If call volume expands to the point where consumers' phones never stop ringing, we are all in a lot of trouble.

Fraudulent telemarketers pose another problem that has the potential to ruin a great business for everyone. We should all operate under the highest ethical standards and support the efforts of law enforcement to root out and eliminate the bad guys forever. There may come a time when the telcos are required to report and license all new telemarketing operations with the government as the phone lines are being installed. Hopefully, we won't reach the point where we need strict governmental regulation to save the industry from itself.

Perhaps all of this will turn out to be a self-correcting problem. If people become less responsive to telemarketing because of overly aggressive practices, only the best and most quality-conscious organizations will survive.

Here are 10 of our predictions for the next 10 years in the telemarketing industry.

1. More than 50 percent of all outbound telemarketing calls will be delivered to an interactive receiver.
2. More than 50 percent of all telemarketing orders will be interactive in nature.
3. Lists with phone numbers and other contact information will become more readily available because of E-commerce. These lists will produce a higher response rate because of an interactive telemarketing capability, which will allow customers to base their decisions on viewing an actual photo or video of the product.

4. The list industry will find it necessary to reassess the value of names generated from different communication sources.

5. TSR appearance will become an important recruiting issue as video is added to voice and customers can see the person to whom they are speaking.

6. Either technology or governmental regulations or both will allow customers to know who is calling before they pick up the phone.

7. Outbound telemarketing technology will catch up with inbound in terms of its ability to access full customer contact history though links to client/mainframe databases.

8. Telemarketing will become a global business with VOIP reducing the telecommunications costs to near zero, and hopefully, language barriers will also disappear with the development of voice-recognition and instantaneous-translation technology.

9. Inbound telecenters will become full customer contact centers capable of responding to customers via all electronic media.

10. Telemarketing will be in a golden age, employing more people than anyone can imagine, and providing an indispensable service for everyone that uses a phone, a computer, or a TV.

Summary

- Access to highly targeted lists will continue to be the single most important issue for our future success. The Internet may well become the single greatest engine for the growth of telemarketing lists in the history of direct marketing.

- Ultimately, the Internet will change everything about telemarketing.

- Convergence and increased bandwidth will allow us to interact with customers in ways we can only dream about now.

- Efficiency in the area of product and service fulfillment will be more critical than ever before.

- The time will come when customers will always know who is calling before they pick up the phone. This will present both challenges and opportunities.
- The pervasive use of cell phones may well increase inbound telemarketing as users find it ever more easy to call toll-free numbers from wherever they happen to be. However this same development could also have some very negative implications for outbound telemarketing. We may need to speak to cell phone users in a different way than we do when we reach them via a land line.
- Increasing bandwidth will ultimately allow for simultaneous communication using voice, video, and text. The implications for telemarketing are enormous.
- Voice-recognition technology coupled with language-translation software ultimately will allow us to break down all of the communication barriers we struggle with today, thereby turning telemarketing into a truly global enterprise.
- Predictive dialing and database-management technology ultimately will allow us to target our campaigns in ways that not only increase response rates, but also limit unwanted calls.
- Governmental regulation is here to stay. It is our responsibility to do everything we can to see that the interests of honest consumers and responsible telemarketers are equally protected, while at the same time making it ever more difficult for dishonest telemarketers to survive.

13

One More Call!
One More Sale!

When I [Richard Simms] started out as a part-time sales rep for DialAmerica in 1982, the mantra in the phone room as we approached the end of each hour was "One more call! One more sale!" A lot of things have changed since then—most notably the development of predictive dialers. I remember hearing in the news in 1983 that the IRS was experimenting with some new technology that would use computers to dial up the phone numbers of delinquent citizens. My first thought was "Wow, if we could get rid of all this paper, we would be much more efficient, and everyone's productivity would go up, even the new reps that hadn't yet honed their selling skills.

A Summary for Success

Even though technology has improved many parts of our business, there are still plenty of programs that fail because someone has made a mistake in the planning or execution of the campaign. Helping clients, marketers, and telemarketing program managers avoid those errors is really what this book is all about.

So here, in a nutshell, is our summary for success.

- Don't be afraid to test. Telemarketing works and can be your most profitable marketing media.

- Pay close attention to the five essential keys to success:
  1. A highly targeted list
  2. Excellent fulfillment, billing and collections, and customer service
  3. An irresistible offer
  4. A quality product
  5. A professionally trained and managed sales force
- Program failures are almost always due to inattention to one of the top four keys. If you are using a good telemarketing organization, you shouldn't have to worry about the fifth one.
- Plan your test carefully. Always start with a small test. Try to expand the selling opportunities as much as possible by including upsells, cross-sells, and downsells into your offer. If you can, pattern your test after a known success formula.
- Get personally involved when you launch your test. Get involved in training. Be available to remote-monitor extensively during the first week of calling. Stay flexible and be ready to make changes to the script, offer, or terms and conditions of the sale.
- Build your inbound, outbound, direct mail, and alternate media schedule as part of a comprehensive plan to leverage each of the media in a way that enhances the profitability of the overall effort.
- When using inbound telemarketing, bring in the technology first, and then put the marketing plan together.
- Always place test orders in the first or second group of orders processed by your fulfillment center. Most of the money is made or lost in how you handle the fulfillment process.
- Be prepared to roll out. It's amazing how often a successful test is not followed by a rollout. Always be prepared for success and have a plan to make money if your test is a winner.
- Understand the basic differences between business and consumer marketing. Don't make the mistake of thinking that you can approach these diverse markets with the same tactics and strategies.
- Continuity offers are a natural fit for outbound telemarketing. Try to organize your product line into club and/or continuity

formats whenever you can. This plan is almost always a winner. Always use telemarketing to reinstate lapsed club members. Always use telemarketing to load up existing club members. Load-up conversion rates are sometimes more than 50 percent, and the people who decline the load-up offer stay in the club, receiving their shipments one at a time as they have been.

- If you are new to telemarketing, always hire professionals to get you started on the right track. A good consultant teamed up with a talented telemarketing agency can make all the difference. Never get caught saying "we tried telemarketing and it didn't work." If it didn't work, you probably did something wrong.
- Remember that customer satisfaction is your best competitive advantage. Embrace quality enhancement as your approach to quality management. Establish your telecenter as a zero-complaint environment. Use predictive dialers responsibly. Set the abandonment rate as close to zero as you can. Follow all laws and regulations rigorously. Maintain do-not-call lists. Adopt a corporate privacy statement.
- Love your customer!
- Make sure that everyone involved is having fun. Think of yourself as a corporate morale officer. Treat everyone with respect. Always stop what you are doing (at least long enough to listen) if someone asks for help. Greet everyone with a smile.

Here's one last telemarketing trade secret: You can "hear" a smile on the phone!

Do-Not-Call Policy

It is the intention of <u>Telemarketing Company</u> and all its managers and employees to maintain the highest standards possible in the course of its business. Toward this end, <u>Telemarketing Company</u> does not intend to violate the privacy rights or wishes of any person who does not want to be called by the organization. The following policy is mandatory in all solicitations and campaigns by our company.

Do-Not-Call Policy

A "do-not-call" is a customer or noncustomer who informs us orally or in written form that he or she does not want further telemarketing solicitation from <u>Telemarketing Company</u>. The specific reason or severity of the tone of the request is not important. ALL REQUESTS WILL BE HONORED.

What to say when the customer requests to be taken off the lists: "Mr(s). _____ , please excuse this call, I will arrange to have your name removed from the calling list immediately."

If the customer states that he or she has already told us to remove the name from the list: "Mr(s). _____ , your name must have been given to me by mistake. I am sorry for this inconvenience. I will have my manager immediately contact our customer service department so that we will not call you again."

Instructing Callers

Telemarketers will be instructed on company policy and provided with guidance on expected reactions and how to make proper entries to affect a consumer's wish to be deleted from future calling campaigns.

Telemarketing Company—Do-Not-Call File

The procedure for our "do-not-call" list file will be as follows:

1. The do-not-call file will be automatically updated daily and used to suppress names on any files <u>Telemarketing Company</u> uses for any campaign.
2. Upon receipt of "*" asterisk lists from Florida/Oregon and the DMA Telephone Preference Service List, the do-not-call file will be updated on an as-received basis to suppress those names from all campaigns.
3. We will request, maintain, and update all suppression lists forwarded by a client.
4. Do-not-call requests that relate to a specific client will be transmitted to that client on a biweekly basis.

Requests for Do-Not-Call Policy

Any customer who requests a copy of this do-not-call policy is entitled to receive it as soon as possible. Any requests for a copy of our do-not-call policy should be answered as follows:

"Mr(s). _____ , we will be happy to send a copy of our do-not-call policy to you. Please allow 4 to 6 weeks for delivery, as the request needs to be forwarded through my manager. Please let me confirm your address. We have it as _____ . Thank you for your interest."

Sample Reports

Example Report: Final Outcome (Refusal) Analysis

Client name: Sample
Project name: Sample
Date: Final Report
List/Key code: Sample

Total Sales	**2,002**	**16.24%**
Already ordered upgrade	2,728	22.13%
Already purchased another product	132	1.07%
Can't afford	59	0.48%
Customer service problem	52	0.42%
Early hangup	274	2.22%
No one responsible for this activity	134	1.09%
Not enough new features/benefits	410	3.33%
Not interested	2,544	20.64%
Not using current copy	350	2.84%
Tech-support problem	29	0.24%
Too expensive	85	0.69%
Uses an outside source	191	1.55%
Won't give credit card out over the phone	410	3.33%
Other refusal reason	332	2.69%
Total Refusals	**7,730**	**62.71%**

Duplicate lead	12	0.10%
Language problem	18	0.15%
No computer	72	0.58%
No CD-ROM	3	0.02%
No longer in business	1	0.01%
Other ineligible	150	1.22%
Total Ineligibles	**256**	**2.08%**

Telephone problem	1,124	9.12%
Wrong number	1,214	9.85%
Total TPS	**2,338**	**18.97%**

Total Leads Used	**12,326**	

SAMPLE DAILY SALES TRANSMITTAL REPORT

Client Sales Transmittal Report

Transmittal Date _____   Transmittal Group _____   Client Name _____

Program	Sales Key	Number of Orders	PI Per Order	Commission
Product A	AA111	70	$28.50	$ 1,995.00
	Program total	**70**		**$1,995.00**
Product B	AA111	54	$33.50	$ 1,809.00
	Program total	**54**		**$1,809.00**
Product C	AA111	40	$13.50	$ 540.00
	Program total	**40**		**$ 540.00**
Product D	AA111	6	$28.50	$ 171.00
	Program total	**6**		**$ 171.00**
	Grand total	**170**		**$4,515.00**

Sample Monthly Transmittal Recap

Product-Key	PI	PI Total	Product Total	5/18	5/19	5/20	5/21	5/22	5/25	5/26	5/27	5/28
Product A - AABB11	$107.50	$ 1,935.00	18	1			6			1	1	4
Product B - AABB12	$107.50	$ 2,150.00	20	8				5	2		6	4
Product C - AABB12	$107.50	$ 1,935.00	18	7			4		2		5	
Product D - AABB13	$107.50	$ 752.50	7	4				2		1		
Product E - AABB13	$107.50	$ 645.00	6		1		5					
Product F - AABB14	$113.50	$ 2,383.50	21	2			5				5	
Product G - AABB14	$ 68.25	$ 1,501.50	22			1	5		8	1	7	
Product H - AABB15	$ 68.25	$ 1,774.50	26	1	1	1	11	7	4	1		
Product I - AABB15	$ 68.25	$ 2,047.50	30			1	7	7		4	9	9
Product J - AABB16	$ 68.25	$ 68.25	1	1								
Product K - AABB16	$ 68.25	$ 2,320.50	34		3		12		6	4	9	
Product L - AABB17	$ 68.25	$ 614.25	9	2				6				1
Product M - AABB17	$ 16.25	$ 227.50	14	1	7		1				5	
Product N - AABB18	$ 16.25	$ 601.25	37	19			3	4	4	8	5	1
Product O - AABB18	$ 16.25	$ 292.50	18		2					9		
Product P - AABB19	$ 16.25	$ 731.25	45	17					1	22	5	
Product Q - AABB19	$ 22.75	$ 796.25	35	16			3		1	15		
Product R - AABB20	$ 42.25	$ 676.00	16	6				2	1		6	1
Product S - AABB20	$ 42.25	$ 591.50	14		1		4		1	6	1	1
Total		**$ 22,043.75**	**391**	**85**	**15**	**3**	**59**	**33**	**30**	**72**	**64**	**30**

Glossary

abandonment rate   The rate of inbound calls that result in the caller hanging up before an agent is available to respond.

account-based marketing   A marketing promotion that generally requires multiple contacts over time to secure an order and requires that the notes from each contact be made available on future contact attempts.

ACD (automatic call distributor)   A machine that receives incoming phone calls and routes them to the proper TSR or IVRU station.

ADRMP (automatic dialing recorded message players)   Auto-dialing machines that play a prerecorded message to anyone who picks up the phone, without the intervention of a live agent.

alternate offer   A secondary offer that is presented to prospects when the initial offer is either inappropriate or is rejected by the customer.

ANI (automatic number identification)   Technology that allows the called party to recognize the phone number from which an inbound call is originating. It is most often used to deliver the caller's previous contact history to the inbound agent's terminal. It is also used by Caller ID to display the caller's phone number on the phone of the person being called.

auto attendant   Call-answering machines that allow callers to route their own call to the correct person without the intervention of a live agent.

b-to-b (business-to-business)   Marketing business products to business enterprises for use in business situations.

back end   Final results of a promotion taking into account the results of the product or service fulfillment, payments, cancels, returns, and bad debt. This term can sometimes be used to refer to the percentage of shipments that have kept and paid for the product or service. (*See* front end.)

bad debt   A customer who receives delivery of a product or service but neither pays for nor returns the shipment.

bill-me option   An optional payment method that involves sending out an invoice and a series of reminders, if necessary, to secure payment for the product or service ordered.

blended agent   A TSR who has been trained to move back and forth between inbound and outbound calls in such a way that each handled may be either inbound or outbound depending upon what is occurring in the telecenter at that point in time. (*See also* universal agent.)

BPA (Bureau of Publications Audit)   An independent organization that audits the circulation claims of controlled-circulation (free to the reader) magazines.

buckslip   A small advertising flier that often is included with other written correspondence such as monthly invoicing or product deliveries.

buyer's remorse   A postsale emotional state in which the customer regrets having placed an order. If given the opportunity, customers experiencing buyer's remorse will likely cancel the order.

call-me button   A website button that customers can click on to request contact with a live agent.

callback verification   A postsale, order-verification process that involves calling customers back on the phone, usually 12 to 24 hours later, to verify the authenticity of the order and the accuracy of the data collected.

Caller ID   Technology that uses the ANI of the caller to display the caller's phone number on a called party's phone.

cancel reinstatement offer   A reinstatement offer that is made to previous customers in good standing (they don't owe any money) who have canceled out of a continuity or club.

cannibalization   Slang term used by marketers to indicate that one medium is capturing customers that might otherwise have been generated by another medium. This term is sometimes used by direct mail marketers who fear that running a simultaneous outbound telemarketing campaign to the same audience will reduce the number of direct mail responders.

cold calling   Making a phone call to a prospect who has not indicated prior interest and has not been exposed to other targeted advertising media, such as direct mail, prior to the call.

collection opportunity   A customer who has received a product or service on a bill-me basis but has not yet paid for it.

commitment offer   An offer that, if accepted, will require the customer to commit to making one or more additional purchases over time to fulfill the terms and conditions for the original offer. This happens most often in negative-option and continuity clubs.

compiled list   A list compiled from publicly available sources such as driver's license records or telephone directories.

confirming retest   A second test conducted to establish the validity of an initial test. The size of a confirming retest is often double (but never more than 10 times) the quantity of names and orders in the original test.

contact rate   A measure of the ability to reach people on the phone over a fixed period of time. It is often measured in leads used per hour (LUPH).

continuity club   An offer structure that starts by delivering a small initial shipment and then delivers ongoing shipments, usually once a month or so.

controlled-circulation magazine   A magazine that is offered free to subscribers as long as they qualify by virtue of their business and job responsibilities.

convergence   A term used to describe the fact that telephones, computers, televisions, and other consumer appliances will be blending together into one appliance in the future.

conversion rate   Orders taken (sales) divided by the total leads used (TLU). It is measured as a percentage and is usually the critical measure of performance for telemarketing campaigns, especially those where the compensation is organized around a PI rate (cost per order) rather than an hourly rate.

co-op advertising   An advertising medium in which a number of different marketers share the cost of sending out a direct mail piece.

cross-sell promotion   A promotion that offers a product similar in nature and compatible with a product that the customer already owns.

CSR (customer service rep)   An inbound agent whose primary responsibility is to handle customer service/support calls. CSRs generally do not handle order taking except on a customer-demand basis.

CTI (computer telephony integration)   The linking of the computer and the telephone so that the voice and data portions of the communication come together to assist the caller and the agent in securing a successful outcome to the call.

decision maker   The person with the authority to make a buying decision.

dedicated environment   A telecenter environment where the TSRs are assigned to work on only one client program. They continue to work on that program exclusively for as long as the campaign remains active. There are varying degrees of dedication. The highest level of dedication would not only have the TSRs dedicated to a single campaign, but would have the rest of the telecenter management and staff similarly dedicated. The goal in this case would be to have no other programs running simultaneously in the telecenter.

demo calls   Demonstration calls made by trainers and supervisors for the purpose of demonstrating proper call techniques to TSRs.

direct-sold buyers   List segment that has been generated from previous purchase history, where the customer bought the previous product directly from the marketer, rather than through a retail or other third-party channel.

disaster recovery   The process of recovering from an incident that caused an interruption of normal telemarketing activities.

DMA (Direct Marketing Association)   Industry association headquartered in New York City that serves the needs of member companies.

DNIS (dialed number identification service)   Technology that recognizes which phone number the caller has dialed to reach the telecenter, thereby allowing the TSR to know in advance which promotion the caller is responding to.

do-not-call requirements   Requirements under the TCPA and Telephone Sales Rule that require marketers to maintain lists of customers who have asked not to be called in the future and to purge those records from future telemarketing campaigns.

do not promotes   Customers who are removed from future promotion lists because of their previous history of not keeping and/or paying for products shipped.

DRTV (direct-response television)   Advertising for a product or service using television as the medium. Responders typically are asked to call a toll-free phone number to place an order or receive additional information.

electronic registration names   Names of customers who have registered the purchase of a product by sending that information to the manufacturer via E-mail or the Internet.

endorsed offer   An offer that carries the endorsement of the company from which the list was secured. (Example: product A from company A is offered to customers of company B, which allows company A to make the claim that product A is endorsed and recommended by company B.)

FDCPA (Fair Debt Collection Practices Act)   Act of Congress that regulates the debt-collection activities of companies.

five essential keys   The secret to a successful telemarketing promotion (see chapter 2).

fixed-length fields   Data records in which each piece of data starts in the same position regardless of how long the previous data components are. (Example: The name always starts in position 1 and there are 30 positions available to record the name. The address always starts at position 31 and also runs for 30 positions even if the name only uses 15 of the 30 available positions.)

fixed record length   Each individual record is always the same number of overall positions in length, regardless of how many positions are actually populated with data.

free trial offer   An offer that includes an opportunity for the customer to try out the product or service for a predetermined period before the sale becomes final and the customer is expected to make a final purchase decision.

frequent rejecters   Customers who have a history of ordering and then returning a product or service.

front end   Referring to the initial results of a telemarketing campaign up to the point of order entry but prior to the fulfillment of the product or service. Front-end results do not include payments, returns, and bad debt. (*See also* back end.)

FSI (free-standing insert)   An advertisement printed on a single sheet of paper and included as an insert with a newspaper or magazine.

fulfillment   The process of delivering the product or service to the customer.

fulfillment house   An agency or business unit that handles the processing, shipping, billing, and collecting of a direct-sold order.

GUI (graphical user interface)   Technology that uses computer icons that allow users to move from one page of data to another by simply clicking.

hard offer   An offer that asks the customer to make a final purchase decision without the possibility of return unless the product or service is defective.

hot transfer   Technology that allows a TSR to transfer a customer call to another person, usually with all of the data as well as the voice portion of the communication intact.

hot-line names   Names of customers or prospects that have just been added to a list (usually within the last three months).

hot-line subs   Term for magazine subscriptions ordered within the last three months.

house file   Names of customers and prospects from a company's own database.

HTML (hypertext markup language)   The language used to build Web pages.

inbound telemarketing   Telemarketing discipline that involves having TSRs respond to calls initiated by a customer/prospect.

ineligibles   Call-outcome category for individuals who are determined to be inappropriate prospects for a particular promotion.

installment billing   Collection process that allows customers to pay for purchases in a number of smaller payments spread out over time.

IVRU (interactive voice response unit)   Technology that allows inbound callers to interact with a computer by pressing the number and symbol keys on their telephone.

lead generation   The process of identifying prospects for a specific product or service.

lead qualification   The process of qualifying suspected prospects for a product or service while generating sufficient interest to warrant a follow-up contact.

level of service   The percentage of all inbound calls that will be answered within a predetermined amount of time. In essence it is a measure of the promptness of response to the inbound call.

list fatigue   A condition that occurs when a list is mailed or called too frequently, which results in many of the prospects on the list declining during multiple contact attempts.

list penetration   A telemarketing metric that measures the percentage of the list universe that has achieved a final resolution.

list selection   The process of selecting names from a larger inventory to use for a specific campaign.

LUPH (leads used per hour)   A telemarketing metric that is used to measure the contact rate of a program. A used lead is one that has achieved a final resolution, meaning it will not be returned to the telecenter for another contact attempt.

mail drop   Usually refers to the date on which a direct mail piece was delivered to the post office for delivery to the customer/prospect.

member save program   An inbound telemarketing program that routes calls from customers who want to cancel a service to specially trained TSRs. These specialists use sales and problem-solving techniques to attempt to change the customer's mind and save the sale.

merge-purge   The process of matching one group of records with another for the purpose of eliminating duplicates.

monitor checklists   Written reports that evaluate how TSRs are handling phone calls from both a quality and a productivity standpoint.

MPS (mail preference service)   A list of people maintained by the DMA who have asked to be removed from as many direct mail lists as possible.

multibuyers   Customers who have made multiple purchases over time.

NCOA (National Change of Address)   A database available to marketers that will update the records of people who have recently changed their mailing address.

negative-option club   A marketing technique that sends out monthly notices advising the customer that a featured product of the month automatically will be shipped unless the customer returns the notice to the club asking *not* to receive the product. If the customer does nothing, the product is automatically shipped.

120-day rule   An industry standard that suggests a minimum of 120 days between successive telemarketing attempts to the same individual.

one-shot promotion   A marketing promotion that involves only one shipment of a product or service.

opt-out   An opportunity for customers to request that their names not be shared with other companies for marketing purposes.

order acquisition cost   The full cost to acquire an order.

outbound telemarketing   Telemarketing discipline that involves TSRs proactively contacting potential prospects and customers from a preselected list using the telephone as the mode of communication.

outside list   A list of prospects that comes from either another company's house file or a compiled list.

outside service bureau   A company that can provide services such as telemarketing, fulfillment, or database management on a contract basis.

package insert   An advertising message printed on a piece of paper that has been included with the shipment of another product.

paid preview offer   An offer structure in which prospects are asked to pay a fee to preview a product for a short period of time. This structure is most often used with professional training video products.

performance-based pricing   A synonym for working on a PI basis where you pay a negotiated commission for orders received in good order at your fulfillment center.

phone screener   A person who intercepts calls made to a decision maker for the purpose of qualifying their importance and relevance to the needs of the decision maker and the business enterprise.

PI (per item or per inquiry)   A commission-based compensation formula for paying for orders generated by an outside service bureau.

positive-option club   Similar in concept to the *negative-option club* except that the product is not automatically shipped if the customer fails to respond to the announcement notice. In this version the customer has to mail back the card to *request* the product delivery. If the customer does nothing, no product is shipped.

predictive dialer   Computer that networks TSR work stations with open telephone lines for the purpose of timing outbound calls and thereby keeping unproductive time between phone calls to a minimum.

premium   A product or service that is positioned as a free gift within the context of an offer. Some premium-enhanced offers require payment for the product or service before the premium may be kept on a no-charge basis.

premium bandit   A slang term that refers to customers who respond to an offer only because they want the premium; these customers have no intention of keeping and paying for the preview product.

price test   A test that measures the response to an offer with different price points as the only variable.

privacy manager   Technology that intercepts calls that do not have ANIs attached and asks callers to identify themselves before the call rings at the called party's location.

quality assurance   A quality-management strategy that attempts to ensure the quality of each call by identifying positive behavior and rewarding it.

quality control   A strategy that focuses on identifying and correcting quality-management problems.

quality enhancement   A quality-management strategy that is more focused on customer reactions and attempts to provide insight on how programs can be improved for the mutual benefit of the client, telecenter, and customer.

recruiting   The effort to draw in new employees into a telecenter.

relationship marketing   A marketing strategy that recognizes the need for the buyer and seller to build a relationship of mutual trust and respect over a period of time before the buyer can be expected to say yes to the offer.

remote monitoring   The process of listening to and evaluating telemarketing phone calls without being noticed by either the TSR or the customer on the other end of the phone.

renewal offer An offer structure that attempts to renew a subscription or continuity membership.

response list A list that has been generated by previous response to a direct marketing offer.

response rate A measure of productivity that is often used interchangeably with *conversion rate*, but can also be used to mean the number of orders divided by the entire universe of names available, not just the leads used.

return The designation that is applied to an order when the customer decides to return the order to the seller for credit or refund.

RFM (recency/frequency/monetary value) A widely recognized matrix used to segment lists and make predictions as to which parts will be most responsive to future offers.

risk-free offer An offer structure that allows customers to try out a product with the assurance that they can return it with no further risk or obligation if it does not suit their needs.

role-playing A training technique that involves TSRs and trainers acting out the parts of callers and customers for the purpose of gaining comfort with the dialogue associated with the script.

rollout The process of calling the remaining names from a list universe after the initial test has proved successful.

seasonality Marketing influences that are connected with the season of the year during which the promotion is being run.

segmentation The process of splitting a list into smaller subsets with the expectation that each segment will have a slightly different response rate.

semidedicated environment A telecenter environment where the TSRs may be asked to handle calls for a small group (two to six) of different programs.

semiduplicate listings Business listings for multiple people within the same organization where the calls are routed through one main phone number.

shared environment   A telecenter environment where the TSRs may handle calls for 10, 20, 30, or more different programs at a time, never knowing from which of the programs the next call will be.

SIC (Standard Industrial Classification)   A numerical coding system devised by the government to classify businesses by the nature of the business activity.

soft offer   An offer that allows the customer to try out the product or service without obligation before making a final purchase decision. (*See also* hard offer.)

space advertising   A paid advertisement that appears in a newspaper, magazine, or other printed media.

SPH (sales per hour)   A telemarketing formula that measures the number of orders divided by the amount of time (in hours) that it took to generate them. This is a prime productivity formula for hourly based compensation telemarketing programs. It is not as important in a PI-based compensation program.

staffing   This is the process of determining how many people are required on the phones to maintain the established service levels or to achieve the program's sales goals.

subscription offer   An offer structure in which the customer pays in advance for a fixed term of service (often a year).

suppression   Names that are withdrawn from the calling or mailing inventories either because they have asked to be removed from the promotion lists or because they have recently received another offer from the same company. These names need to be "rested" before they can be promoted to again.

taped confirmation   The process of creating an audio record of the conversation between a TSR and a customer once the customer has said yes to the offer and the TSR is delivering the dialogue from the confirmation section of the script.

TCPA (Telephone Consumer Protection Act of 1991)   The first federal law designed to regulate the activities of legitimate telemarketing organizations.

telemarketing   The business of using the telephone to establish a direct one-to-one communication between a seller and a buyer for the purpose of moving goods or services from a producer to a customer.

Telemarketing and Consumer Fraud and Abuse Protection Act of 1994   Federal legislation designed to protect consumers from telemarketers who use deceptive sales practices.

Telemarketing Sales Rule ("The Rule")   Regulations written by the FTC (Federal Trade Commission) to implement the *Telemarketing and Consumer Fraud and Abuse Protection Act of 1994*.

telephone problems   An outcome designation for used leads that are determined to be either wrong or disconnected phone numbers.

teleweb   A term coined by Bob Doscher (as far as we know) that is used to describe the convergence of televisions, telephones, and the Internet.

third-party verification   The process of transferring a live phone call to an independent outside verifier to authenticate the validity of the order being processed.

TPS (telephone preference service)   A list maintained by the DMA of people who have asked to be removed from as many outbound telemarketing lists as possible.

training   The process of teaching people to accomplish the task of speaking with callers in such a way that the goals of the program can be achieved.

transmittal   A batch of orders that are being delivered to a fulfillment center for processing that will lead to product or service delivery.

TSR (telephone sales rep)   A person employed for the purpose of making or receiving calls from prospects and/or customers.

unconditional satisfaction guarantee   Part of the terms and conditions of an offer that guarantees satisfaction regardless of circumstances. This is usually an indispensable component of any outbound telemarketing offer.

universal agent   A TSR who has been trained on both inbound and outbound telemarketing programs but is assigned to work on one or the other for extended periods of time. Unlike a *blended agent* this person will not be expected to move back and forth between inbound and outbound with each call.

upgrade offer   An offer structure most often associated with computer software promotions where customers that bought previous versions are contacted with an offer for the newest version.

upsell offer   An offer structure that allows the TSR to offer a customer an additional product once the customer has said yes to the primary offer.

used lead   A record (customer name, address, phone number, etc.) that has been removed from the callable inventory and will not be returned to the telecenter for additional contact attempts as part of the campaign in progress.

verification audits   An after-call quality-management process that sends all of the orders generated by the TSRs to a separate staff for the purpose of verifying authenticity of the orders along with the accuracy of the data collected.

VOIP (voice over Internet protocol)   A technology that allows the caller to make free long distance calls over the Internet rather than via standard telephone company switches and lines. The only cost associated with these VOIP calls is the regular monthly ISP access charge.

zero-complaint environment   A quality standard for telemarketing that has a zero tolerance for complaints.

Index

About the Authors

Robert S. Doscher is a graduate of Northeastern University where he attained a BS in marketing in 1967. He received his MBA from Rutgers University in 1969.

Bob has almost 30 years of experience in the publishing and direct-marketing industries and has been president and CEO of Response Innovations, Inc., for the past 20 years. Response Innovations is a full-service advertising agency with an office in Hershey/Hummelstown, Pennsylvania. Response Innovations' client list includes many Fortune 500 organizations as well as leading publishing and direct marketing organizations.

Bob has held positions with Time-Life, *Reader's Digest*, and the Chilton Company where he was vice president and general manager of Chilton Trade Book Publishing. He also was vice president of direct marketing at Western Publishing—the publisher of Golden Books.

Bob has extensive publishing, direct marketing, market research, and new-product development experience. He has been involved with the development of more than $500 million of new products during the past 10 years. Bob has taught at Penn State University and periodically presents his "4-Hour Direct Marketing MBA" seminar throughout the United States.

Bob can be reached at (717) 566-3849 or through E-mail at resp-mailo.44@prodigy.net. You can view the Response Innovations' Website at www.responseinnovationsinc.com

Richard Simms graduated with a degree in chemistry from Duquesne University in 1972. He joined DialAmerica Marketing in 1982 as a part-time telemarketing sales rep (TSR), was promoted to part-time phone room supervisor in 1983, and accepted a full-time position with DialAmerica as an account executive in 1984.

Over the past 15 years, Rich has built an impressive account résumé that reads like a who's-who in direct marketing. He has worked on programs for such major firms as Chase Manhattan Bank, Columbia House, Grolier, Intuit, the *New York Times*, Scholastic, Standard & Poor's, Sony Computer Entertainment, and Time-Life Books, among many others. Rich is a recognized pioneer in outbound telemarketing for computer software products. He is currently responsible for new client development in DialAmerica's software and video division.

Rich is quite active within the Direct Marketing Association (DMA). He has served on the operating committee of the DMA's marketing council. He has been a member of the Children's List Legislative Coalition, which helps formulate the DMA's children's list privacy positions. He has also served as a member of the DMA's telemarketing Program Advisory Committee (PAC), where he has helped to plan seminar topics and speakers for the DMA's annual telemarketing conferences. Rich is a member of the American Teleservices Association (ATA) and a member of the American Marketing Association (AMA). He is also a regular guest lecturer on the subject of telemarketing at Western Connecticut State University's direct marketing degree program and is a much sought-after speaker on telemarketing at a wide variety of industry seminars and conferences.

Rich can be reached at (800) 531-3131 or through E-mail at rich_simms@dialamerica.com. You can view DialAmerica's website at www.dialamerica.com